Martyrs

They Died for Christ

Bob and Penny Lord

Journeys of Faith
1-800-633-2484

Other Books by Bob and Penny Lord

THIS IS MY BODY, THIS IS MY BLOOD
Miracles of the Eucharist
THE MANY FACES OF MARY
a Love Story
WE CAME BACK TO JESUS
SAINTS AND OTHER POWERFUL WOMEN
IN THE CHURCH
SAINTS AND OTHER POWERFUL MEN
IN THE CHURCH
HEAVENLY ARMY OF ANGELS
SCANDAL OF THE CROSS
and Its Triumph
THE ROSARY
The Life of Jesus and Mary

ISBN 0-926143-12-3

Table of Contents

Dedication

"Woe to you! You build the tombs of the prophets, but it was your fathers who murdered them. You show that you stand behind the deeds of your fathers; they committed the murders and you erect the tombs. That is why the wisdom of God has said, 'I will send them prophets and apostles, and some of these they will persecute and kill'; so that this generation will have to account for the blood of all the prophets shed since the foundation of the world."   *Luke 11:47-51*

To write this book, we needed to live with the brave brothers and sisters, to take on their joys and sorrows, the physical and spiritual suffering, they endured for God, for Church, and for those who will have to draw on their strength one day, hundreds of years later. We want, first, to dedicate this book to those Martyrs about whom we have written, who give us courage, to stand up for our Church.

Our Lord said, *"But when the Son of Man comes, will he find faith on earth?* We say *"yes!"*, because, Lord, You have raised up two dry Martyrs who were born to pave the way for Your Second Coming. They are Pope John Paul II and Mother Angelica to whom this book is specially dedicated.

Our Pope, John Paul II, truly a *dry Martyr.* If anyone stands out as a modern day hero of the Church, he does. We always seem to be dedicating our books to our Pope, which is as it should be. He has given us, the laity, the boldness to evangelize the brothers and sisters who have lost their way.

Mother Angelica - We also always seem to be dedicating our books to a personal heroine, our Mother Angelica, another *dry Martyr*, a woman with great focus, and determination. Mother Angelica has stood against the powers of hell, with the Eucharist and Mother Mary as her Shield and Armor. She goes against the satan of television, and turns it around to praise and glorify the Lord.

iv

Closer to home, there have been a great deal of people who saw the importance of this work, gave willingly of their time and material.

Fr. Harold Cohen, Closer Walk Ministries - If anyone should know about the North American Martyrs, the Jesuits who came to bring God to our country, Jesuit Fr. Cohen did, and shared diaries on the Jesuits about whom we wrote.

Maryknoll Missions - Maryknoll, New York - The Archives department was extremely helpful in getting us out of print books, written about our Maryknoll Martyrs.

Monsignor Dominick Grealy - Knock Shrine, Ireland - He got us involved with the Irish Martyrs in the first place, and recommended *Veritas* and others who generously supplied the reference material we needed to write on those Martyrs.

Luz Elena Sandoval, and *Brother Joseph*, the core of our Community, and Ministry. The Lord made us *one*, knowing we would get the job done. Because of their undying commitment to the Lord, His Will was done, once more.

Debbie Callens - Our own Miss D., who researched the libraries, called all parts of the country, got half-tones made, cooked for the community many nights, when we burned the midnight oil to meet the deadline for the book.

Lura Daws - Our one year old convert - Lura is madly in love with our Church and our Ministry. She takes care of everything while we're on Pilgrimage, Lectures, Conferences and writing books. She does it very well, in fact.

We dedicate this book to the many supporters we have, who buy our books and watch our TV programs, who come to listen to us at Conferences, and go with us on Pilgrimages. You make it possible for us to fulfill the mandate the Lord has given us. *God bless you!*

Thank you, dear daughter Sr. Clare and grandson Rob for always being there for us, with your love and understanding. You are and always have been part of the fiber of our lives. And we love you!

Introduction

Our Lord Jesus always works through my wife. I have to believe that His mandate to us, "*Unless you come as little children*" and "*Suffer the little children to come unto Me.*" has to apply to my wife. She has the beautiful faith of a child. He speaks to her; she listens; and she acts on what He says. Either He doesn't speak to me, or my brain is too clogged with garbage to listen. Thank God for Penny. He told her to have us write our first book, *This Is My Body, This Is My Blood, Miracles of the Eucharist*, when I would have thought that was the last thing we should have done. That book is a best seller, which put us into a completely new Ministry, and it was because she listened to the Word of the Lord.

Even before we finished writing the *Scandal of the Cross and its Triumph* in 1992, Penny was getting the message to write about the Martyrs in the Church, those selfless brothers and sisters who gave their lives for this beautiful Church of ours, that it may survive, that it may spread to the four corners of the earth, that Jesus' message, "*Go out to all the world and proclaim the Good News*" may be carried out.

Also, in 1992, we made a 13 part television series, *The Many Faces of Mary*. During the taping of this series, we had to travel all over Europe and into Mexico, in the course of just a few months. In Zaragoza, Spain, we were honored to interview the Archbishop, Elias Yanes Alvarez. He told us briefly about the *Martyrs of Zaragoza*, young men who died for their faith during the Spanish Civil War. Within a few days of this interview, we went to Knock, Ireland, to make the program about Our Lady of Knock. Monsignor Grealy, the custodian of the Shrine, told us about the *17 Irish Martyrs* who were being beatified in September, 1992. And then, on our trip to Our Lady of Guadalupe in December, 1992, we were introduced to *the three young Martyrs of Tlaxcala, Mexico*, who were beatified with Juan Diego in 1990. The Lord spoke to us again, when we appeared on Mother Angelica Live. A telephone caller asked the question, "*How were the Martyrs of the early Church able to withstand the cruel torture they had to endure?*" "*How was Maxmilian Kolbe able to take another man's place, and be willing to die, during the Nazi annihilation of prisoners at Auschwitz?*" "*How did Joan of Arc manage to pray, while being burned at the stake?*" We didn't have the answer. Thank God we had Mother there. She zeroed in on the answer immediately. She said, "*They were given Signal Grace. That is a special grace given to those who have to perform special tasks for God, or undergo severe anguish for God.*" I recall that Mother was extremely serious that evening. Her eyes were sad; her jaw set.

No matter where we turned, the Lord was pointing out Martyrs to us. We knew that this was what He wanted from us this year. We knew the Lord wanted the world to know about those who had given up their lives, for Him, and for His Church which they had embraced as their own. But we weren't sure why. We knew that one reason had to be the dissimilarity between those who are willing to die for Christ in His Church, and those who are not even willing to live for Christ in His Church, for those who take it so for granted, that it has very little meaning to them. It's just something they do, someplace they go on Sunday.

It wasn't until we began the chapter on the Martyrs of North America, that the whole reasoning behind it came upon us full force. I would say coincidentally, but I became aware a long time ago that there are no coincidences with the Lord, unless they are *Holy Coincidences.* So, to rephrase, Holy coincidentally, we began writing the chapter about the American Martyrs around the 23rd of January, the anniversary of the Roe-Wade Decision, which legalized abortion in our country. And on the 23rd of this January, 1993, the twentieth anniversary, our new President Clinton issued Executive Orders wiping out all bans on federal aid regarding abortion, which had been instituted during the previous twelve years.

It was in this context, and against this background that we began to write about those people of the early days of our country who struggled against unbelievable odds to bring Jesus to the people of this new land. We had to read about those who left other countries to make a new life in this country, because of religious persecution and atrocities they suffered in their native land. It was with some irony and a great sense of loss that we compared their courage and bravery, and commitment to their God, with what seems to be a complete lack of religious rights in this country today, this *free* country founded under God. It was very depressing. We heard our pro-life leaders conceding that we could not expect any help from our government for religious freedom. We would have to convert men's hearts, rather than expect justice through legislation. And we were ready to do that, and we are ready to do that. But we really felt defeated.

And then came January 25th, 1993. That is the Feast Day honoring the Conversion of St. Paul. Our minds and hearts clicked in on this *totally impossible situation,* Saul the Christian persecutor. His very name made the Christians shake with fear. They fled for their lives from this self-appointed defender of the Jews against this "*New Way*", these Christians. Nowhere were they safe. He tracked them down in Jerusalem. When that seemed to get the desired results, he spread out his operation to areas outside Jerusalem, Damascus, for example.

Saul, the Christian killer, was on his way to Damascus, in hot pursuit of all those followers of Jesus who had fled Jerusalem. They would not escape him. He had the law on his side; he had the government behind him. Nothing could stop him; but something did stop him. That something was the end of Saul, the Christian Killer, and the beginning of Paul, the most powerful Apostle our Church has ever known. *Jesus knocked him off his high horse to get through to him.* If Saul could be converted, who cannot be converted? Who can withstand the power of God? The battle cry of the mighty Archangel Michael, roars down through the celestial galaxies, *"Who is like God? No one is like God!"* We have weapons, family. We have prayer, which is the most powerful weapon available on the face of the earth and has always been from the beginning of time. Our cry should not be, *"Well, when all else fails, pray."* No, our battle cry should be, *"Our sword is our prayer."* Each prayer raised up to heaven is another sword in the hands of the mighty Angels. And whether you believe it or not, no one, not on earth, nor in heaven, or in hell, can come against the power of prayer.

We believe this was the light at the end of the tunnel, the reason the Lord wanted us to write this book, at this time. We believe we are to show the people of God the price we have paid, not only in this country, but all over the world, the blood which has been shed so that we can be Catholics. We must know how precious our Catholic Church is. We must fight every element within and without, who would destroy the people of God. We cannot fight among ourselves. We have a greater enemy, who is determined to gobble all of us up, and spit us out at the gates of hell.

We are in serious times. We've been in these times before; we're in those times right now. The attacks against the Catholic Church, have become fierce. You can't turn around without seeing a new, blatant attack mounted against the people of God. Sometimes I feel as if we are with Jesus in the Garden of Gethsemane. *"This is your hour and the power of darkness."* or when He said to Pilate, *"If My kingdom were of this world, my soldiers would be all around me to protect Me, but My Kingdom is not of this world."* Our Lord Jesus, our Mother Mary, our brothers and sisters the Saints, our cousins and guides, the Angels, are all crying out to us to save our world. Our Lady has been said to be appearing all over the world, to hundreds of thousands of people with one message, *Repent and Reconcile. Stop killing one another.* It's not just the United States. We're not unique. We're just a part of world genocide. But we have to focus our country on the Martyrs who bought this land with their blood, and be an example to the rest of the world. We can only do it together. *"A house divided against itself cannot stand."* Nor can a country, nor can a people. We are the people of God. We have been given a very clear cut mandate. *We must unite now!*

The Martyrs of Ireland

Ireland is an enchanted land, famous for its shamrocks and harps, leprechauns, shillelaghs, and green-eyed coleens, lightly sprinkled with freckles on skin as white as milk. It is called the Emerald Isle, and the national color is green; Ireland is lush green, almost tropical in certain areas. The Irish people are always pictured as being gay, musical, with the love of all things festive. In our mind's eye, we see them as being Bing Crosby or Barry Fitzgerald, of "Going My Way", which is lovely.

They have grand traditions, such as the monkeys left over from the time when St. Patrick chased the snakes out of Ireland using monkeys. There are those antagonists of Ireland, and all things Irish, who would demean God's special children by the derogatory moniker *Monkeys*, because of this tradition of St. Patrick. There is a possibility that it wasn't the best idea for St. Patrick to use monkeys as a means to accomplish this task. He may not have been thinking of the hazing the Irish people would be receiving in centuries down the line. But keep in mind, he may not have been Irish originally. There are rumors that he may even have had Roman roots, which might account for the ongoing battle between the Irish and the Italians. It may have taken St. Patrick all his life to be trained properly in the ways of being Irish. We do know that when he entered the gates of Heaven, he was definitely Irish.

But God's beloved children of Ireland are a paradox in terms. Those who only see the surface of the Irish people, don't know about the years of suffering, persecution, famine, Martyrdom, and near annihilation of them as a people, all for their Faith. When they joke that there are more Irish in Boston than in Ireland, there is somewhat of a note of melancholy, mixed with the joke. Those who left for a better life in the United States, did no favor to those who remained. It just made their struggle more difficult. Most people don't know about the brave men and women who stood up against the powers of Hell, and survived only because of their great faith in their Catholic Church, and their complete dependence on the Mother of God.

Possibly this is why, when we wrote about Our Lady's Apparition at Knock, Ireland, on August 21, 1879, we thought her reasoning for not speaking to her people was because she had no complaint. We felt she was commending a faithful people for a job well done. We still feel that way, but we know that Our Lady had much more to say than she was given credit for. But all of that was covered in our book on the *Many Faces of Mary, a Love Story*.

"There have been reports in 1985-6 that Our Lady has appeared to different people in various parts of Ireland. At a little shrine devoted to our Lady of Lourdes in Cappoquin, Waterford County, which we visited in 1984, a year before the reported apparitions, Our Lady allegedly complained about the loss of Faith that was being experienced by the people in Ireland. We are not going to attempt to speculate as to the veracity of these reports. We will say, however, that if they were true, they give more credence to the silent apparition of Mary at Knock in 1879."[1]

In 1980, we were in Assisi. We were bemoaning the outcast state of vocations in the United States. We asked a well-known Franciscan Priest, who had become a dear friend over the years, to pray for vocations in our country. He leaned over to us, and said, very seriously, *"You Americans are too fat. You will not see vocations until you become lean, like the Irish and the Polish and the Mexicans."* We could not understand what he meant, or how we could lump these three diverse ethnic groups together. But since that time, and especially during the research of this book, we have

---

[1]The Many Faces of Mary, a Love Story - Bob & Penny Lord, 1987

found that *powerful* common denominator that links the three together.

Irish and Mexicans and Polish have one outstanding trait in common. You might think to yourself, what a combination. And you would be right. We believe, however, that our marvelous Pope John Paul II picked up on this over thirteen years ago. It might be why he loves those three cultures so much, why he can relate to each of the other two ethnic groups. This marvelous trait, which the Lord has been able to work with down through the centuries is *Holy Stubbornness*. They are bullheaded when it comes to their Church. Proof of that is how they have held up under extreme persecution during various crucial periods in their history. Without that gift from the Lord, none of these three groups of Powerful Catholics would exist as a people or as Catholics today. Thank You Jesus; praise You Jesus.

The Struggle of the Irish People

The Irish people had been considered highly intelligent and extremely spiritual. Ireland was called the Land of Saints and Soldiers. Many of their young men became Priests and brothers, and traveled all over Europe, as well as up and down the coasts of the United States and Mexico, evangelizing the natives. There is a great tradition that the Mexican god, Quetzacoatl, the fair skinned god who came from the sea, to Cholula in 700 A.D., and taught them a religion similar to Christianity, was the great Irish Saint Brendan, who, not coincidentally, was born near Knock. During the period from St. Patrick's conversion of the people of Ireland, to Henry VIII's great sin, there was not a great deal of religious persecution to be suffered by the people of the Emerald Isle.

Until the satan of *lust* took over Henry VIII's heart, he was known as *Defender of the Faith*, a title given him by the Medici Pope, Leo X. He received this honor for his book, defending the Seven Sacraments against Martin Luther. But when Henry asked the Pope to grant him a divorce from his first wife, Catherine of Aragon, in order to marry Ann Boleyn (*who would leave her head on the chopping block in the tower of London anyway*), the troubles began. The Pope could not possibly grant a divorce to Henry VIII, and so this Defender of the Faith, became Persecutor of the Faith. He broke off with Rome in 1529, instituted his own State Religion, and proceeded to plague the Church. Because of the power structure of the British Isles, whichever way the English went, so went the Irish. And so this dear faithful people found themselves under English Protestant rule, without any voice in the decision at all.

Henry was cruel, but his successors were even worse. It was almost as if they had to outdo Henry. Queen Elizabeth began putting great pressure on the Irish with her Act of Supremacy in 1560, which stated very simply, she was in charge, and anyone who disobeyed her laws, especially ecclesiastical laws, was guilty of Treason.

Now, it was not considered a major offense on the books, but because the Irish immediately and with unanimity, refused to accept Elizabeth as head of the Church, and deny the Pope in Rome, the country was in a state of martial law most of the time. This being the case, the door was wide open as to what punishments could be inflicted on the Irish. In addition, it was strongly implied that anyone who was outside the established Church, that is the Church of Henry and Elizabeth, was not a loyal subject, and as such, could be persecuted without any other reason. The fact that Pope Pius V excommunicated Elizabeth as a heretic, in 1570, didn't help matters any. Elizabeth got back at him. In 1585, a law was passed which *stated that a Priest was guilty of treason, merely by his presence in the country.* Most of the people of England had accepted the new rule fairly readily, but the Irish would never budge. You see that *Holy Stubbornness* clicking in. The Lord works well with that.

The situation went from bad to worse, reaching a breaking point when Oliver Cromwell took control of England. He was determined to destroy these people. He instituted a plot for the methodical and systematic annihilation of all Catholics in the little country of Ireland. The Penal times began. Brutal torturous inhuman penalties were inflicted on Catholics. If it was possible, Cromwell was more wicked than Henry and all his followers. He thought the Church of England, which was persecuting the Catholics, was too much like the Catholic Church. It was too soft on the Irish. He was determined to make them bend or break.

It was at this time that the Lord gave these dear people His greatest gift to them. The blanket of Holy Stubbornness came over the populace, giving them strength. Uprisings began. The government didn't know what to do. They never expected the people to react that way. Before the end of the Sixteenth century, many uprisings had to be put down by the government. The penalization became very hard. They were determined to break this community of Faith. But the powers that be were told loud and clear by the people that they were not going to give up their Catholic Faith.

The uprisings were even brought to the level of Crusades. The Irish believed they were justified in declaring war for the preservation of Catholicism in their land. They were even able to muster aid from foreign countries, most notably Spain. These dear zealots for the Faith envisioned a victory akin to the Battle of Lepanto in 1571, in which the Turks were defeated by a Rosary Crusade, during which an image of Our Lady of Guadalupe was at the forefront, at the mast of the lead battleship. But that gift was not to be given to the faithful brothers and sisters of Ireland. For them, their very existence as a people of God was at stake. To the other powers who had been their benefactors, it was a matter of politics. The Spanish in particular, hated England and would do whatever they could to embarrass the monarchs. But eventually, most drew away from the situation, including two Popes. These dear people, the brothers and sisters of Ireland, were abandoned, left alone by all, except for the greatest help they could possibly have asked for, Our Lord Jesus and His Mother Mary.

The Holy Spirit inspired the Pope, and members of the Council of Trent that warships and battles were not the way to win the war for the Irish people. Strong Catholic Priests and Bishops in the country, using the greatest weapons we have ever had, *the Eucharist, the Mass and the Rosary*, would do what cannons and guns could not do, melt men's hearts and pave the way for the emancipation of Catholics in Ireland.

[Author's note: *On January 23, 1993, the 20th anniversary of the Roe-Wade decision, newly elected president of the United States, Bill Clinton, signed an executive order, removing all bans which had been put on abortions in the United States. We watched the reactions on Television from Pro-life people all over the country that evening. It seemed that everyone felt completely defeated and abandoned. Then a woman from the Pro-Life movement in New Orleans made a profound statement. She said, "We can't expect any help in legislation for the next four years. We can only pray to change mens' hearts."*]

We believe the same can be said of the philosophy of the Holy See in the Sixteenth century, as proclaimed by the powerful Council of Trent. This reform in the Church philosophy brought about a renewal in the Church. A great wave of young men who had left Ireland to study for the Priesthood and religious life in Europe, came back and converged on their homeland as Priests and brothers. But it also brought about the beginning of the Irish Martyrs, these unselfish men and women who stood up to the powers of hell, and did not waiver in their loyalty to the Lord. Many no sooner stepped foot on Irish soil, than they were arrested and put to death. Others infiltrated the country, began their ministry, and became Martyrs as a result, later on. We will never know just how many Irish brothers and sisters were murdered for the Faith. There are so many stories of the bravery of these dear people of Faith, who stood up against the powers of hell for what they believed in. Many of the victims of this genocide by the British were presented to the Church for beatification. However, there were just too many Martyrs and not enough valid records. When the Irish initially rejected the King's Religion, they were declared non-persons, and therefore all records of births, deaths and Baptisms were repressed. The Church could never have opened the causes equaling the actual numbers of brothers and sisters who died because they numbered into the hundreds of thousands. Therefore, in her great wisdom, Mother Church picked seventeen people from the various periods of the Penal Times, and investigated their causes. They were beatified in September, 1992.

We want to share with you, these brothers and sisters. Because we believe that each of the Martyrs were as important as the others, we will mention them by the date they gave up their lives.

†

Blessed Patrick O'Healy, and Blessed Conn O'Rourke, 1579

Of the seventeen Martyrs beatified in 1992, Fathers Patrick O'Healy and Conn O'Rourke were the first to be put to death.   Both men were members of the Franciscan Observants, an off-shoot of the Franciscan Order, which embraced the original rule of Father Francis.

St. Bernadine of Siena is known as the Second Founder of the Strict Observance of St. Francis.   Bernadine was a strict believer in the original rule of St. Francis, which was not being practiced by the Franciscan community by and large.   They contended from the time of Francis that it was too strict.   There were a small group of stalwarts who still practiced the original Rule, but they were very small. Bernadine became their champion and trail blazer.   He traveled the countryside, recruiting fervent young men to the Strict Observance of St. Francis.   Patrick O'Healy and Conn O'Rourke were two such men.

Patrick O'Healy was born in or around 1545.   But like most of the young men of that time, who were fervent for the Faith, he went to Europe to be trained as a Franciscan and Priest.   He was educated in Catholic Spain for the most part. But we first hear of him in Rome in 1575.   He attached himself to a great crusader for free Ireland, James Fitzmaurice, who started an actual crusade against Queen Elizabeth, the heretic. He was in Rome, seeking support from Pope Gregory XIII. We're told by the biographer, that Fitzmaurice received a Papal Blessing, and not much more. The following year, Fr. Patrick was ordained Bishop, and appointed Bishop of Mayo. This was a great blessing and honor, but it was also a death sentence. If and when he should return to Ireland, he would immediately be hunted, and when caught, executed, and he knew that. So he was in effect, a Bishop in exile. He went with Fitzmaurice to Spain, where their greatest support was found. They were attempting to get more help from King Philip. Although King Philip hated Queen Elizabeth, he was cautious. He didn't just go bounding into situations where Angels fear to tread. He wanted to help the Irish, but felt the need to look at the entire situation first.

Patrick was in Spain, in his capacity as Bishop of Mayo, but felt he was spending more of his time lobbying for war than in the spiritual development of his people. He decided to leave politics up to Fitzmaurice and King Philip, and he headed back to Ireland. He went by way of Paris, where he met up with a fellow Franciscan Observant, Conn O'Rourke, who came from Breifine, the same area of Ireland as he. O'Rourke had followed a similar path as Patrick, being educated in Europe and joining the Franciscan Observants. Together, strengthened by the blessings of the Council of Trent, and the teachings of Father Francis, they gave each other the courage to head back to their homeland to feed their flock. They went to Brittany, France, where they were able to get a ship back to Ireland. It was 1579.

We just want to make a point about the Observants, Franciscans and otherwise. Many of the religious orders had softened in the wake of Francis and Dominic. The Rules had been compromised; the friars became more worldly. But in times of crisis, the Lord always sends us powerful men and women, to strengthen us, and focus us. Fervent young men cast aside the watered-down versions of the Rules, and searched for the meat, the original Rules. This is what they brought with them to Ireland, and created what has been called the Observant Reform. Thanks be to God, the movement lasted longer than the poor, fervent Martyrs who brought it over.

As soon as Bishop O'Healy and Fr. O'Rourke landed in Ireland, they immediately attempted to preach to the people. They tried to get support from various families of nobility in Ireland. We learn that Conn O'Rourke was from noble lineage, having been born a member of the ruling house of Breifine. We're not sure if he thought that would do him any good, but it seemed likely they were heading in that direction, trying to recruit support and protection from people in power.

It's known they looked for the help of a certain Earl of Desmond, but were unable to find him. He seemed to have disappeared during the three days they were in his area. After they left the area, he returned. They were arrested shortly after their attempt to make contact with the Earl. This occurred while they were going through Limerick, on the way to Breifine.

What happened next gets a little confusing, only in that it became mixed up with an attack by Fitzmaurice and Spanish troops in July of 1579. Reports stated that Bishop O'Healy and Fr. O'Rourke were part of that ill-fated attempt to liberate the country. None of it was true, but it had a great influence on the court. Most likely Bishop O'Healy and Fr. O'Rourke were tried by a military court, with the charge of treason. Now, this by itself would not have been enough to execute them under British law. Even if it were enough, Fr. O'Rourke never had anything to do with Fitzmaurice or his plans for a revolution, but it couldn't be proved. The country was under martial law, which gave Lord Drury the right to act as judge, jury and executioner. When we look through his words, he made all kinds of allegations, including threats about being "*the Pope's Prelates and agents....*" The actual charge on which they were convicted was, refusing to take the *Oath of Supremacy*, which would have been grounds enough for execution. They went to the gallows together, praising Our Lord Jesus and the Church in Rome.

It is believed that these two zealots for the Church, Bishop Patrick O'Healy and Fr. Conn O'Rourke were executed on the road from Limerick to Cork, in a place called Kilmallock. They never did get to their own County Mayo. There are those who would say their mission was never completed; their lives were wasted; they died failures, by never having brought the Faith to these dear people. Remember, they were very young men. O'Healy was 34 years old, and O'Rourke could not have been much more. They had not been back on their native soil for more than a few months when they were executed. What could they possibly have accomplished?

They accomplished what only God could have done. A spirit was instilled in the people. Spurred on by their courage, young men were willing to live and die for their Church and their country. Could those who remained do less? Could they backslide, give in, turncoat, and go over to the other side? You see, it was that easy throughout. *You must not forget that!* All it took was to pledge allegiance to the religion of the Crown, and life would be easy. And many were tempted to do that. Life was too hard as it was. But then they looked at the sacrifice of Bishop Patrick O'Healy and Fr. Conn O'Rourke, and their spirits were lifted, and they were given renewed courage. That's how the Irish people got through it.

Blessed Matthew Lambert, Baker
Blessed Robert Myler, Blessed Edward Cheevers,
Blessed Patrick Cavanagh and two Sailor companions - 1581

As we research the Martyrs chosen by the Church to represent the hundreds of thousands who were victims for the Lord, we find some very strange stories, so strange that we cannot deny their authenticity. They had to be true. Such is the case of the five men mentioned above. They really didn't do anything. They only tried to help two who *did* something.

We've mentioned the James Fitzmaurice uprising in the section above, about Bishop O'Healy and Fr. Conn O'Rourke. He's not really to blame for all of this; it's just that he spearheaded a movement which all the people wished they had the courage to support. Fitzmaurice and his companions were the ones who made it happen. These others did what they could to help in whatever way they could. With that in mind, we will begin.

Viscount Baltinglass was a member of the Fitzmaurice Crusade. He had held forth in the Crusade, and when all was lost, tried to get out of Ireland. He knew it was immediate torture and death, if he was found. He suspected that he could not attempt to get out through Dublin, because the British had a search party out looking for him. He and his chaplain, Fr. Rochford, a Jesuit, went down to Wexford, which is on the southeastern tip of Ireland, right next to Waterford. They felt this was their best chance.

They appealed to a simple but loyal man, Matthew Lambert, a local baker, to give them a night's lodging while they tried to put their escape plan into effect. Matthew was a good Catholic, but he didn't quite understand what the conflict between the Church and the Queen was all about. He knew there was a problem, but he could never figure out why there was a problem. That's not to say he wouldn't have helped the patriots anyway. He fed the men and gave them shelter for the night. He also contacted **Robert Myler, Edward Cheevers, Patrick Cavanagh** and two sailor companions, to help him in trying to get the fugitives out of the country.

A plan was devised in which Viscount Baltinglass and Fr. Rochford would go down to the port of Wexford, and board a ship for Europe. The authorities caught wind of the plot, and before the fugitives even arrived at the port, the baker and five sailors were arrested, and thrown into jail. They were charged with treason. Now we don't know what happened to Viscount Baltinglass and the Priest. Did they ever get caught? We never hear another word about them. All we know is the police took it out on these poor innocent men who were just trying to help others.

When the men were questioned about their role in the conspiracy, their innocence came forth in full bloom. Matthew Lambert said he was a good Catholic and loyal to the Queen. When the interrogators asked how he could justify the one with the other, his answer was:

"I am not a learned man. I am unable to debate with you, but I can tell you this. I am a Catholic, and I believe whatever our Holy Mother the Catholic Church believes."[2]

Matthew Lambert, Robert Myler, Edward Cheevers, Patrick Cavanagh, and the other two unnamed sailors, were tortured, hung, then drawn and quartered.[3] Before the sailors were executed, they were tortured cruelly. They declared their loyalty to the Catholic Faith until their death.

†

Blessed Margaret Ball - 1584

We can see why this woman's cause was to be among those chosen for beatification. It is so outrageous, it's difficult to believe that it could happen. Margaret Ball was the wife of a prosperous and important merchant, Bartholomew Ball. They were completely faithful to the Church, and had raised their children to be the same.

They spent much of their time supporting the struggle of the Catholics in Dublin. She had only one black sheep, a son Walter, her oldest. He had turned Protestant, with a vindictiveness that was not to be believed.

From the time of her husband's death, she devoted herself and all her possessions and influence in defending the Church, and protecting those who were in danger because of their beliefs. Her home became a haven for

---

[2]The Irish Martyrs - Msgr. Patrick Corish P. 17

[3]There are two definitions for Drawn and Quartered - 1. To execute by tying each arm and leg to a different horse, and then driving the horses in four different directions. 2. To eviscerate (disembowel) and cut into pieces after hanging.

Priests who came into the city. They would celebrate Mass; they would have meals there and free lodging. Oftentimes, she would have her son Walter come and dine with the Priests. She was praying desperately for a conversion. It did not come in her lifetime.

Eventually, she was caught, and carted off to prison, with one of the Priests who had celebrated Mass at her home. But being a woman of status in the town, she was able to use her influence to be released. Then she went back to what she had been doing, and was caught again. This went on and on. It was a round, round robin between her and the authorities.

Now here's the sad but true, and very ironic part of our story. Her son Walter was elected to the post of Mayor of Dublin in 1580. *He gave an order for her to be arrested!* At his command, she was dragged through the streets. She was put in jail, and never released again. She was sixty-five and in poor health when she was arrested.

She was subjected to the worst possible conditions. No one, not even a peasant from the lowest standard of living, would have survived as long as she did, she from the *upper class* of Dublin. Her only consolation was her prayers. She saw many Priests and religious come and go during her time in the castle at Dublin. She was very loved by many of the people of Dublin. It grieved them so when they saw her wasting away.

But she had the great gift of *Irish Stubbornness*. She could have left in a minute. All she had to do was deny her loyalty to the Pope. *Nobody cared if she meant it; just say it.* Take the Oath of Supremacy to the Queen. They begged her to free herself, regularly. Not her son, but her jailers. Her son knew her better. We don't know if he ever visited his mother while she was in jail. How would he have been able to live with himself, looking at his own mother wasting away in a prison, and him the cause of her death. We can just picture the great party that was given for him when he arrived at the gates of Hell. We're sure, though that his dear mother, nestled in the bosom of Our Lord Jesus and our Mother Mary in Heaven, must have wept for her son.

†

Blessed Bishop Dermot O'Hurley - 1584

Dermot O'Hurley was a product of the strong stock of County Tipperary. We have first hand knowledge of the inhabitants of Tipperary. We have been privileged to visit with, and experience the beautiful people of this part of God's country. We saw them through the eyes of our Pastor, our Irish Monsignor, Tommy O'Connell, born in Cahir, county Tipperary.

He took us through southwestern Ireland, introduced us to his country and his people, the brothers and sisters who make up the texture and fiber of Ireland. We have been able to see the strength of these people of God, especially when it comes to their Faith. And so it comes as no surprise when we learn that there was an Irish Martyr from this part of the country. It stands to reason.

Dermot O'Hurley would be what we call a *Reluctant Saint*. He never asked to be a Priest, or a Bishop, or an Archbishop. He was minding his own business when the Lord came along, and asked him to say Yes. If he committed any crime at all, that would have been the extent of it. He said *Yes* to the Lord, as did so many others down through the history of our Church.

He was born in 1530 in Tipperary, in a small village called Emly. He was the apple of his parents' eyes. He was sent to Louvain University in Belgium, where he graduated with honors. He received a Masters in Art, and went on to become the dean of the law school there, which is quite an honor. Nowhere do we hear anything of a religious nature about him. This is not to say he was a bad person; he just went about living his life. He had to have been aware of what was going on in his homeland, which must have given him reason for great sorrow. It may also have accounted for his not returning for 30 years.

He left Louvain in 1576, and went to France, settling in Rheims, near the Belgium border. He stayed there for about four years, until 1570. For some unknown reason, he went to Rome. There may have been some natural reason for bringing him there. Italy was a great center for the arts, and much of it was in the area of Rome. We know the Lord had His reason for bringing Dermot to Rome. He spent the next 11 years in Rome, having nothing at all to do with anything spiritual, as far as we can discern, or anything to do with his country. There's no question that he knew about the Crusade planned by James Fitzmaurice, and his frequent trips to Rome. But there's nothing to indicate that they knew one another, or had even met, much less had any goal in common.

However, in 1581, Dermot O'Hurley was told by Pope Gregory XIII that he was to be Archbishop of Cashel, in his home province. *The man wasn't even a Priest!* But he said *yes.* There was an urgency on the part of Mother Church to have him take over the reigns of Cashel in Tipperary. From the time he said yes to the Pope, which was in the summer of 1581, it only took *two weeks*, from July 29 to August 13 for him to go through the procedure of Ordination. Then, it took a month, from August 13 to September 11 for him to become Archbishop of Cashel.

To the best of our knowledge, he returned to Ireland almost immediately. He was a very above-board person. He had no desire to deceive anyone. He had a respectable position; he was an Archbishop in the Roman Catholic Church. Was he taking into consideration that it was illegal in Ireland to be a Roman Catholic Priest of any kind, much less Archbishop? He walked around freely, cautiously, but not covertly. To give him credit, he had been absent from his homeland for thirty years. He had lived in total freedom those thirty years. He had been a highly respected professional for most of that time.

He did not try to hide his identity. He stayed with a nobleman, Baron Thomas Fleming. He was recognized by the baron's first cousin, who was chief justice of the Common Pleas, in Dublin. Word got back quickly to the powers in Dublin, and the Baron was threatened, if he didn't turn over Archbishop Hurley, he would be jailed as a conspirator, giving aid to traitors. Meanwhile, Archbishop Hurley went to Munster, another part of the area, to enlist the aid of a local Earl, and to advise the Queen's Archbishop that his interests were not political nor deceitful. He was only interested in the spiritual welfare of the people of Cashel.

We have to believe that the Angels were protecting Dermot O'Hurley every step of the way. He said all the wrong things to all the right people, and still had not been jailed. It wasn't until Baron Fleming tracked him down, and begged him to go to Dublin, and tell the powers that be, that he, Fleming, was not guilty of treason, that Archbishop O'Hurley put himself in an impossible situation. He agreed to go, and indeed did. He was immediately imprisoned, and incarcerated in Dublin Castle, charged with treason and conspiracy to overthrow the Queen's government.

We have to bring you up to date on the Crusade situation, which was the main cause for believing everyone of a religious nature in Ireland was a Papal ploy. James Fitzmaurice attempted his attack on Ireland on July 18.

However, a month to the day later, Fitzmaurice was killed. Now this was two years later, but there was still a great deal of suspicion about anyone or anything that had to do with religion. The government had reclaimed its hold on the people, but they were sure that there were plots all around, groups trying to overthrow the government. They were sure that Archbishop O'Hurley was a spy. They were convinced that he had information about what the next plan was against the throne. Actually, the poor man had no information, but they couldn't believe that. The way he was ordained and made an Archbishop in six weeks was extremely suspicious. And so it began. He was not put on trial. There was good reason to believe he would never be convicted. So he was just kept in the Dublin Castle and tortured, for how long, we don't know. At one point, it was suggested that he be transferred to London, where they had some really good torture equipment, but that was rejected. They did the best they could with what they had to force the information by means of acute suffering, out of a man who clearly had no information.

The longer they kept him in the Castle, the more embarrassing it became for the government. They were beyond putting him on trial. They couldn't even allow him to be brought out in public, he was so disfigured. One of the tortures was to put his legs in metal boots, filled with oil, and placed over a fire. They literally cooked his legs, until the flesh fell off the bone. The government had to get rid of him. An order of execution was given, and he was rushed through the procedure. Early in the morning on June 20, 1584, he was brought out to College Green in Dublin, and hung. Before he died, he was able to make a last statement to some people who were not expected to be there at such an early hour. He said:

"I am a Priest anointed and also a Bishop, although unworthy of so sacred dignities, and no cause could they find against me

that might in the least degree deserve the pains of death, but merely my function of Priesthood wherein they have proceeded against me in all points cruelly contrary to their own laws."[4]

These final words of Archbishop O'Hurley ricochet down through the centuries as a stinging condemnation to all murderers, torturers and strong-arm men who choose to hide behind propriety and legality. *"They have proceeded against me in all points cruelly contrary to their own laws."* He was saying what many of the oppressed have said all through this book: the oppressors have made laws to suit themselves, and then broken their own laws if they don't fit into a particular scenario. Henry VIII did it in England and Ireland, Plutarco Calles did it in Mexico, Hitler did it in Germany, Stalin in Russia, Mao Tse Tung in China and on and on. When will it stop, dear Lord?

†

Blessed Fr. Maurice MacKenraghty - 1585

Details about the life of Fr. MacKenraghty are sketchy, at best. He was born in Kilmallock, where Bishop Patrick O'Healy was executed. He came from a good family. His father was a merchant, a goldsmith. The first we really hear of him is when he was acting as chaplain for the Earl of Desmond, who was on the run.

Desmond had been a revolutionary, who had taken part in an ill-fated attempt by Spanish and Italian forces, and was trying to find sanctuary anywhere. He was trying to lose himself in the area around Clonmel. He had felt he could

---

[4]The Irish Martyrs - Msgr. Patrick Corish Pg 13

get some help from the good Irish people there, but they had suffered severely, during and immediately after the uprising, and wanted nothing to do with any revolutionaries or crusaders.

That was with their mouths. With their hearts, the Catholic loyalty was growing, even if it was an underground movement. They would help wherever and whenever they could. Fr. MacKenraghty was separated from the Earl of Desmond. He was not a military man; therefore he didn't have the shrewd knowledge of maneuvering necessary to stay out of the hands of the enemy. He was caught in September, 1583, and put into prison at Clonmel. The Earl of Desmond was killed in November of that year.

It was strange that Fr. Mackenraghty was not executed right away. They usually got rid of Priests, Bishops, brothers, anyone of a religious affiliation. Possibly because it was in Clonmel, which was a sleepy little town in Tipperary, rather than in Dublin. Also, Fr. MacKenraghty was virtually a local boy, as Kilmallock was but a short distance from Clonmel. We don't really know why they allowed him to stay alive for almost two years after he was apprehended, but they did.

His downfall came when one of the merchant class of the Irish of Clonmel wanted to have a Priest celebrate Mass for him and his wife and family on Easter Sunday. He bribed the jailer at Clonmel prison to let the Priest go just for Easter Sunday. He paid a tidy sum for this privilege. All the money was to go to the jailer. Everything worked out as planned, with one exception. On that day, the head of the army, Lord President of Munster, came to Clonmel. The jailer feared for his life. He told the Lord President about the Mass that was to take place in the village. While the Priest was celebrating Mass at the home of the Catholic merchant, the Lord President and his troops broke into the house.

Fr. MacKenraghty was able to hide himself. He might have escaped, except he heard the official tell the Catholic merchant, he would be executed if the Priest were not found. Fr. MacKenraghty immediately gave himself up and was returned to prison. It was almost as if they had forgotten that he was even there until this incident came up. Naturally, now they had to do something with the Priest. First they asked if he would take the Oath of Supremacy. If he did, he would be pardoned, and released from prison. He couldn't do that. He was condemned to death and hanged in Clonmel on April 20, 1585.

It's strange, the way the events of the Martyrdom of Fr. Maurice MacKenraghty came about. Would they have allowed him to live out his life in prison if he had not gone to celebrate Mass? Was the jailer, who was probably a local boy, sympathetic to his brother-in-Christ, not necessarily to his cause, but the fact that he was a fellow Irishman, and there was something sinful about killing one of your own, especially a Priest? Was everyone just a little tired of all the murdering of people who were most likely kin? We have to wonder. How do we feel when we kill our own unborn children by abortion?

†

Blessed Dominic Collins - 1602

Dominic came from a well-to-do family in Youghal, County Cork. His brother served a term as Mayor as did his father. They were of the merchant class. Dominic was born in or around 1566. The town was an important port town in the south of Ireland. The people of the town didn't want trouble with England. They were very happy with their lives. They were loyal to the throne, but not happy with the idea that their religion had been changed from Catholic to the Queen's religion. They maintained their loyalty to the Pope, but we don't think they were bothered that much by the government, because they were not rebels, plus the area was lucrative for both the Irish and the English. So it seemed that while hell may have been breaking loose throughout Ireland, this little hamlet was being spared.

A Jesuit grammar school even opened up in Youghal, when Dominic was about 11 years old. The Priest, Robert Rochford, who later became the chaplain for Viscount Baltinglass[5] a few years later, was one of the two who began this school. In addition to teaching the young people their reading, writing and arithmetic, the Jesuits also gave them a spiritual foundation in the true Church. Much of this was unhampered by the government, which affirms that they were not being harassed much. Life was good for the little town of Youghal.

That is, until 1579, when the Earl of Desmond[6] began his revolutionary activities against the Crown of England. We're not sure if he was sincere in his claim that he was fighting for the religious freedom of Ireland, or whether it was that his lands were in jeopardy of being taken over by the advance of royalty. The people of Youghal wanted no part of revolutionary activities. They sympathized with his religious beliefs, if indeed that was the motivation behind his aggression against the British. In truth, they were afraid that in joining with him, they would have lost everything they had, including, possibly, their lives.

The Earl of Desmond repaid the people of the town for what he considered gross cowardice, by attacking Youghal,

---

[5]See the account of Matthew Lambert, the Baker, and the five sailors from Wexford

[6]See the account of Fr. Maurice Mackenraghty

destroying just about everything in his path. He wreaked far more havoc than the British would have, if they had attacked the little town. The upshot was that most of the people left, and went to other places. As we mentioned earlier in this account of the Irish Martyrs, Desmond was killed; all his ambitions were crushed; but it didn't end there. Life became difficult for the people, as the government took on a very strict and suspicious posture, in order to avoid a repercussion of what had happened with Desmond and Fitzmaurice.

There was not much left for Dominic in Youghal. The town was in ruins for years after the damage done by Desmond. If that was not bad enough, he had the strict Rule of the government to contend with. He had to do the same as all the young people of his station. He left Ireland and went to Europe. We don't think he went for religious reasons. He didn't go as a playboy, however. As a matter of fact, he had very little when he began his adult life. But he did have those Irish good looks, a great personality, and many noble qualities. He found himself in the military. He looked great in a uniform. There was a war going on in France between Catholics and Protestants. He fought on the Catholic side.

He prospered in the military. He rose from the ranks, becoming a captain of a calvary company, and eventually governor of a territory captured in battle. He was becoming jaded, however, with the military. He could see that he had put his faith and efforts into man, and man was deceiving him. This was to be proven to him, time and time again. He went to Corunna, in northern Spain, to meet up with Irish soldiers stationed there, so he thought. In reality, the Lord had moved him in that direction, so that he would be able to meet Fr. White, a Jesuit, who would be very instrumental in his life.

Fr. White had founded a college in Salamanca, which is deep into the central section of Spain. The purpose of the college was to teach young Irishmen who were interested in the Priesthood. Remember, anyone who wanted to practice or know anything about his Catholic Faith was exiled from Ireland. To find colonies of Irish in different towns in Spain was not unusual, especially since Spain was sympathetic to the cause of the Irish people.

During Lent of 1598, Fr. White went to the military installation where Dominic was stationed, to hear confessions, or so he thought. The Lord put him in the path of Dominic. He recalled their meeting:

"When I spoke to him, he gave thanks to Our Lord for meeting a Priest who was a member of the Society of Jesus and a fellow countryman. He told me that for more than ten months, he was unable to feel any joy or inward peace by reason of a struggle with Our Lord who was urging him to choose a different walk in life and leave the world and its vanities."[7]

Dominic shared his desire to enter the religious life. To Fr. White, this seemed like an impossible goal. He was too headstrong, too excitable, too worldly to be *a religious*. Fr. White gave him the worst recruiting speech possible. He told Dominic about all the difficult and undignified chores, he would have to carry out. We have to remember that in Fr. White's eyes, here is a high-ranking officer in the military, asking to be accepted into a religious order. The religious life is full of menial tasks, at best. As much as Fr. White would love to have Dominic, he didn't think he could weather the storm of religious life. Fr. White's feeling was he would rather pass on allowing Dominic to enter the community, than have him leave sometime in the future. Of course, he didn't know with whom he was dealing. That

---

[7]Dominic Collins, Irish Martyr, Jesuit Brother - Forristal, Desmond

headstrong, passionate young man was very much like St. Paul the Apostle. When *his* shortcomings were turned around for the Lord, they became his greatest assets. And so it was with Dominic Collins.

He stayed at the college of the Jesuits in Santiago de Compostela in Spain for about two years. He was really put through his paces there. No sooner had he arrived than the plague broke out. He worked overtime and doubletime trying to help those stricken with it. But it was what Dominic needed. He was able to absorb the religious life while working at breakneck speed. Jesus knew it was the only way to get Dominic's attention.

A new offensive was being launched by the Spaniards to aid the people of Ireland against the Throne of England. Groups cropped up all over the countryside, trying to sew the seeds of insurrection. The government was having a difficult time fighting it. Dominic found himself among Priests and Bishops, who were going to Ireland to try to bring the Faith to spiritually starved community there. But the main thrust of the journey was war. They had a plan to liberate Ireland from the military hold of the British. Remember, Dominic had nothing to do with any of this. A Jesuit Priest, Fr. Archer, had requested him as a companion. He was more than happy to be returning to his homeland, although he was more than a little nervous about going as a Jesuit *brother*. However, this is the only way he could have gone home. *That's who he was now!* But the point here is he had nothing to do with the military plots against the government.

The attempt failed badly. It doesn't even make any sense to lay blame. It won't do any good. However, what it accomplished was to make the peoples' plight even worse than it had been. What might have been a victory for Ireland turned out to be a sound defeat, and all the Irish retreated back to their villages. Dominic went with a group to a castle in the Beare Peninsula. It was strategically a good place for the Irish to defend themselves, but they were so outnumbered they could not last against the British. In addition, it seemed like the people, they were supporting, had abandoned them. The Priest, Fr. Archer, got into a boat and headed back to Spain to procure reinforcements which never came. Another man, O'Sullivan Beare, was said to have over a thousand troops near the castle, and never sent them in to help the troops which were trapped there.

The bottom line was that the British broke through, and massacred all in the castle, except Dominic Collins and two others. The enemy had a reason for not killing Collins outright. He was a Jesuit, and they thought they could get information about what was called "The Popish Plot". We know that Dominic had no information to give the British. But they were sure he did. They tortured him ruthlessly. Their main goal was to get him to renounce the Faith, his loyalty to the Jesuits, and to the Pope in particular. They also thought it would look good if he were to do battle on their side. So they would torture him, then stop, and offer him all kinds of good things. He would refuse. They would continue with the torturing.

They even sent his family to try to persuade him to give up his loyalty to the Pope. His brother had been Mayor of Youghal just the year before. He had a lot to lose if the British were to punish him for his brother's obstinacy. The family even asked him to fake a conversion. He could always renounce it later, saying he was under the pressure of torture. He refused.

There is a little Irish pathos in the way in which Dominic Collins was executed. He was brought back to his hometown of Youghal for the execution. He wore his Jesuit black robe. He was allowed to talk to the people. He sounded like St. Stephen the Martyr, as he was being stoned to death. He prayed before the gallows: "*Hail, holy Cross, so long desired by me.....*" Then he turned to the crowds, and praised Our Lord Jesus for the life he had given him, the Jesuits, and on and on. One of the bystanders remarked that Dominic sounded as if he were going to a banquet, upon which Dominic replied: *"For this cause, I would be willing to die not once but a thousand deaths."*[8]

The crowd clung to his every word. Sobs could be heard, coming from the heart. The executioner was so moved, he *refused* to hang Dominic. The crowd cheered. Dominic continued preaching to them. The situation was getting completely out of hand. The British didn't know what to do. Even *some of them* were sympathizing with Dominic. Finally, they grabbed a fisherman who was on his way home. They forced him to execute Dominic Collins. He asked Dominic his forgiveness, which Dominic gladly imparted to him.

The fisherman put the noose around Dominic's neck. Dominic prayed the Psalms. As the ladder was pulled away from Dominic, he had just finished praying, *"Into Your Hands I commend my spirit."* With that, he died.

It was possibly the biggest mistake the British could have made. He was immediately proclaimed a Martyr and Saint, and venerated by the people of Youghal first; then his fame spread all over Ireland. Even in Spain, at the Jesuit community where he had served, the name of Dominic Collins and his actions were known and applauded. Miracles and cures have been attributed to the intercession of Dominic Collins. He was surely given the gift of *Holy Stubbornness.*

---

[8]Dominic Collins, Irish Martyr, Jesuit Brother - Forristal, Desmond

Blessed Bishop Conor O'Devaney
Blessed Fr. Patrick O'Loughran-1612

The British felt the need to crush any resistance in Ireland; they had to plug up any hole. They felt confident that all political resistance had been quelled, but they had to concentrate on killing religion in the country! All the battles, and all the executions and exiles had not put an end to that. Rather than teaching the people a lesson by the executions, the British had created Martyrs, which was just the opposite of what they were trying to accomplish. But the powers that be were still not convinced that making an example of Catholic Priests and Bishops would not be a good way to stamp out religion in the country. However, it had to be clearly stated that the execution of the Prelates of the Church was not for religious reasons, but for reasons of treason against the throne.

A scheme was concocted. A law had been imposed on the English, which was different from Elizabeth's Act of Supremacy. It was put into effect during the reign of Charles I (1625-1649). It was called the Oath of Allegiance. Most subjects in England accepted it; however, others would not. But no one had been chastised for not having taken the oath. It was never imposed on the Irish. But the English believed that if it was imposed on the Irish, charges of treason would be easier to make, and enforce. They had to get it through the Irish Parliament, which they felt would be extremely difficult, because they were all Catholic. But the Oath was misleading in that the Irish did not understand the full consequences of the law. The Irish Parliament passed it, not really knowing what they were passing. Now the British only had to find some good examples, where they could apply the law.

One of only two remaining Bishops in Ireland was in prison in Dublin. His name was **Conor O'Devaney**. He was the Bishop of Down and Connor, which had been a stronghold of the Irish resistance, until it was pretty well crushed by the British. Conor O'Devaney had been protected to a degree by the heads of the Gaelic clans in the territory. When they left, he was completely vulnerable. Eventually, he was arrested, and brought to the castle in Dublin.

Conor was born of a class of people in Ireland, called "*erenagh*". These were laymen who held property for the Church. You might say they were agents for the Church. They upheld and maintained Church property, such as schools, and hospitals. They were very close to the Church. Traditionally, the children of *erenagh* families very often became *religious* of one kind or another. Conor was one of these children. He became a Franciscan Observant in Donegal, and later went to Europe for his seminary training, and ordination. He became a Bishop in Rome in 1582. He returned to Ireland, to the diocese from which he had left. He was now Bishop of that diocese.

He had never taken any active part in the uprisings, as had many of his fellow clergy. He wanted to be a good

Bishop to the people. But after he was arrested in 1611, and the Oath of Allegiance was put into effect, he was considered a perfect example to use against the Irish. He was given the opportunity to take the Oath. Naturally, he refused. He was put on trial for treason.

Fr. Patrick O'Loughran was a somewhat different story. Born in 1577, he, too was of an *erenagh* family, which made him automatically suspicious. He was from a different section of Ireland, Donaghmore in county Tyrone. In his family, there had been so many Priests, they were considered chaplains to the O'Neill clan, who was the moving force behind the last uprising Ireland made against the British at the end of the sixteenth century. Patrick O'Loughran did not take part in this battle. He was chaplain to O'Neill.

When O'Neill went into exile at the end of a severe defeat, Fr. O'Loughran went with him. There are bits and pieces of information about him during his time in Europe. He was known to have gone to Rome, and also the Netherlands. But we don't hear anything solid about him until he returned to Ireland in 1611. It's not known for sure even why he chose to return to his native country, other than the fact that he was an Irishman, whose people were in Ireland. He was committed to minister to them, no matter what the cost. And the cost for Patrick O'Loughran was his life. He was arrested almost immediately, upon arriving in his native land.

O'Loughran was   ordered to take the Oath of Allegiance. He refused. It was decided that Fr. Patrick O'Loughran and Bishop Conor O'Devaney be made examples. They would be executed for treason, because they didn't take the Oath of Allegiance.

Even with their new Oath of Allegiance, it would have been very difficult for the British to prove a case of treason against them. However, it was what we would call a *"Kangaroo court"*. It was a set-up deal. Charges were made in their local courts, which were already pre-determined to be guilty. It really wasn't even necessary to go through the charade of a trial. The results, however, were rushed to Dublin, where the two were imprisoned, so that charges could be made there. Neither man was allowed a lawyer. *They didn't even know what they were being charged with, until they got to court.* They didn't stand a chance.

But Bishop O'Devaney did exactly what the judges didn't want done. He attributed the cause of his arrest and trial to be the fact that he was a Catholic Priest, rather than for treasonous acts for which he was being charged. The Bishop was brilliant in turning the whole case around. Anyone with an ounce of intelligence could see that he was being tried for being a Priest. But the jury had been rigged. The verdict came in guilty, and the two were condemned to be hung.

Things got even worse for the British, as the two men were marched to the gallows on February 1, 1612. A crowd which began at a few hundred, mushroomed into a thousand, and then into several thousand. Fear ripped through the police and government officials. They weren't sure if they could control the crowds. In addition, conversions took place at the gallows. People who had gone over to the British, disclaimed their oaths, and proclaimed themselves Catholics again.

Government officials begged the two prisoners to confess their guilt of treason, take the Oath of Allegiance, and they would be set free. But they could not. They had been given so much courage by those who followed them, who had declared their allegiance to the Church, nothing could have stopped them from giving their lives over to the Lord. They could not have accomplished so much for the Lord, if they were converting sinners for the next hundred years. They knew that this was the reason they were Priests;

this was the reason they were born. They were witnessing triumph before their very eyes, the triumph of the Cross.

The situation was completely out of hand. Bishop O'Devaney asked to pray. The prayer became a long homily to the people, encouraging them to keep the Faith, no matter what the cost. He again reiterated his innocence, and that of his colleague, Fr. O'Loughran. The crime was not treason; the crime was being a Catholic, and a Priest at that. Now the government wanted to get this over as quickly as possible. At four o'clock, the Bishop put the cloth over his head, the rope over his neck, and his hands out to be tied. As the executioner was ready to perform his act, a beautiful gift from the Lord was given to the assembled faithful. The clouds opened up, and a bright red sun lit up the scaffold. It remained until the Bishop was hung. Then the clouds covered over the sun.

After the execution of the two Priests, the executioner drew and quartered them. The crowd went wild. They charged the scaffolding, in an attempt to get relics. They knew these two men were Saints as they were being executed. Everybody wanted something for themselves. *The head of the Bishop was stolen!* There are reports that the head of Bishop O'Devaney has never decomposed. These have not been confirmed, however.

The government was completely defeated. They had made more of a situation than they had hoped to resolve. Rather than make an example to those who were hesitant about signing the Oath of Allegiance, they created two powerful Martyrs. Reports of miracles attributed to the two Martyrs took place almost immediately. The situation was worse than it had been before they attempted to repress the religion of the Irish people. The government official, whose job it had been to carry out this execution, reported sadly to his superiors in London that the guilty ones, rather than becoming examples to the people, were considered by all as

Saints and Martyrs. Their fame spread all over Ireland, and indeed, into Europe. Jesus knows how to use His people, how to inspire His people, and how to get the most out of His people. Every time a brother or sister gave up his or her life for the glory of God, for the Kingdom, the rest of the country was strengthened. God is in charge; God is always in charge. Praise be to God.

†

Blessed Francis Taylor - 1621

Francis was one of the elite in Dublin. He came from a wealthy and influential family of merchants. As a young man, he went out on his own, and did very well. At one point in his life, he was elected Mayor of Dublin. He kept his Catholic traditions.

The new mayor had gone over to the Church of Ireland, which was the *Protestant* Church. No Catholic wanted to run for mayor, because they were afraid they might be asked to take the Oath of Allegiance, which they would not do. They knew that could have been a trip to the Dublin Castle, followed by the gallows. Dublin was being represented by two Protestants. The government was attempting to dispose of the Irish Catholics in Parliament, or any government positions.

The Catholics knew they couldn't live with this. They had a meeting. They put up two Catholics as representatives, and held an election. One of them was Francis Taylor. The government reacted immediately. They declared the election and appointments illegal, and had an election of their own. According to the Catholics, by the elections, they were merely replacing two posts left open by Catholics with Catholics. The Protestants disagreed. The upshot was that the Protestants arrested the two men, in addition to other Catholics. It was shocking to all in Dublin that a man of Francis Taylor's station had been arrested. No charges were ever filed against Francis Taylor. No trial was ever held. Francis Taylor was left in the Dublin Castle for seven years, under the worst possible conditions. There were rumors, implications that he was stripped of all his possessions, and unofficially condemned to a life of imprisonment. Information filtered out of the prison that he died on January 30, 1621.

There's a very interesting, but sad point to be made about Francis Taylor, and many of the Irish Martyrs. They were loyal to their Church and their countrymen; they really weren't the ones who were causing all the problems with the British Government. We're not suggesting that those who were in the vanguard were not heroes of the first degree. We're just saying that many of those who were imprisoned were guilty of loyalty to the Church and their God, and for that they were executed by and large. They were not arousing the people to revolt against the government. They did, however, pay the price. And with their Martyrdom, they would for all time arouse the Catholics to be faithful to their Church. We're sure that Our dear Lady, and all the Angels, were waiting for them when their earthly struggle was over, to bring them personally to her Son, Our Lord Jesus, and then to their special place in Heaven. Praise You, Jesus. Thank you, Mother Mary, all the Angels and Saints.

Blessed Fr. Peter Higgins - 1642

The fate of Fr. Peter Higgins, Dominican Priest, was ironic, in that he may have been killed because he helped Protestants, if you can believe that would be possible. We have to remember that over 100 years had passed since the beginning of the persecution of the Irish people. It was getting to be tiresome to some in England.

A lot of things were allowed to pass, based on who was in charge at the time. Since there was no outright rebellion against the crown of England or threat of uprising, there seemed to be an unofficial, unstated tolerance towards Catholics who did not make waves. If they worshiped quietly, secretly, without any fuss, the powers that be were willing to let it slide.

Peter Higgins was a Dublin boy. He was born about 1600, and as a young man, studied under Dominicans who operated out of the backs of houses in Dublin. The front of the house might have been used by a professional man, or an artisan or craftsman, and in the back, these Dominicans lived and taught the Faith, as well as their own charism, based on the spirituality of St. Dominic. It is believed that young Peter was invested into the Dominican Order at one of these Mass-houses, as they were called. Now remember, all of this was under pain of death. The house would be confiscated or burned, the owner sent to prison or worse, and the religious immediately hanged, if they had been caught. This was the world in which Peter grew up.

But there was a great deal of excitement involved. We can't paint a totally dismal picture of their lives. As we research these persecuted, the Irish, the Mexicans, the Polish, we find that their lives were exciting, exhilarating. They wouldn't have had it any other way. Everything they did was a heroic act, offered up for God and country.

[Author's Note: In our book, *The Many Faces of Mary*, we shared about one of these Mass-Houses in Dublin. We'd like to insert that little section for you here, so that you can get some idea of how the Faith was practiced at that time.

"There is a beautiful church in Dublin, called "The Church of Adam and Eve". During the days of persecution, when it was illegal to practice their religion, the Church of Adam and Eve was a pub, called the Adam and Eve pub. Dubliners frequented this pub by the droves, especially on Sunday. Irishmen going into a pub seemed a natural enough thing to the police, so they never questioned the crowds that went into the bar. The people walked in the front door of the Adam and Eve pub, and out the back door, to an underground church. Mass was celebrated under the guise of bringing the family to the local pub. It's very possible that after the Mass, they might have stopped off for a pint; as long as they were there, it would be a sin to waste the visit. They took their lives in their hands by disobeying the law in this way. But it was so important to these beautiful people, they took the chance, knowing He would protect them."[9]]

†

There were a cluster of Mass-houses in the Catholic ghetto in Dublin. When Peter was old enough, he went overseas to learn more about his Faith. He was ordained a Dominican, and joined the community in Spain, somewhere around the year 1627. He stayed in Spain, working with the local Dominican brothers for about six or seven years. In the early 1630's, he returned to his homeland. He went to Naas and ministered there.

---

[9]The Many Faces of Mary, a Love Story - Pg 120

Now, let's think for a moment. Dublin was a large city. It was easy for these brothers to get lost there, to slip through the hands of the police. But in these little villages, like Naas, which was about twenty miles west of Dublin, everyone knew everyone else, and their business as well. We're not suggesting that the Dominicans in *Dublin* were not brave men, but the Dominicans who chose the smaller hamlets put themselves in more of a direct danger of being found out. Such was the choice of Fr. Peter Higgins, Order of Preachers.

He began working near the original Dominican Abbey in Naas, which, of course, had been closed when the situation became dangerous. The Abbey was located almost next door to the parish church, which was Protestant. But Naas was strongly Catholic, so there was a great deal of confidence that Peter and his companions would be safe.

There was a group known as the *"Old English"* in Ireland. These were English who would not buckle under to the religion of Henry VIII, or his daughter, Elizabeth I. They maintained their Catholicism, although they were victims of the same persecution as the Catholics. Then there was the *"Old Irish"*, those who would not take the Oath of Allegiance, and maintained *their* Catholic Faith. They found themselves in league with the Old English, who had never been their friends. You see how the Lord works, bringing people together, for His glory.

An uprising took place in 1641, in which the Old Irish and the Old English became allies, strange bedfellows that they were. The uprising was against some injustices they both felt they had suffered. They banned together as Catholics, and persecuted the Protestants. This was a real switch. The Protestants fled from the area, Ulster, into Dublin. They were desperately seeking help and shelter. In the middle of this, we find Fr. Peter Higgins. His ministry in Naas, was about twenty miles southwest of Dublin. As they were fleeing into Dublin, they stopped on the way at Naas. Fr. Higgins aided the Protestants by hiding them from the Irish rebels, a complete turnaround from what had been happening.

A minister, William Pilsworth, was having a difficult time fleeing from Naas to Dublin. He had ten children. Just the logistics in moving them was difficult. The family found themselves hiding from the Catholics, who were out for blood. A letter from a friend in Dublin, asking Rev. Pilsworth to join in a search for one of the Catholic leaders, Fitzgerald by name, was intercepted.

Pilsworth was immediately taken prisoner by the Irish rebels, and brought out to the forest for execution. The Irish were not out for blood, just for the sake of killing. Therefore, they gave Reverend Pilsworth a trial. They could not honestly find him guilty of any crime. So he was given the choice of giving up his religion, and embracing Catholicism, or be hung. He chose the gallows. He truly believed his Protestant religion to be the just religion.

As they had hoisted him on a horse, with the rope around his neck, they shouted *"Preach here!"* They had good intentions to give the horse a smack, upon which he would go flying off, leaving Reverend Pilsworth hanging by the neck, until he was dead. That was the plan, but that was not how it worked.

A Dominican Priest arrived on the scene, and began begging for the life of the Protestant Minister. Reverend Pilsworth had never seen Peter Higgins before. But because of his plea, the Protestant minister was freed. A time would come when Reverend Pilsworth would have to do the same for Peter Higgins.

A false rumor began that a plot had been hatched by Catholic Priests to annihilate every Protestant in Ireland. The British sent a new governor to Ireland, a cruel man, Sir Charles Coote. He was out to break the back of the conspiracy, no matter what the cost. Coote was actually enough reason to cause any rebellion. He was out to destroy Catholics. He immediately went after any Catholic Priests he could find. But there was a just young man, James Butler, who was in charge of the Army. He was only interested in justice, not persecution. So here we have a Catholic Priest, who is helping Protestants and a Protestant commander-in-chief of the Army, who is being lenient to Catholics.

When James Butler and his troops recaptured Naas, Fr. Peter Higgins went to him and identified himself. He explained how he was helping the Protestants. He was not part of the reported plot. He professed loyalty to the King. James Butler promised Fr. Higgins a fair trial, if one should come up. However, his boss, the infamous Governor Coote came in on the heels of James Butler, and insisted that he arrest Fr. Higgins on suspicion of *anything*, especially the fact that he was a Catholic Priest. He quoted a 1641 law which stated that all Priests had to leave the country, under pain of being judged traitors. James Butler countered that that was *British* law, and had nothing to do with Ireland.

The governor Coote seethed at being blocked by one of his own officers, even if he was right. There was no morality involved here, so though justice was not being served, the governor insisted Higgins be arrested, and put in Dublin Castle. Fr. Higgins was confused. He couldn't figure out why he had been arrested. He had actually helped the Protestants. Many others, Protestants that he had helped, as well as Catholics, felt the same way. Letters were written by prominent people, whom Higgins had saved from the gallows. The pressure was on for the government.

A scheme was concocted by Governor Coote. It was a calculated risk, but he was pretty confident how it would turn out. A proposition was given to Fr. Higgins. They would not only free him, but reward him for the good deeds he had done for the Protestants of Ireland. *All he had to do* was to renounce his loyalty to the Pope and his Church, and embrace the Church of England. He told his captors to present the paper to him on the gallows. He would make his decision there and then.

On the morning of March 23, 1642, Fr. Peter Higgins was brought to the gallows. Coote and his cohorts felt they had a good thing in this Priest. If he were to denounce the Church from the gallows, which they were very confident he would, that would be a coup for them. As per the plan, he was brought to the gallows. He took the document as it was handed to him. He read it to the people, and then rejected it. To paraphrase his statement,[10]

"See here the condition on which I am granted my life. They want me to deny my religion. I spurn their offer. I die a Catholic and a Dominican Priest. I forgive from my heart all who have conspired to bring about my death."

He threw the document to a friend, and signaled the hangman to do his job. As he went to the Father, he praised Our Lord Jesus. A Protestant Minister rushed through the crowd. It was Reverend Pilsworth. He yelled at the top of his lungs, *"This man is innocent! This man is innocent! He saved my life!"* He hoped that he could stop the Priest from falling through the trap in the gallows. But it was too late.

Now Fr. Higgins was not supposed to be executed. Governor Coote had no authority to do what he did. When questioned, nobody wanted to claim responsibility for it. But the young military officer, James Butler, was bound to get to the bottom of it. He accused the lords of the county, who proceeded to blame it on Sir Charles Coote. He argued that he had nothing to do with it. However, nothing ever came of the charges. Fr. Higgins was just another Irish Catholic

---

[10]The information we have comes from a book *"Two Dominican Martyrs from Ireland"*, written in 1992 for the Beatification. Their resource for the statement made by Fr. Higgins comes from what an eye-witness recalled ten years later.

Priest who got caught up in the fight for his Faith. It was possibly the strangest twist of events in our research of the Irish Martyrs. But God worked powerfully through the sacrifice of life of this dedicated son of Ireland.

†

Blessed Bishop Terence Albert O'Brien, O.P. - 1651

Terence O'Brien was born the year after Peter Higgins, 1601. The only difference was that he was from Limerick county, which is quite a distance from Dublin. He most likely studied with the Dominicans in Limerick, and then joined the community in 1622. The situation was the same in Limerick as in Dublin. Brave lay people risked their lives, and those of their families to set up a series of Mass-Houses, in which the family lived in the front of the house, and the Dominicans in the back. It was here that Terence passed his first year, his novitiate, as a Dominican.

We don't know when he left Ireland to go to Europe. We do know he was ordained in Spain in 1627. The Irish had set up two communities in Spain, where they could work, and also train brothers and Priests for missionary work back in Ireland. Terence didn't stay very long after his ordination. He returned to Ireland.

Things were not that bad in Ireland at that time, during the reign of Charles I of England. He slackened the *enforcement* of the actual laws, although discrimination was a way of life. So in the early days, Terence was able to practice his ministry fairly openly. However, with the rebellion of 1641, which was the cause of Fr. Peter Higgins losing his life, the penal laws were put back into practice, full swing. But then two years later, in 1643, the Lord gave the Irish a diversion. King Charles I got into a war. He had no time or men to police Ireland. They had a period of a few years where they virtually ran their own country without any interference from the British. A Catholic Confederation was formed, which handled the governing of the country.

It was during this time, 1643, that Fr. Terence became the provincial of the Dominicans. In his position, he was invited to Rome in 1644, to attend a general chapter of the Dominicans. It opened on Pentecost Sunday, May 14. Fr. Terence shared the tribulation of the people of Ireland, as well as the wholesale massacre of religious which had taken place. He mentioned in particular, Fr. Peter Higgins, a fellow Dominican, who had been a Martyr for his Faith in 1642. While in Europe, Fr. Terence visited Dominican communities in Lisbon, Portugal.

In 1647, Terence was ordained Bishop of Emly. Something we have to consider here is this business of being made Bishop. Many Bishops and Archbishops were taken from the ranks of the religious orders. There were good reasons for that. There were not very many secular Priests, because the Diocese as we know it today, didn't exist. Most vocations came from the Orders. With the Council of Trent, and a renewal of the Church, many religious orders grew in Ireland. The spiritual perspective of the Faith took on greater meaning.

But when these dear men were promoted to higher ranks within the Church, their lives took on more jeopardy. They became visible, whether they wanted to be or not. By the very token of being, first a Priest, and then a Bishop, or Archbishop, they really took their lives in their hands. This is why we're seeing many of these Prelates being raised up in this Beatification Process of the Irish Martyrs. The Bishops were the first line of defense, which the enemy had to smash.

Either they had to kill them, or better yet, they had to break them, make them renounce their Church. Their names were put on a list. Whereas clergy may have been exempted from mercy generally, Bishops were exempted *by name*, and searched for *by name*.

Only a year into his ministry, Bishop Terence was forced to make a stand, which put him in even greater danger. The Catholic Confederation was falling apart. The British, for their part, were looking at Ireland again. The Confederation agreed with the Protestant Viceroy, Earl of Ormond, to a cease-fire. The Papal Nuncio of Ireland, Archbishop Rinuccini, was furious. He immediately condemned it, and directed all his Bishops to do the same. The Bishops, Terence included, not only endorsed the condemnation, but excommunicated anyone who upheld the truce. But it was too late. The damage had been done. The Confederation fell apart. The Papal Nuncio, completely broken, left for Italy shortly thereafter, in February 1649. Terence, and the other Bishops, were left behind.

We don't know whose timing was bad, the Papal Nuncio, or Cromwell. Whatever the case, they both acted about the same time. King Charles I was executed on January 30, and Oliver Cromwell formed the Commonwealth of England immediately thereafter. He was the worst scourge on the Irish people. He instituted the Puritan philosophy of living, which he fully intended to impose on England and Ireland. He hated Catholics with a passion. He was determined to rid the British Empire of them. The only real holdout was Ireland. He was committed to purge that little island of any last remnant of Catholicism.

To that end, he committed money, troops, whatever it took. He crushed the Irish people as much as he possibly could. He put his son-in-law, Henry Ireton, in charge of bringing Ireland into line. If it was possible, Ireton was worse than Cromwell. One of his own people wrote about that time:

"It is an unlawful war, a cruel and bloody work to go to destroy the Irish natives for their consciences and to drive them from their natural and native rights...The cause of the Irish natives in seeking their just freedoms, immunities and liberties is the very same with our cause here."[11]

The Bishops had to flee their dioceses to avoid the persecution under the ironhanded rule of Cromwell. They sought sanctuary in Galway. A meeting was held in Clonmacnoise,[12] reputed to be one of the holiest places in the country. They prayed a great deal. They asked Our Lord Jesus for the wisdom and inspiration, the courage to hold fast to their beliefs. They may have reminded themselves of a statement made by St. Columban to Pope Boniface IV: *"We Irish....are disciples of Sts. Peter and Paul...; we hold unbroken that Catholic Faith which we first received from you."*

They issued a statement condemning Cromwell's rejection of the Mass.[13] They begged the people of Ireland to stick together, forgetting any animosity they may have held against one another, to pray, pray, pray, and fast as if their lives depended on it, because they did. One of the Bishops to sign this decree was Terence Albert O'Brien. The statement found its way all over Ireland. It was just a matter of time. He was a doomed man. Cromwell made a stinging reply to the deposition of the Bishops, to the degree

---

[11]*Two Dominican Martyrs of Ireland* - Page 45

[12]One of the oldest monasteries in Ireland. It is reputed to be the great learning place from which disciples went all over the world, evangelizing in the name of Jesus.

[13]In response to a plea for liberty of conscience for Catholics, Cromwell made the following statement: *"I meddle not with any man's conscience. But if by liberty of conscience you mean a liberty to exercise the Mass, I judge it best to use plain dealing and to let you know, where the Parliament of England has power, that will not be allowed."*

that if the people were going to take the counsel of the
Prelates, he washed himself clean of the blood that would be
shed, and would, with great joy, exercise great severity on the
Bishop.

Cromwell did exactly what he said he would. He turned
on the hot water, until it came out scalding. When he left
Ireland in May 1650, he advised Henry Ireton to finish the
war, whatever it took. Cripple the few cities which were
strongholds of the Catholics. Ireton did this with great
pleasure. He aimed his sights on Limerick. After a military
mistake, Ireton converged all his forces on Limerick. The
people knew they didn't stand a chance. They asked for
surrender. Ireton, cruel and hateful to Catholics, wrote in
his articles of surrender, *"That all such persons now in the city
as shall desire to live peaceably and submit to the Parliament of
England, (except the persons excepted in the second article
foregoing, and except all clergymen, Priests and friars of any
order) shall upon their application to that purpose, have
protection to live quietly."* If Bishop O'Brien didn't get the
hint, he was excluded from the list *by name.*

On Wednesday morning, October 29, 1651, Ireton and
his troops had but to march through the gates of the city.
There was no opposition. He focused immediately on the
clergy. They systematically murdered all the Priests in
various ways. But they hadn't found the Bishop. Ireton
wanted the Bishop.

Bishop Terence Albert O'Brien hadn't taken part in the
surrender of the city. He stayed behind to care for the sick
and dying. They needed him more. He anticipated the
soldiers coming for him. When they did, he surrendered
without resistance. On that very day, he was tried, convicted
and sentenced. He would be hung the following day. He
was charged with stirring up the people against the
government. Bishop O'Brien turned on Ireton, and accused
him of complete lack of humanity and justice. He

prophesied that Ireton would soon have to answer to God for his actions.

The following day, October 30, 1651, Bishop Terence O'Brien, Dominican, Priest of the people, was brought to the gallows, and hung. There are reports that Ireton hated Bishop O'Brien so much, he had his body hang on the gallows for three hours. The body was beaten beyond recognition, until it was just a bloody pulp. His head was cut off, and hung on the gate of the city. It did not decompose, and so after a few days, they had to take it down. It never accomplished what Ireton set out to achieve. Terence O'Brien wouldn't even give his executioner the satisfaction of rotting away. Two weeks after the hanging of the Bishop, Ireton contracted the plague. He was dead within fifteen days. *Don't mess with the Lord!*

†

Blessed Fr. John Kearney - 1653

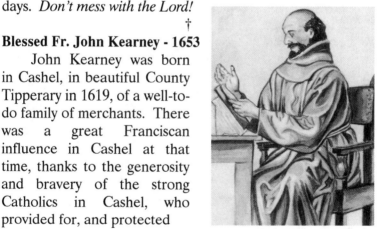

John Kearney was born in Cashel, in beautiful County Tipperary in 1619, of a well-to-do family of merchants. There was a great Franciscan influence in Cashel at that time, thanks to the generosity and bravery of the strong Catholics in Cashel, who provided for, and protected the Franciscans in their midst. John was naturally drawn to them. He had a vocation from his earliest days, even though he was a very normal boy, getting into scraps and being punished. It was a time of gallantry. Many of his playmates only thought about being soldiers, wearing uniforms, and firing muskets, driving the dreaded English out of their country. Many nights, the children would listen at the door of the kitchen when they were supposed to be in bed. They would hear the adults talking about the terrible situation in the country, and what they wanted to do about it. Phases of the revolution may have been conceived in the kitchens of the homes in Cashel.

But John spent most of his time learning from the Franciscans in their Mass-house, in back of a villager's home. When it was determined that he was going to follow in the footsteps of St. Francis, he left the country, as had all the young men before him in search of a vocation. He was sent to an Irish Franciscan college in Louvain, Belgium, named after St. Anthony, one of the great Franciscans of all times. In 1642, at the tender age of 23, he was ordained a Priest. He stayed on in Europe for two years, returning to his native land in 1644.

He was almost killed on the way home, as he went through England. He was captured by the enemy. Remember, it was treason to be a Catholic Priest in England at that time. In 1653, the English law of 1585 was extended to Ireland. It became *treason* in Ireland also, *just being a Catholic Priest!* The Lord still had much work for Fr. John to do, and so he sent His Angels to rescue John, much as He had rescued St. Peter the Prince of the Apostles, before him, because he, too still had work to do. He escaped, and made it back to his hometown, Cashel.   Rather than being discouraged or frightened by having been prisoner of the British, he was excited by his miraculous escape. It became a war story he shared with the Friars.

At the time when Cromwell attacked Limerick City, 1650, John had been ministering fairly openly to the faithful in Cashel and Waterford, which was no great distance from Limerick. He continued his work, being a brave young man that he was, all of 31 years old. But now he had to confine his activities to clandestine meetings in guarded locales. He played cat and mouse with the police and government soldiers for the next three years. His life reminds us a great deal of Blessed Miguel Pro, the Martyr of Mexico, who ministered under the noses of the police and government soldiers by the use of elaborate disguises. We're not told how John Kearney managed to slip through the intricate road blocks put up by Cromwell and Ireton, but he did.

When the Lord felt it was time for John to glorify Him through the giving up of his body for the Faith, He allowed him to be captured, in the spring of 1653. He was brought to Clonmel, not far from his home. Here he was to be judged, sentenced, and executed. How many times had he visited Clonmel in his short life, ministering to the *Catholics there!* What fond memories he had of his exciting life, his Ministry, his love for the people of God, this strong stock of Ireland.

He was tried and convicted, almost in the same breath. As far as a sentence, he was given three choices. The *first*, and most preferred by the government, was that he renounce his Faith, and his allegiance to the Pope, and embrace the Faith of the State. In that case, he would be freed, probably given some kind of reward, and sent on his way. His *second* option was to leave the country in exile, never to return. This was very ironic. He was being told by foreigners, the British, that he would have to leave his homeland, and never return. How could they tell him to leave the land of his birth? But that's what the Irish people were up against. His *third* option was to hang for his treason. John Kearny, possessing Signal Grace, and *Holy Stubbornness*, chose the third. The next day, he proclaimed his guilt of being a Catholic Priest, thanked Our Lord for the gift, and gave his life over to his God. He was 34 years old. As the trapdoor opened, and the noose tightened around his neck, ending his life on earth, we can just hear Jesus whispering in John's ear, *"This day, you will be with Me in Paradise."*

†

Blessed Fr. William Tirry - 1654

William Tirry's life and death was most unusual. He was a contemplative Augustinian, who spent much of his time in prayer and meditation. He maintained an active ministry, but more and more people came to him. He was always on the go, running from one place to another. He is a remarkable Saint.

He was born of a very well-to-do Cork family. They were actually Old English, who worshiped as Catholics, but came from English roots. They were the ones who refused to accept King Henry VIII or Elizabeth as head of the Church. William's family was well known in Cork, and had been for hundreds of years prior to his birth. Many of the Tirrys had served as mayors of Cork, or in high government positions. They were well respected, as was William. He had an uncle who was a Bishop, also named William Tirry.

He was a very reserved youth. He spent much of his time in seclusion, praying, or reading about the Faith and the lives of the Saints. He was well educated, which would fit in with his station in life. He learned English and Latin, most likely Spanish, and Gaelic, the Irish language. When William expressed his desire to become a Priest, he was sent overseas to study. There were more reasons for that than meet the eye. The most obvious was that there was more access to seminary training in countries like Spain or Belgium, because they were free to worship. The atmosphere lent itself to meditation, contemplation, and study. In addition, the young men who attended these Catholic seats of knowledge, were surrounded by Our Lord Jesus in every way. If just made their walk towards their vocations easier.

We know William moved around a lot in Europe. He studied in Valladolid, Spain, in Paris and in Brussels. He was ordained in 1636, and returned home to Ireland in 1637 or 1638. He worked with the local Augustinian community in Cork. But because of his high visibility, being one of rank, he had to maintain a low profile. Often, he spent months away from the city, working first for his uncle, the Bishop of Cork and Cloyne; then when things became hot, as chaplain for his cousin, and tutor for his cousin's children. He expanded his ministry to other members of his family, although they were distant relatives. He acted as spiritual director and tutor for many of those who lived in proximity to where he was. It was during this time that he met Mrs. John Everard of Fethard, who was to give him sanctuary for the last four years of his life.

In 1646, things in Ireland began to open up for Catholics. It was only a temporary thing, but it gave the Augustinians, and Fr. Tirry in particular, the opportunity to come out from hiding and practice their ministries in relative freedom. This was because the King of England, Charles I was engaged in a war, which took his attention and his troops away from Ireland.

This openness was good for the Priests, but on the other hand, it presented its problems. When Cromwell took over, after defeating Charles I and executing him, finding out who the Priests and Bishops were in Ireland, and where they were located, was a fairly easy task, because they had come out into the open.

During that time, Fr. William was assistant to the Augustinian Provincial, Fr. Denis O'Driscoll for almost three years. They moved all around the country in their capacity, but their headquarters was in Fethard, in Tipperary. When things began to deteriorate badly in 1649, Fr. Tirry was assigned as prior to an Augustinian abbey in Skreen. He never made it there, however, because Cromwell came in with full force, and forced every religious into hiding. Fr. William went to his relative's home, Fr. Everard in Grove, near Fethard. They worked with the people in the local community, and those who would come from far and near to be ministered to by Fr. Tirry.

This is where it gets really exciting. While Fr. Tirry never left this area, his reach expanded to many areas outside Tipperary. He began to be known as a very spiritual Priest, a gifted confessor and counselor. Especially in the time that they were entering into, it was extremely necessary for the people to have someone they could come to. Fr. Tirry's days were so busy, he had to cut down on his sleeping time, in order to accommodate his schedule. His *"house imprisonment"* reminds us of St. Paul's time in Rome, when he was first arrested and put under house arrest for two years. He ministered more to the people of Rome from that one house than he was able to do running all over the city. The same applied to Fr. Tirry.

But four years was too long for a Priest to stay in one place during that time. The law of averages was against him. Someone was bound to turn him in, for the thirty pieces of silver they would be paid. This is exactly what happened to Fr. Tirry. Someone in the town told the soldiers where to find him. On March 25, which was Holy Saturday, in 1654, just as he was about to begin the celebration of the Mass in the home in which he was hiding, the soldiers broke in. He was vested up, and ready. That was a severe strike against him. In addition, they found papers on his desk, which were against the Protestants, and in defense of the Catholics. This was as bad, or even worse. At any rate, Fr. Tirry was brought to Clonmel and put in prison.

The end of Fr. Tirry's life was unique. In prison, he had four other Priests, who were also arrested, as companions. From the time he was put into jail, he was the unofficial spiritual director of the prison. He led the others in prayer;

he consoled them. He brought the Eucharist into prison with him. For all the time he was incarcerated, he and the other Priests received Our Lord Jesus in the Eucharist. On the day he walked to the gallows, he was fortified with the Body of Christ.

He forced his brother Priests, by his example, to concentrate more on their *spirituality*, and less on their *corporality*. He became their role model. Also, interestingly enough, he was the only one of the five Priests to be executed. The other four were exiled from the country.

Fr. William was held prisoner in Clonmel for five weeks. This was unusual, in that prisoners were usually judged and sentenced the same day, and executed the next day. But Fr. William Tirry had a reputation, and it was not one for which he was hated, but one for which he was held in awe by the public, the Priests, the police, and the prisoners. His reputation for holiness preceded him. The biographers are even confused as to why he was treated so well. But in the jail, he was afforded every courtesy. The only possible explanation we can give is they must have seen the aura of Jesus emanate from the eyes of the Priest. During those five weeks of captivity, people came from all over, to have their sins forgiven, to receive counsel from the good Priest. *And nobody stopped them!* God is so powerful; God is so good.

Fr. Tirry's trial was a farce, at its best. The saddest thing was that the Priest defended himself with all his heart, truly believing that somehow, possibly because there was a jury of good men, justice might be served. The truth of it is that as the jury left the courtroom to deliberate on the verdict, the head jurist asked of the colonel in charge if Fr. Tirry should be found guilty. He nodded a definite yes.

Of all the executions we have described in this chapter on the Irish Martyrs, none comes close to what happened with Fr. Tirry. He was allowed to process from his cell to the gallows in full Augustinian vestments. While he was handcuffed, he was not pushed or pulled or manhandled in any way. Just short of the scaffold, he stopped and knelt. The other man, who was to be hung at the same time as Fr. Tirry, was to be first. He was a layman, Peter Power. While Mr. Power was being executed, Fr. Tirry knelt, and prayed for the soul of Mr. Power.

When it was his turn, he began walking up the steps of the scaffold. He looked at the crowd of people looking up at him. There had to be at least a thousand. As he mounted each step, he gave a teaching to the people. He taught on the Ten Commandments, and the Seven Sacraments. He shared especially on the Eucharist, and on the Pope, to whom he gave his spiritual allegiance.

A very unusual thing happened. During Fr. Tirry's preaching, a Protestant minister began arguing with him from the crowd. He was no match for the wisdom and infused knowledge Fr. Tirry had been given from the Lord. Not only the people were swayed by Fr. Tirry's convincing explanation of the Eucharist, but many of the Protestants appeared to be in accord with the Priest. Finally, in a fit of panic, the Protestant Minister asked the soldier in charge to move along with the execution. He was truly fearful that he was losing his people. But the Marshall wouldn't have any of it. He allowed Fr. Tirry to talk as long as he wanted.

As a last blessing, Fr. Tirry forgave those who had turned him in, as well as those who were involved with his execution. He asked for absolution from any Priest who may be in the vicinity. Then he gave the signal to the executioner, and the sentence was carried out. As the pressure from the noose tightened around his neck, blood flowed out of his nose. People ran up onto the scaffold, trying to catch some of it in their handkerchiefs, to keep as relics of a Saint. They tried to tear some of his clothing from his body. They knew they had witnessed the execution of a

Saint. They were sure he would remember them if they prayed to him for his intercession.

There is proof of this happening! The Priest who was with Fr. Tirry to the end, Canon Conway, was exiled from Ireland. He brought with him, relics of Fr. Tirry, to give to the Augustinians in Brussels. During the voyage over the sea, a violent storm broke out. All feared for their lives. They were sure the ship was going down. Prayers were offered to the Saint who had died only days before. Fr. Conway took out the relic of Fr. Tirry, and prayed for his intercession. As quickly as this had been done, the sea calmed, and the storm subsided. We had been given a sign from Heaven that one of Our Lord Jesus' favorite brothers, one of Our Lady's special sons, had come home, and he was working for the Kingdom in Heaven.

†

There are hundreds of thousands of brothers and sisters in Ireland who gave their lives for their Faith. These are only seventeen of those heroes, on whom the Church was able to get enough information to put through the Cause for Beatification. They are called the **Seventeen Martyrs of Ireland**. They are standing in for the rest of their brothers and sisters whose names are not written in our Calendar of Saints, but are surely numbered among those *"who washed their robes and made them white in the blood of the Lamb."*[14] These seventeen were beatified in September, 1992. But we cannot end the book on the Irish Martyrs without sharing with you the only Irish Martyr canonized to this date. His name is St. Oliver Plunket. He is said to be the last man to have been executed for the Faith.

†

---

[14]Rev - 7:14

St. Oliver Plunket - 1681

Oliver Plunket was born in 1629 in Oldcastle, county Meath, into the turmoil that was Ireland's heritage. It was during the dreaded persecution, the people suffered at the hands of their closest neighbors, the British. He was educated at the Benedictine Abbey in Meath by his kinsman, Patrick Plunket, who later went on to become the Bishop of Meath. Oliver was a brilliant boy. He came to the attention of the Pope's envoy, Fr. Scarampi, who brought Oliver back to Rome to finish his education in the Faith. He was ordained from the Irish College in Rome, in 1654. This was just about at the height of Cromwell's massacre of the Irish People. Prudence dictated that Fr. Plunket remain in Rome. He could do more alive working in Rome, than he could dead in Ireland.

Oliver waited until his superiors felt it was the right time for him to return to his native land. In the meantime, he earned degrees in canon and civil law, and became the Roman representative to the Irish Bishops. But he was just preparing for his work, which he knew would bring him ultimately home.

In 1669, the Primate of Ireland died in exile in France. Oliver was chosen by the Pope to replace him. He went to Belgium to be ordained, and installed as Archbishop of Armagh, which would be considered Northern Ireland today. He entered the country incognito in 1670, but within six weeks, the power of the Lord through this committed soldier, was felt notably. He went on a stampede for the Lord.

Within six weeks, he baptized ten thousand Irishmen. In five years, he had confirmed more than fifty thousand. He traveled all over his twelve diocese province, bringing the Faith back to those who had lost it, bringing back courage to those who had had it beaten out of them, bringing back the spirit to his Priests, whose fortitude had been beaten out of them. The Mass was celebrated again, in this land of hopelessness. Their God had not left them orphans. He would be with them until the end of time, and Archbishop Plunket was His man in Ireland, the man to make it happen.

The Lord uses who He will, and puts them into the positions, He wants them in, so that they can be used by Him. In the instance of Oliver Plunket, he came from a very noble and influential family. A lot of the things he was able to get away with were because of favors owed to various members of his family. Another thing we have to remember is that all this work he did, was without churches. *He had no churches!* He had the fields, and that was all.

Celebration of the Mass in the Penal Days

We're not sure if the tradition of the Altar Rock was begun during the time of Oliver Plunket. The practice was begun when it became illegal to celebrate Mass in Ireland. So it might have begun long before Oliver Plunket. The Priest and the congregation would go out into the fields, and find a flat stone, like a table. The Priest would celebrate Mass on that stone, while some of the community would stand watch. If the police or soldiers raided the Mass, everyone would flee in different directions, so the least amount of people would be caught and punished. There was a good reason for this. In Ireland, during that time, if a Mass was celebrated in a house, for instance, the Priest would be killed; the people would be jailed; the house would be confiscated or burned.

Archbishop Plunket had to do a lot of his traveling in disguise. According to his own writings, he used every possible form of camouflage imaginable, to wind his way past road blocks, armed guards, vicious dogs, and soldiers whose greatest joy would have been to capture the *"criminal Bishop"*, and have him tortured and killed. But the Lord had powerful work for Oliver Plunket, and so he just kept going. His philosophy was that he would go at breakneck speed for the Lord until He was finished with him. Then, when his job was over, the Lord would just take him home. As St. Bernadette of Lourdes said of herself, *"The Blessed Virgin used me like a broom. What do you do with a broom, when you have finished sweeping? You put it back in its place, behind a door!"*[15]

There was a great deal of excitement during those days. Oliver Plunket gathered followers all around him. They wanted to be part of what was going on. Their lives took on new meaning. They felt there was a reason for their existence. Everything became important. A network of believers was begun. God was forming an army of this staunch Irish flock.

Even the hardships they had to endure took on a heroic glint. You have to remember that Plunket came from a very well-to-do family. He never had to do without anything in his life. All of a sudden, he found himself sleeping under the stars, in the freezing cold, with rain and hale as his companions. There were times they passed days on end in barns, with only the body heat of the animals to keep them

[15]Laurentin, Rene - *A Hundred Years Ago, Bernadette* - 1979

warm. But it was okay. It was great. Life was worth living. And they always knew that the more successful they were in their mission for the Lord, the closer they were to having a noose squeeze the life out of them. But that was all right too. They wouldn't have changed a minute of their lives.

This is what enthusiasm and courage Oliver Plunket was able to instill in his little province in the northeastern part of this destitute country. For ten years, he played his cat and mouse game with the authorities, all the while, teaching his followers how to do the same. He got caught in the middle of a political scheme, which was designed to kill more Catholics in Ireland. An Englishman called Titus Oates, who must have had some influence in England if people were willing to listen to his nonsense, falsely accused the Pope, King Louis XIV of France, and the Jesuits of concocting a plot to invade Ireland, and liberate it. According to his logic, the next step would be to invade England. Enough people believed it so that every clergyman in England and Ireland had to hide for fear of being caught. But not Archbishop Oliver Plunket.

He went to Dublin to visit his relative, Bishop Patrick Plunket, who was dying. Oliver was arrested in Dublin, and thrown into the Castle. They decided to try this new plot, concocted by Titus Oates on Archbishop Plunket. The government lined up a long list of lying witnesses, and trumped up charges. They were also able to put together a variety of defrocked or dissolute religious who had been disciplined by the Archbishop over the ten years. There is always someone who hates you. A Priest once told us we have enemies we don't even know. The same was with Oliver Plunket, multiplied a thousand fold.

The phony trial didn't make it. It was just too loose, too bizarre. Not even the witnesses for the crown showed up. And so, it fell apart. Well, they still had Oliver Plunket. They were not about to let him go. They sent him over to

London, where they could start up the trial all over again, with more of a stacked deck. Oliver Plunket was brilliant, but he didn't stand a chance. He was not allowed to bring over witnesses from Ireland. He was not allowed to cross-examine any of the people, the Crown put up. It was a total travesty. But it cost Oliver Plunket his life. He described the proceedings in a letter to a relative, Michael Plunket.

"On the eighth of this month I was brought to trial, accused of introducing the Catholic religion, of preparing 70,000 men for rebellion, collecting money for them, exploring the fortresses and forts of Ireland, and of destining Carlingford as the landing-place for the French. I applied for time to bring my witnesses from Ireland, but in vain. I argued that the pretended crime having been committed in Ireland, it should be there discussed, or that at least a jury should be brought then, who would be better acquainted with the circumstances and condition of those concerned; but everything was denied to me.

"Two Franciscan friars were the principal accusers against me, the one named John MacMoyer and the other Hugh Duffy, and a certain Priest of the MacClanes. Four seculars (laymen) also appeared against me, viz., two of the O'Neills, a certain Hanlon and Florence MacMoyer. As to these four, I never saw them in my life....

"When I alleged that no one was ever known, when accused before the tribunals in Ireland, to have been afterwards summoned to answer the same charges in England, the judge eluded my argument...Sentence of death has been passed against me....and thus those who beheaded me in effigy have now attained their intent of beheading the prototype....My conscience never reproached me with being guilty of any conspiracy or rebellion, direct or indirect. Oh, would to God that I were as free from every other stain and sin against the divine precepts as I am from this. Therefore it is necessary for all my friends to pray for me, as I confide they will."

Oliver Plunket died a brutal, horrible death. He was tied to the tail of a horse, and dragged through the streets of the town, to the hanging place. His actual execution is too cold-blooded to even describe. It is only another example of man's heartless inhumanity to man. It has been echoed through the pages of this book.

Oliver Plunket was canonized at St. Peter's Basilica on October 12, 1975 by Pope Paul VI. As part of the canonization, His Holiness said the following:

"He would not compromise with truth or condone violence. His constant plea was for pardon and peace. He would not substitute another gospel for the Gospel of love and peace. His words of love and pardon rang from the scaffold on which he was about to hang. They were words of blessing and forgiveness: 'I forgive all who had a hand directly or indirectly in my innocent blood'. O what an example, especially for the Irish people of whom he was one and to whom he ministered."

We are told that Oliver Plunket was the last of the Irish Martyrs. And yet, even as he was being canonized in 1975, a war was raging in his Province, Armagh, which is today in Northern Ireland. The people of Ireland have suffered greatly to be Catholics. No wonder Our Lady didn't have anything to chastise them for when she visited them in Knock in 1879. She was congratulating them for a job well-done, for being a faithful people in a completely deceitful world. It is now the 1990's, the last decade of this millennium, and nothing's changed. The locations may change, the faces and names may change, but the suffering and agony goes on. The brave men and women of Ireland are still being persecuted, not in quite the same way as those who went before them, but as long as they maintain their Faith, and exercise their God-given gift of Holy Stubbornness, they will pay the price. And they are willing to make that sacrifice. *Erin go Bragh!*

English Martyrs

Those who would destroy our Church, have forgotten the price we have paid for her. This is a story of men who would not compromise their Church, not even for the King and country they dearly loved.

How does a just king, a loyal *Defender of the Faith*, turn on all that he vowed to protect, betraying Church and country? Was it the limitless power he had, the power to decide between life and death, that gave birth to him placing himself above his Pope and Church? Was it the example of other Henrys before him? This chapter is about one man's infamy and the powerful men and Martyrs God raised up to defend His Church. But before we speak of King Henry VIII, and the Martyrs who died rather than deny the Church, we want to touch briefly on some of his predecessors.

Henry II, Emperor of the Holy Roman Empire who became emperor in 1056, at the age of six years old, fought against Pope Gregory VII. The Pope excommunicated him. What did that Henry do? He went to Canossa, Italy where the Pope was living. It was winter and there was snow on the ground. He stood outside the Pope's castle donned in coarse sackcloth, for three days in the bitter cold. The Pope forgave him and took him back into the Church. This Henry's reign was filled not only with battles against the German Kings and the Pope but against his own sons.

Had he taught them, through his disobedience to the foster father that Jesus had left, the successor to Peter, the Pope, they did not have to respect and obey him, their earthly father? And so, once again, disobedience breeds disobedience and division. A new Henry would disobey. But he would not beg forgiveness, and the innocents would suffer.

St. Thomas Becket - Martyr of the Middle Ages (1118-1170)

Thomas Becket was born on the Feast Day of St. Thomas the Apostle, in 1118. He lost both his parents when he was twenty one. He was educated with the Canons regular. At twenty-four, he obtained a position in the home of the Archbishop of Canterbury. He received minor orders; the Archbishop was so fond of him, Thomas obtained many favors. He was ordained deacon, in 1154, and  then the Archbishop appointed him Archdeacon of Canterbury. Now, this was an important position, second only to that of a Bishop or Abbot. The Archbishop entrusted his most delicate affairs to him to manage, seldom doing anything without asking his advice. He sent him to Rome on a very important mission. Thomas Becket never gave the Archbishop cause to regret the confidence he placed in him.

Thomas Becket was the kind of man, monarchs liked to have around them. He spoke frankly, had the gift of discernment and an understanding so profound, he was always able to answer difficult questions plainly and simply. It was his diplomacy that swayed Blessed Pope Eustace III to discourage the succession to the throne to Stephen's son, making the crown secure for Henry of Anjou. Later as King

Henry II, he would appoint Becket, at age thirty-six, as his Chancellor. Thomas Becket not only served the King well and faithfully, but became his intimate *friend*. They are said to have had *"one heart and one mind"*. He influenced King Henry to bring about much needed reforms. But their friendship went beyond their common interest in affairs of state. They were friends who enjoyed one another; they laughed together; they had fun together.

Thomas Becket had an entourage almost as large and grand as the King himself. As Chancellor, he led a predominantly secular grandiose existence. He was proud and arrogant. But there was another side to Thomas Becket, the man who went on retreats, would subject himself to heavy penitential disciplines, was spotted praying during his nightwatches. His confessor said that at the beginning of his his career Becket's life was blameless, even under the most menacing circumstances and enticements.

The Archbishop of Canterbury died in 1161. King Henry wanted to raise Becket to that position, but he protested that if he became Archbishop they would lose their close friendship; their friendship would turn from love into hatred. He told his friend and king that, as Archbishop he could not condone the things he does against the Church. King Henry would not listen to any of Thomas Becket's arguments. But Becket was resolved, until Cardinal Henry of Pisa, legate from the Holy See overruled his objections as over scrupulosity. He was elected in 1162, and set out to Canterbury from London. On the way, he reached out humbly to several of his Priests from his church to alert him when they detect any faults in his character or conduct.

He was ordained Priest on Saturday of Whit-week[1], and on the octave of Pentecost, he was consecrated Bishop of Rochester. Something happened to Thomas Becket when

---

[1] The week of Pentecost

he received the pallium from Pope Alexander III. By the end of the year, there was a visible change. He wore a hairshirt next to his skin. No more fancy clothes for him. He donned the plain cassock of a Parish Priest. He rose early in the morning and read Holy Scriptures. At nine each morning, he sang Holy Mass, or was present when another Priest celebrated. He gave twice the alms to the poor, his predecessor had given. He took a nap in the afternoon and when he dined with guests and his household, instead of music, a spiritual book was read. Although he was generous with portions for his guests, he ate moderately. He visited the infirmary and the monks who worked in the cloister, each day. He personally screened and interviewed candidates for the Priesthood. He became a Priest and a Bishop!

Although he resigned as Chancellor, after he was raised to Archbishop, he and the King remained the good friends they had always been. Until they had their first disagreement! It was customary for each landowner and farmer to pay two shillings a year for each hide on their land to the local sheriffs of the counties, for protection against unsavory local officials. It was graft of the worst kind. This sum was then ordered to be paid into the the King's exchequer. The Archbishop argued that this was a voluntary payment and could not be exacted as revenue by the crown. He added if the sheriffs defended the people, they would pay, otherwise no! The King was furious and swore: *"By God's Eyes, this shall be paid!"* to which Becket retorted: *"By the reverence of Those Eyes, my lord King."* Henry did not press on, but a chasm grew between them that would become too wide to cross.

There were many battles fought, as the friend became more and more the Bishop. When a cleric was accused of wrong-doing, the Archbishop insisted they be tried before his court. The King accused him of showing clemency because he was a Priest. October, 1163, the King called the Bishops to a Council and ordered all clerics, accused of crimes, to be handed over to the civil courts to be tried and punished. When the Bishops began to weaken, Archbishop Becket pressed them to remember they were pledged to protect their Priests, insuring they would be treated fairly, that they were sons of the Bishops and if punishment was to be enacted, it was the place of their Bishop to do it. The King ordered all the Bishops to observe his mandates. St. Thomas and the other Bishops agreed but with a qualification: "*saving their order*". The King took this as a refusal, and the next day ordered Thomas Becket to relinquish certain castles and honors bestowed upon him as Chancellor.

The King, remembering their friendship, tried in vain to get Becket to change his stand, and accept his conditions. For awhile, because of little encouragement from Pope Alexander III, Thomas Becket agreed to accept the royal customs.   But when he read the provisions of the constitutions which contained the royal customs, he refused once again to affix his seal to the documents.   Areas he strenuously objected to were: *No prelate could leave the kingdom without the royal license, or appeal to Rome without the King's consent, no one could be excommunicated without the royal will.* It went from bad to worse, but the crowning blow was that clerics convicted and sentenced by ecclesiastical courts had to be turned over to the civil jurisdiction of the royal officers, and would be exposed to possible double punishment.

There was no chance of reconciliation between Becket and the King. The King made false claims of money due the crown which he had already discharged. He added fines for Becket not appearing in his court. It went on and on. When he was ordered to pay up or face judgment, Becket said he would not be judged by anyone but by the Pope who solely had jurisdiction over him. He left the court with shouts of

Traitor! following him, and some from fellow Bishops who chose to serve "*man rather than God*".

Becket left for France where the Pope was staying. The Bishops and members of the King's court arrived before Becket and having accused him, left before he reached the Pope. When Becket arrived, he showed the Pope the sixteen constitutions. The Pope not only agreed they were intolerable but severely chastised Becket for compromising in the first place. Becket kneeled before the Pope and accused himself of having received the See of Canterbury uncanonically. Although it was against his will, he confessed he shared in the sin, and removed his Bishop's ring, and left the Pope's presence. The Pope called him back and reinstated Becket, only now canonically, as Archbishop, insisting that for him to refuse would be to abandon the cause of God.

Becket went to a Cistercian Monastery to do penance for his sins. In the meantime, the King confiscated all his property and that of his family, friends and domestics. He sent them to France so that Becket, seeing them, would be moved and return to England and the King's judgment. In addition, the King advised the general chapter of Cistercians that he would confiscate all their property, within his realm, if Becket remained at the Monastery. The Abbot can hardly be blamed for kind of hinting that perhaps Becket should leave the monastery. After nearly six years of haggling, with the King of France now brought into the struggle, King Henry and Thomas Becket met and reconciled.

The streets leading to Canterbury were lined with cheering faithful welcoming their Archbishop back. But Becket had made enemies of the other Bishops and they would not rest until he was removed. At the court of King Henry, someone exclaimed, there would not be any peace for the realm while Becket lived. And then, King Henry in one of his uncontrollable rages, repeated "*Who will rid me of this turbulent Priest?"* The words no sooner out, he, in his heart, knew he would regret them over and over again. His words would soon become a reality.

The Archbishop received a letter warning him of his danger. Four knights arrived from England, and insisted he remove the cinctures from three of his Bishops. When he refused, they threatened and swore they would return. And return, they did, but not before the Archbishop's men hustled him off to the Church. The frightened monks in the Church bolted the door quickly behind the Archbishop, locking out some of their monks. The Archbishop insisted they unlock the doors and allow the monks to enter. He remonstrated them, saying: *"This is a church, not a castle"*. Petrified with fear, all fled, leaving the Archbishop alone, with only one monk staying behind. The knights, joined by a sub-deacon, shouted *"Where is Thomas, the traitor?"* Becket replied he was no traitor, but an Archbishop and Priest of God. One of the knight's response to his question *"Reginald, you have received many favors from me. Why do you come into my church armed?"* was for the knight to swing his axe menacingly at the Archbishop. St. Thomas spoke: *"I am ready to die, but God's curse be on you if you harm my people"* One of the knights drew his sword and struck St. Thomas' head and blood ran down his face. St. Thomas cried out: *"Into Your Hands, I commend my spirit!"* They struck him again with the sword, bringing him down on his knees. He gasped: *"For the name of Jesus and in defense of the Church, I am willing to die."* With that, he fell forward, and a knight struck him another blow, severing his scalp. The sub-deacon scattered his Archbishop's brains with his sword, and the cowards ran out shouting: *"The King's men! the King's men!"*

For a long while, no one dared touch the Archbishop's body. But he would not be left for long. Before dawn began to cut through the dark night, people began calling him Martyr and Saint. They dipped cloths in his blood that would be used as relics, and miracles began to happen immediately. The indignation over an Archbishop being murdered in his own church spread throughout Europe, and there was wide-spread clamoring for the canonization of Thomas Becket

The indignant, outraged people of the world demanded no less than a most humiliating form of public penance for King Henry. The King, for his part, although he never meant for Becket to be killed, grieved and fasted for forty days. July 1174, eighteen months after Thomas Becket was solemnly canonized as a Martyr by Pope Alexander, King Henry went to the Cathedral where his friend and Archbishop had been slain, and humbly did public penance.

July 7, 1220, St. Thomas' body was solemnly processed from its tomb in a crypt to a shrine behind the main altar. This became one of the most visited shrines by pilgrims of the Christian world.

The feast of St. Thomas of Canterbury, as St. Thomas Becket is known, has been kept throughout the Church from the very beginning, and in England he is venerated as protector of the secular clergy.

†

King Henry IV. The rulers of England declared themselves the rightful rulers of France and by 1422, England had overrun most of northern France, including Paris and were heading southward. The ruler of France was the weak King Charles. But the Lord raised up a Saint who would become a Martyr, sold out by the French King she had helped and by another King Henry's decree. She, like the other Martyrs in this book had heard the word of the Lord and said *Yes*! **St. Jeanne d' Arc** was burned at the stake.[2] It was during the reign of King Henry IV that a Saint was put to death for listening to the Lord. 500 years later,

---

[2]see chapter on Joan of Arc

she was officially proclaimed a Saint by the Church she loved.

What was the legacy and example left by the English King? More Martyrs to be perpetuated by his successors. And so, once pandora's box of power was opened, another King Henry would dip into it, and hate and division would be the sad struggle of England and her cousins on the British Isle for centuries. The Martyrs in this book followed the *love* perpetuated by their King, Our Lord Jesus Christ and His successors, and we, their heirs, can do no less.

King Henry VIII. On May 30, 1431, Jeanne d' Arc died and by 1491, a new King would be born who would be responsible not only for the Martyrs we will speak about in this chapter but be the catalyst for the ongoing Martyrdom of so many more. Some of these you will read about in our chapter on the Irish Martyrs.

King Henry, when you faced Our Lord Jesus, which were the crimes revealed that so deeply touched you that you condemned yourself?[3] Was it the men who had dearly loved you and you condemned to death because they could not be a party to your sin? Or was it the rift and division caused by your avarice and selfishness that would pit brother against brother for centuries and centuries, the bloodshed never ending?

The saddest reaction to King Henry's action was the part he would play in leading his faithful innocent subjects unknowingly away from their beloved Church. They never knew what hit them! They loved him! They trusted him! He was their king! The people of England have always loved the Monarchy, willing to accept whatever hardships necessary for King (or Queen) and country. They had been so proud when King Henry VIII was proclaimed "*Defender of*

---

[3]It is said that when we stand before Our Lord Jesus, all we have done will be revealed and then He does not condemn us, but we condemn ourselves.

the Faith" by Pope Leo X. They would never be able to accept that he would do anything against them and their immortal souls, no less attack the Church he had pledged to defend.

When did it all start? When did the *"Defender of the Faith"* turn from a loyal son of the Church to Heretic-Schismatic? When his brother King Henry the VII died, King Henry married his widow, the Spanish princess - Catherine of Aragon. They had a daughter - Mary (who would later become Queen of England). But that was not good enough for the King. He wanted a son who would some day carry on as King of England. When Catherine failed to give him sons, he decided to divorce her and marry Anne Boleyn. He asked the Pope to nullify his marriage to Catherine, declare it illegal, that it never existed. Of course, the Pope refused. Now, that was not easy to do. King Henry had defended the Church against Luther, saving the faithful of England from falling into heresy. But, the Pope had no choice. Jesus had said it, and he had to obey: *"What God has joined together, let not man put asunder.*[4]*"*

When the Pope refused to condone his plan, King Henry the VIII set up his own church and declared himself Head of his newly founded church, the Church of England.

King Henry VIII married the English Anne Boleyn, who later proved disappointing by giving Henry a girl instead of a boy. Her name was Elizabeth. She would later become Queen Elizabeth I. After three short years, poor Anne Boleyn lost favor with the King. She had failed to give him any sons. He accused her of misconduct and had her beheaded!

He then married Anne Seymour who finally gave him the son he so ardently desired. The baby was named Edward. He later became King Edward VI. Well, Anne

---

[4]Mark 10:9

Seymour did not live long enough to suffer the fate of those others who had not met the King's expectations. She died giving birth to Edward.

Henry was to go through wife after wife, dissolving marriage after marriage by simply declaring it never existed - nullifying it, or by beheading the wife who lost favor. But as our Lord would have forgiven Judas if he had only repented as Peter had, Our Lord sent men to King Henry to stand firm in trying to keep him from doing this heinous act that would reverberate so much pain and division. They were sent to him to save his soul. But the self-indulgence and gluttony he practiced, putting himself before and above others, would become an addiction that could not be satisfied or arrested. One of the men Our Lord sent was John Fisher.

†

St. John Fisher - Cardinal and Martyr (1469-1535)

We are in the year 1469. The Church would be attacked brutally, once again, and God would raise up Saints who would defend the Church and shed their blood, if need be. John Fisher was to be one of those Saints. He was born into a poor family. He lost his father when he was very young; yet he entered Cambridge University at the age of fourteen.

He was a fine scholar, excelling in school. So outstanding were his accomplishments, he was ordained a Priest, by special permission, when he was merely twenty-two years old.

King Henry VII was king. His mother met John Fisher and when she soon became aware of his piety and wisdom, she chose him to be her spiritual director. Through John Fisher's influence, the King's mother spent her remaining years dedicating her life to God. She encouraged students eager to learn. She used her wealth to help them financially, as well. Through him, she also became patroness of Cambridge University.

In 1504, John Fisher was elected Chancellor of Cambridge. His great works and pastoring skills came to the attention of King Henry VII who recommended he be ordained a Bishop. He was only 35 years old. Now, John Fisher did not want to take on this added responsibility, fearing it would take away from his commitment to Cambridge. But we have an expression "*Doers do*". If you want a job done, call on someone who is busy. John Fisher never neglected his duties at Cambridge and yet spiritually ministered to his diocese tirelessly and wisely. Neither of his appointed tasks suffered because of the other. When Luther and his schismatic doctrines were infiltrating London and the universities, John Fisher wrote many volumes successfully refuting Luther's heresies. His books were the *first* published defending the Church against Luther's attack on the Faith.

When King Henry VII and his mother died, St. John Fisher sadly preached at their funeral Masses. With King Henry VII's death, *King Henry the VIII* became the new monarch. He recognized the outstanding qualities his mother and brother had experienced and he proclaimed John Fisher the finest prelate to be found in any kingdom in the world!

†

Upon his brother's death, King Henry the VIII married his brother's widow - Catherine of Aragon, taking her as his first wife. Everything went well, until she made the fatal mistake of giving birth to a daughter (who would later become Queen Mary I). This became a giant problem! She had not given the King a son! Out she goes! He decided to divorce her and take a new wife, Anne Boleyn. The Pope refused the King's request to have the marriage nullified, and King Henry VIII left the Church and began his own church, *The Church of England*. Now, he would be free to marry Anne Boleyn, and he would have the male heir he desired.

John Fisher was chosen to defend Catherine. He stood before the court and ably presented the argument that the marriage was valid and could not be nullified by *any* power, human or divine. He gave St. John the Baptist as an example, who had been beheaded because he had come against King Herod who had defiled the sanctity of marriage. When this reached the King, he became furious! The case went to Rome. John Fisher no longer had any connection with it.

You would think that would be the end of it, wouldn't you? After all, John Fisher had done all he could to stop the King from sinning against God and His Church! He had defended the Sacrament of Matrimony! But now, the next step, Our Lord would call him to, was to defend the rights of the Roman Catholic Church, and the Pope. In order for his subjects to accept him and his new Church, the King knew he had to have the clergy behind him. After all, to the people, they were their *teachers* and were respected as the faithful passers down of the Lord's Word and Church. King Henry issued a decree forcing his Priests to pledge loyalty to the Church of England and to King Henry as the rightful head of the Church. John Fisher denounced the courts that were passing down these dictates from the King. He could not stand silent while the King and his courts denied the Roman Catholic Church as the true Church and the Pope as the rightful head of the Church. As a member of the House of Lords, he denounced the measures that were being instituted against the clergy down through the Commons, loudly crying out: "*It is nothing but* **'Down with the Church!'**"

He persistently denied the King's claim as head of the Church in England. His friends tried to warn him to back off, a little. He couldn't! Twice he was imprisoned; they tried to poison him; he was shot at through his window in his study. They even tried to smear his name.

Things never stand still. Bishop Fisher was summoned to appear at a meeting concerning a bill which would declare that children resulting from the King's marriage to Anne Boleyn would be rightful successors to the throne of England after his death. Although so ill he fainted on the way to the meeting, Bishop Fisher attended. It would have been a valid excuse to not go, and probably save his life. Because, with every motion against the wishes of the King, he was driving another nail into his coffin. Now, like Saint Thomas More, John Fisher did not object to the succession in itself. But unlike the other Bishops of England, he refused to take the oath, as it declared recognition of King Henry as *supreme head of the Church*. He did not condemn his fellow Bishops for taking the oath, saying: "*Their conscience will save them, and mine must save me.*"

The King removed him as Bishop and had John Fisher imprisoned in the Tower of London, on April 26th, 1534. On May 21st of the following year, Pope Paul III raised him to Cardinal. This infuriated King Henry and hastened the end of John Fisher. Furiously, he barked: "*Let the Pope send him a hat. I will make sure that when it comes, they will have to place it on his shoulders, as he will no longer have a head to set it on.*" On June the 17th, he was brought before thirteen commissioners and a jury of freeholders[5]. The physical abuse showed tragically on his entire body. He looked closer

---

[5]freeholders: those holding estates or offices for life which have been passed down to them, and would be passed down to their heirs through inheritance.

to eighty-six than his sixty-six years.   His health, already weakened by his austere life, had seriously deteriorated during his stay in the Tower of London.   But that did not stop him from being his cheerful self, as his indictment was read.   There was a peace that emanated from him, his eyes glowed as he appeared to be looking beyond them to his Source of true Peace, his Lord.

Although quite lengthy, in essence, the indictment called him a traitor, declaring that he maliciously and falsely stated that "*the King, our sovereign lord, is not supreme head on earth of the Church of England*".   When he was finished reading the charges against Bishop John Fisher, the court clerk demanded: "*What say you?   Are you guilty of high treason?*"   John Fisher, with a voice that belied his feeble frame, answered strongly and resolutely "*not guilty*".

Now, the King had sent his personal solicitor general - Richard Rich to speak to John Fisher in the Tower, before the trial.   Now, he was the *sole* witness testifying against Bishop Fisher.   It was he who had stated that Bishop Fisher had maliciously made statements by which he now stood accused of treason.   John Fisher spoke directly to him.   He stated, if he had expressed his feelings, on King Henry VIII as head of the Church in England, as Richard Rich had accused him of doing, he had not spoken with treason in his mind or heart.   He reminded Richard Rich that he knew well that he, the king's solicitor had come to him, *privately*, as a representative of the King.   And that he had told John Fisher that the king had sent him to ask John Fisher "*for his (the king's own) conscience*", what Fisher truly believed about his supremacy.   He asked him if he did not recall how he had assured the Bishop that his words would not be held against him, and that his answer would be transmitted strictly to the King and no one else.

Although John Fisher argued brilliantly before the commission and the jury that he could not be judged based on this testimony, as it was based on *advice and counsel* given solely to the king, it did not sway the commissioners or their verdict. Even his argument that the testimony of one man was not sufficient to prove him guilty of treason, fell on deaf ears. The commissioners insisted, in the case of a king, it was not up to the law, but to the consciences of the jury (all of which would not have dared to find Bishop Fisher anything but guilty, if they did not want to join him). It had been a long accepted conclusion that the King's will was the law, in any case. You see, he already had set himself as divine!

The commissioners berated Bishop Fisher for his *obstinacy* in opposing the king's claim as head of the Church in England. They said that he alone, of all the Bishops of the realm, stood against Parliament and their ruling on the King's supremacy. Bishop Fisher retorted that he stood with all the Bishops of the Catholic *world*, and all the faithful of the One, Holy, Universal Roman Catholic Church, in swearing allegiance to no one but the Pope as head of the Church.

The twelve jurors returned after a short time of deliberation, with the verdict: "*guilty of treason*". When asked if he had anything further to say, John Fisher replied:

"*If what I have spoken is not sufficient then I have no more to say, except to beg Almighty God to forgive those who have condemned me, as they know not what they have done.*"

The lord Chancellor pronounced sentence:

"*You shall be led to the place from where you came, and from there shall be drawn through the city to the place of execution at Tyburn, where you shall be hanged by the neck; and being half alive, you shall be cut down and thrown to the ground, your bowels to be taken out of your body and burnt before you, while still alive; you are to be decapitated, your head separated from the rest of your body which then will be drawn and quartered, after which the King will decide where your head and four quarters of your body will be set up. And God have mercy on your soul."*

Some of the judges cried when the sentence was read.

Before being taken back to the Tower, John Fisher addressed the commissioners one more time, formally stating that not King Henry or any other sovereign can ever be head of the Church in England or anywhere else. Four days later, the King issued orders for his execution, but not according to the prescribed sentence but by beheading. The next morning, the lieutenant of the Tower came to Bishop Fisher's room. He was sleeping peacefully.

The lieutenant awakened him and told him he was to be executed that morning. The Bishop asked the lieutenant to convey his thanks to the King for ridding him of all this worldly business. He then calmly asked him the hour of his execution. When the lieutenant replied it was to be at nine in the morning, Bishop John Fisher asked him what time it was. Upon hearing it was about five o'clock, he requested he be able to sleep an another hour or two, as he had not slept much during the night. He assured him that it was not out of fear of dying, he wanted to sleep a little more, but because of his infirmity had left him weak, he would need to, if he was to be able to walk to his death. The lieutenant shared that the King had expressly ordered the Bishop to say little, and nothing that might lead the people to believe that the King was acting wrongly. The Bishop assured the lieutenant that no one would mistake his words or their meaning, not the King or anyone else.

Two hours later, the lieutenant returned and awakened the Bishop for the last time. The Bishop called to his manservant and asked him to help him up. He ordered him to remove his hairshirt and hide it. He dressed carefully, donning his very finest clothes. When his manservant questioned him on why he was taking more care dressing, today, than at other times in his life, that after all, the clothes he was wearing would be soon destroyed, he replied it was his wedding day, the day he would be united with the Bridegroom His Lord and Savior for all eternity, and he wanted to look his best.

Bishop Fisher took his New Testament that had been always by his side and making the sign of the cross, he motioned to the lieutenant that he was ready. Because he was too weak to walk, they carried him out of the Tower on a chair. When they reached the place of his execution, he stood up from his chair, unaided, and looking up toward his Savior, His Mother and the whole heavenly court of Angels and Saints, and opened his Bible for the last time. He prayed: *"Oh Lord, this is the last time that I shall ever open this book. Please comfort me so that I, Thy poor servant may glorify Thee in my last hour."*

Upon opening his Bible, what passage would appear to him, but:

"Now this is eternal life: That they may know Thee, the only true God and Jesus Christ Whom Thou has sent. I have glorified Thee upon the earth; I have finished the work Thou has given me to do. And now glorify Thou me, Father, with Thyself, with the glory which I had, before the world was, with Thee." (John 17: 3-5)

When they tried to help him ascend the steps to the gallows, he refused, insisting he be allowed to go to his Lord under his own power. He mounted the steps with a spring to his step that belied his frail frame. As he climbed, the sun broke through the clouds and began to illuminate his face. There was a glow about him. As he reached the scaffold, he raised his arms, he said: *"Draw close to Him and receive His Light and you shall never be discouraged."* The executioner kneeled down and asked his forgiveness. The Bishop consoled: *"I forgive you with all my heart, and I trust you shall see me overcome this storm lustily."*

When he was stripped of his gown, his frail body looked like a skeleton. He turned to the people:

"Christian people, I have come forth to die for the Faith of Christ's holy Catholic Church, and I thank God that so far, I have not feared death. I now entreat you all to help and assist me with your prayers that, at that very moment and instant when death strikes its blow, I may in that very moment stand steadfast, without weakening in any one point of the Catholic Faith, free from any fear. And I beseech Almighty God of His infinite goodness to save the King and this realm, and that it may please Him to hold His holy Hand over it and send the King good counsel"

He knelt down on both knees and prayed. After he recited the *"Te Deum"* and the psalm *"In te Domine speravi"*, the executioner bound a handkerchief over his eyes. Then this holy Priest and Bishop raised his hands and heart to Heaven, said a few prayers, and laid his holy head on the block. When the executioner's ax struck him, severing his head from his body, the blood of this Martyr burst forth with the powerful passion with which another sacrificial Lamb had given up His Life that His Church might live. And the earth was covered with blood, once more. And the Church was nourished by that blood, and she lives today because a man chose to die rather than deny His Lord and His Church.

Henry's anger and hate followed the Holy John Fisher, Priest, Bishop, Saint and Martyr to the very end. He had the Bishop's body *dumped* into a grave without a shroud, without a Catholic burial, and his head impaled for fourteen days on London Bridge so that all who passed could see. They recounted, it was as if he was still alive, his face had such a peace about it. Then, the King had his head thrown into the river to make room for his friend Thomas More's head.

May 1935, almost four hundred years after his death, John Fisher, and his friend and fellow Martyr Thomas More, solemnly joined the number of Saints who had lived and died for their God and Church. Throughout England and Wales, and parts of Scotland, July 9th is celebrated as the Feast Day of these two Martyrs, till today. And King Henry the VIII?

Saint Thomas More - Martyr (1478-1535)

God was to raise up two Thomases in England, one who would give his life to stave off royal aggression against the Church for three hundred and fifty years, only to see that aggression rise again and require another Thomas' Martyr's blood to try to save the faithful children of God from separation from their and His Church. It would seem, for the foolish, it was in vain, the second time. But, as we see whole congregations, with their pastors, coming back home to the Roman Catholic Church, we cry out:

Martyrs of God, rest in Peace, the Cross is coming together. Division is at an end! Alleluia!

Both Thomases: Thomas Becket and Thomas More were Chancellors; each loved God more than his earthly king. There are many parallels. They just take place at a different time in Church and World History. Thomas Becket was born between the twelfth century and the turbulent tide of the Renaissance! Thomas More was born during a time of deceptive, devastating Revolution (erroneously called the Reformation), with protest, politics and disobedience. Thomas Becket was a churchman; Thomas More a layman. God would use these two loyal sons of the Church.

Thomas More was born February 6, 1478. His father was a lawyer and judge. He fared so well in school, at age thirteen, he was sent to Oxford where he entered Canterbury College. Thomas' father was strict with him, giving him money only for the merest necessities. Although, I am sure, the young Thomas was not too happy with this discipline and austerity, it served him well, as he matured. Thomas did very well at the university, but after two years, his father called him home. He studied for the next five years and in 1501 was admitted to the bar. He, three short years later, entered Parliament. He was brilliant, successful and popular.

This did not seem to satisfy him, though. He felt drawn to the life of the Carthusian Monks. He even thought of becoming a Friar Minor of the order of St. Francis. But he could not hear the Lord calling him to either the monastic life or to the secular Priesthood. He ardently loved the Priesthood. But he wanted to be sure, he would not be anything but faithful to God in whatever vocation He called him to. He said, to be an unworthy Priest was the last thing he would ever desire. In 1505, he married.

He was highly regarded as a man of the world, but he had none of that contempt for ascetism[6] that was so prevalent in the Renaissance. From the time he was eighteen years old, he wore a *hairshirt*[7], used the *discipline*[8]

---

[6] The religious doctrine that one can reach a higher religious life by self-discipline and self-denial.

[7] the name given to a shirt made of coarse animal hair, worn by many of the Saints who desired to do a form of continual Penance. Although it is prescribed for certain religious orders, it is not to be undertaken unless by consent of your Spiritual Director. Other forms of Penance are being supplanted for the hairshirt, more in keeping with the times, our culture, and our life style.

[8] discipline - name of the small whip or scourge used by some austere religious orders in penitential practice as a means of bodily mortification. - Catholic Encyclopedia

on fridays, assisted at *Daily Mass* and recited the *Little Office*[9] every day. His controversial friend Erasmus[10] said of him that he never knew anyone so indifferent to food.

Thomas married Jane Colt, the eldest daughter, although he was attracted to her younger sister. But because he knew, it would bring grief and shame to Jane, if her younger sister married first, he married her. He was never sorry for his choice and loved his wife dearly. They had four children. Their home was a place filled with people of learning and accomplishment. It would appear it was only for the elite or *the Highbrow*. But that was not the case. He, his family and all their servants prayed together each night, before retiring. They all ate together at mealtime and heard Holy Scripture read and explained. They all shared on the Word, and what it meant in their lives. Thomas had a profound sense of humor. His home was a place of joy and fun, but he did not allow card-playing or rolling dice.

He bequeathed a Chapel to his Parish Church and even after he became Chancellor, he sang in the choir, wearing a surplice, like the other members of the choir. Whenever there was a woman in labor, whether in his home

---

[9]prayers in honor of the Blessed Mother, that contain the same elements as the Divine Office, only in shorter form. It is the daily office recited in common or privately by some orders of sisters and lay brothers, and is obligatory for some tertiaries. It has become popular amongst the laity and is often recited by members of Sodalities of the Blessed Mother.

[10] Erasmus went to school in a monastery and became a Catholic Priest. He later studied in Paris. When Martin Luther came out against the Catholic Church, and started what became the Protestant Churches, Erasmus agreed that there were problems in the Church, but that Luther went too far in breaking from the Church. Erasmus remained in the Church, although he wrote a book about what he thought was wrong with the Catholic Church. He wrote many other books, but he was more interested in helping people understand the philosophies of Ancient Greece and Rome than in religion. This was the thrust of that period of the Renaissance.

or in the village, More would begin praying and would not stop, until someone arrived telling him that she had successfully given birth. He would visit the poorest of the poor, taking the alleys, less he be detected. He was truly a living example of the Gospel which tells us to not let our deeds be known in the light of day.

He often invited his poorer neighbors to dine with him and his family. He rarely invited the rich and most never the nobility. Now this did not preclude him from inviting great minds, or Martyrs-to-be like John Fisher or controversial figures like Erasmus. St. Thomas More defended his friendship with Erasmus: He did not find the "*shrewd intent and purpose*" he found in Tyndale[11]. He said that rather, he found that "*Erasmus detested and abhorred the errors and heresies that Tyndale plainly taught and abided by*". And because of this, he said, Erasmus was his friend, still. But, as we will see later on, if he had not truly believed this, if he thought that Erasmus had gone against the Church, More would have defended the Church against him, as he would against King Henry VIII.

More's idyllic life soon came to a crashing end. His wife Jane died, leaving him with four small children. He remarried within a few weeks, a lady seven years his elder, a good housewife, with lots of good common sense, someone he could trust with his children. Although she could not take the place of his love - his Jane, their life was a good one.

Having heard of him, King Henry VIII and his Cardinal Wolsey, one of the most important men in the realm, were

---

[11]Tyndale was a Catholic Priest who translated the New Testament and parts of the Old Testament from Latin into English. He came into problems with religious authorities over some of his translations and religious views contrary to Church teaching. Rather than obey, he became a heretic and was imprisoned and burned at the stake, in 1536, through the efforts of Henry VIII. His translations are the foundation of The King James (Protestant) version of the Bible.

determined to have More's services at court. Thomas More was not too enthusiastic about it. Although he was not diametrically opposed to the position, he was not looking forward to being in Court with the King and his entourage, stating that the "*good life*" was definitely not there. But he obeyed his sovereign and was so well accepted and trusted, he, after many advancements, became Lord Chancellor, replacing the now disgraced Wolsey[12].

More's advice was held in high regard; he proved himself an able and prudent judge in deep and important matters that would arise at court. He was able to see both sides of a question and tried to satisfy both sides, but never by compromising his values. He was considered by all "*a gentleman of great learning in law, art and divinity, as good a courtier as a Christian man and saint can be, and that does not mean that he was not a very good one.*"

King Henry was very fond of St. Thomas More and this affection was shared by Thomas for his King. But he had no illusions about his King. Now, when Thomas More was appointed Chancellor, he had been busy writing against Protestantism, particularly in rebuttal to Tyndale and his writings. Thomas More's attitude toward heretics was moderate, hating the heresy but not the heretics. He was very cautious about the laity reading the Bible in the vernacular, as he judged, it could lead to misinterpretation. He strongly advised no such books be read without the Ordinary's approval.

When King Henry VIII demanded the clergy acknowledge him as "*Protector and Supreme Head of the*

---

[12] Although Cardinal Wolsey was at once the most powerful man in England next to the King, he came into serious disfavor with the King when he failed to get the Pope's approval of the dissolution of the King's marriage to Catherine of Aragon, and his marriage to Anne Boleyn. The King had him arrested, but he died before he was able to go to trial.

Church of England", Thomas More immediately wished to resign as Chancellor. But he was persuaded to remain, in order to give his attention to the matter of the King's annulment to Catherine of Aragon, or as it was called "*the King's divorce*". St. Thomas More upheld the validity of the King's marriage to Catherine, but requested he be allowed to stand aside from the controversy. When he was asked to present the case to Parliament, he refused to render his opinion. As we all try to do, he was trying to skirt the issues, but he would soon find it to be impossible.

In 1532 the King imposed a decree forbidding the clergy to prosecute heretics, or to hold any assembly without his permission, a clear interference of State and Church, a matter resolved centuries before by the Church that the state could not interfere with the Church and its matters. Then he had a bill passed in Parliament that the *firstfruits* due the Holy See was to be withheld. Now, St Thomas More could not sideswipe *this* issue. This went way back to the Law of Moses which stated that the *first produce of man and animals, and whatsoever was sown in the field was to be given to the Lord*[13]. (Ex. 23:16) St. Thomas More openly opposed all these measures, and the King was furious! On May the 16th, after having served only three years, St. Thomas More handed in his resignation as Chancellor, and the King accepted it.

Without his earnings as Chancellor, he and his family were reduced to poverty, with barely enough to eat. But they never lost their joy. **St. Thomas More refused to go to the coronation of Anne Boleyn**. His enemies, those who had envied him and his former position with the King, took this opportunity to taunt him, accusing him as they did St. John Fisher of all sorts of crimes. Praise God, the Lords insisted

---

[13]This Old Testament law has been ascribed to the physical support to be given to the Church and her Priests in present times. However, now it pertains to the monetary offering given by the faithful.

on hearing St. Thomas More's defense themselves, so the King retracted the charges. But the time was now approaching when nothing would help St. Thomas More.

March 30, 1534, a law was passed requiring all subjects of the King to take an oath recognizing the succession to the throne, of the King and Anne Boleyn's offspring. King Henry added, this was to nullify his union to Catherine of Aragon, that it had never been a *true marriage*, and that "*no foreign authority, prince or potentate had any authority to repudiate this*". To refuse to take this oath or to oppose it in any way was an **act of high treason**. This came on top of the Pope, the week before, declaring the marriage of King Henry and Catherine to be valid and irrevocable. Many Catholics took the oath with this reservation: "*as far as it be not contrary to the law of God.*"

April 13th, Sir Thomas More and Bishop John Fisher refused to sign the oath. St. Thomas was remanded to the custody of the Abbot of Westminster. A lord close to the King tried to dissuade him from taking any drastic action against Sts. Thomas More and John Fisher. But he refused to compromise, and the oath was once again tendered to Thomas More and John Fisher. They refused to sign! They were both imprisoned in the Tower. St. Thomas spent the next fifteen months, there, writing loving, faith-filled letters to his family. They begged him to do as the King ordered. But all their pleading fell on deaf ears.

February 1, 1535, the **Acts of Supremacy** were to go into operation. This gave the King the title of "*only supreme head of England*". When, in April, Cromwell came to St. Thomas, asking him his opinion of the bill, he refused to give it.

May 4th, his daughter was allowed to visit him for the first time. They witnessed the first three Carthusian monks and their companions go to their Martyrdom. When Cromwell and others returned and again taunted him to comment on the statute, they made sport of him because he remained silent.

June 19th, the second group of Carthusian Monks were Martyred.

June 19th, Bishop John Fisher was beheaded on Tower Hill.

June 28th, Sir Thomas More was indicted and tried in Westminster Hall. By this time, he was too weak to stand, and had to sit during the proceedings. The same witness that had falsely accused St. John Fisher of speaking against the King, falsely testified against St. Thomas More, alleging that he had spoken to him against the Acts of Supremacy. As had St. John Fisher, St. Thomas maintained that he had remained silent and had not shared any opinion with Rich or anyone else. He was found guilty and condemned to death. Now, something you have to understand, this was not legal! So, as the Church is attacked and we lose our religious rights, our other rights will follow!

At last, St. Thomas More spoke up! He had not before, afraid he would not be up to Martyrdom; fearing he was a weak sinner, he did not want to tempt the Lord. But now, at last, he spoke. He proclaimed that no temporal lord (sovereign) could or ought to be head of the Church. He told the lords that he would pray for them; and as St. Paul had persecuted St. Stephen and went on to become a Saint, he would pray that someday they would all rejoice in Heaven, together. He said his last farewell to his son and daughter.

Early Tuesday morning, on the July 6th, Sir Thomas Pope came to warn him that he was to die at nine o'clock that morning. St. Thomas More thanked him and told him she would pray for King Henry. He held his weeping friend in his arms, consoling him. The words I hear echoing through the Tower are: "*Lord make me an instrument of Your Peace...Oh Master, grant that I may never seek so much to be consoled as to console, to be understood as to understand, to be loved as to love with all my soul.*

Dressing in his finest clothes, *love* walked to the scaffold on Tower Hill, consoling people on the way, never once angry or sad. He even joked with the executioner to make him feel better. When it was time for him to speak, he asked the people for their prayers that he would be worthy to die a Martyr's death. He told them, he was dying rather than deny the Holy, Roman Catholic Church. He said that *"he was the king's good servant, but God's first"*. He said the Miserere; he kissed the headsman and assured him, he was willingly dying for the Faith. And this, from a man who did not think he would have the courage to face his executioner. He covered his own eyes and adjusted his beard. And he was beheaded. He was fifty-seven years old.

His body was buried somewhere in the church inside the Tower and his head placed where St. John Fisher's head had been. He was beatified with other English Martyrs in 1886, and canonized in 1935. It has been said that even if he had not died a Martyr, he would have been declared a Saint. *He was from first to last, a holy man, who lived his prayer:*

"Give me, good Lord, a longing to be with Thee; not for the avoiding of the calamities of this wicked world, nor so much for the avoiding of the pains of Purgatory, nor of the pains of Hell neither, nor so much for the attaining of the joys of Heaven..., as even for a very love of thee."

The American Martyrs

The United States is a country founded under God, as a haven against religious persecution, for the singular purpose of free expression of our love for our God. There can be no question about that. The country is spotted with Biblical names in honor of God. All you have to do is look at the names of the cities scattered all over the country, especially in the south, southwest, and west, but even in states like Pennsylvania, New Hampshire, and Ohio. Names like Sacramento, Los Angeles, San Francisco, Santa Fe, Santa Ana, Santa Monica in the west, and Ephrata, St. Mary's, Maryland, Bethesda (*in Arkansas, Maryland and Ohio*), Bethlehem (*in Georgia, Indiana, Connecticut, New Hampshire, Pennsylvania, and Ohio*), St. Lawrence, St. Michael, St. Thomas, Nazareth (*in Kentucky, Pennsylvania and Texas*), Jerusalem (*in Arkansas and Ohio*), in the East and southeast. The list goes on and on.

Our rich history is filled with undeniable signs, proof positive from the Lord that it was indeed His will that this New World be consecrated to His Name, for His glory and for His people. There are no coincidences with God. The Heavenly mandate to evangelize new lands, to proclaim the Name of Jesus, was given to the Catholic Queen Isabella, and her husband King Ferdinand, to institute, in thanksgiving to Our Lord for having delivered Spain from the Moslems after seven hundred years of captivity.

Think of it, my brothers and sisters, for seven hundred years, the name of Jesus could not be spoken in that country. When the Lord gave Spain liberation, the joy of the monarchs and the people was so great, they would have done anything to show their appreciation to their God, and so they eagerly and gladly undertook the venture.

The name of the man whom God chose to bring light into the darkness was Christopher, *Christ-Bearer*, who truly believed his mission was to bring Christ to far off lands. On the voyage across, each morning, a hymn was sung to Our Lord and Savior,

> *Blessed be the light of day,*
> *and the Holy Cross, we say,*
> *and the Lord of Veritie,*[1]
> *and the Holy Trinity.*
> *Blessed be the immortal soul,*
> *and the Lord who keeps it whole,*
> *Blessed be the light of day,*
> *and He who sends the night away.*[2]

The first place in the New World where Christopher Columbus set foot, he named *San Salvador*, after our Savior, Jesus Christ. He prayed at that spot, "*O Lord, almighty and everlasting God, by Thy Holy Word Thou hast created the heaven, and the earth, and the sea; blessed and glorified be Thy Name, and praised be Thy Majesty, which has deigned to use us, Thy humble servants, that Thy Holy Name may be proclaimed in this second part of the earth.*"[3]

Columbus never accomplished what he set out to do, but he was an instrument of the Lord. He opened the door for Spain to send Evangelists in the form of Franciscan Missionaries. The Lord had a plan for this New World, and He would have His way. He had to put up with the frailties and shortcomings of human beings, but they would get the job done for Him.

For the next thirty nine years, not much apparent headway was made in bringing the Kingdom to the pagans. On the contrary, to the human eye, things went downhill in the New World. It seemed like everyone had forgotten the

---

[1]Truth

[2]The Light and the Glory, Peter Marshall, David Manuel, Revell Publications - 1977 - Pg 38

[3]The Light and the Glory, Peter Marshall, David Manuel, Revell Publications - 1977 - Pg 41

pledge the Catholic Queen, Isabella, now dead, had made to bring the light of Jesus to the darkness of these pagan lands. The Spanish who came to the New World, were on their own agenda, and that agenda was singularly focused on greed and licentiousness. The name of the game was pillage, rape and rampage, in the name of gold and lust.

And so our dear Mother Mary had to intercede. In 1531, on a cold December morning, she gave us a miracle through her apparition to an illiterate Indian convert, Juan Diego, which would mark the seal of the beginning of God's reign in the New World, bringing about reconciliation between the Spaniards and the Indians. Conversion came about in massive numbers. Eight million Indians were converted in seven years. We had Pentecost every day for seven years. The people of the Americas were given a mother in the person of Our Lady of Guadalupe. She opened the doors from which all graces flowed. She gave the missionaries the impetus they needed.

The Franciscans and Dominicans poured into the New World, most notably to Mexico and Central and South America. There was a great battle they had to fight, which, strangely enough, was not only with the fierce, savage Indians, but the greed of the conquistadores. They were two separate cultures, neither of which understood the other. Neither ever trusted the other, with good reason. They were exposed to the worst of each culture, and so you have a tiny idea of the situation the Lord was up against in this New World.

The Indians had learned of the gross cruelty inflicted on their brothers by the gold-crazed Spaniards, and waged war on all Europeans in the New World. Some of the Indians didn't need encouragement; they were bloodthirsty killers, and cannibals. But there were other natives who had befriended the Spaniards, who were treated terribly by the settlers. The situation between the Indians and the

Europeans was coming to a head. War and massacre was sitting on the horizon, waiting to happen. If not for Our Lady's intercession, all Europeans would have been annihilated in the New World.[4]

The Missionaries evangelize the United States

Spanish Missionaries looked north to Baja (Lower) and Upper California, New Mexico and Arizona. With Blessed Junipero Serra spearheading the mission, the unknown lands north of Mexico were settled. The task of Friar Serra and his successors was more difficult in this land north of Mexico than it had been in Mexico and Central America. We're told that the Indians were more civilized in Mexico and Central America, than they were in what is now called the United States. Serra and his followers had to bring these tribes together, form family, community. One of the greatest feats Our Lord Jesus accomplished through Blessed Serra and his followers was in how they taught the Indians to help themselves. *"If you feed a man a fish, he will be hungry soon after. But if you teach him how to catch fish, the man will never be hungry."*

With much hardship, the Spanish Franciscans not only evangelized California, but set up settlements in which the native Americans were able to become self-sufficient. The Franciscans taught them how to farm, how to read and write, how to express themselves in art, as well as how to worship our God. Each mission from San Diego to San Rafael was designed to be one day's journey by horse or donkey, from the other. In this way, the missionaries could visit each of the settlements, without having to be out overnight.

---

[4]Those who shed their blood for the kingdom in Mexico are covered in the chapter about the Martyrs of Mexico

The North American Martyrs - 1642 - 1649

We, the people of the Church, and of this country, paid an extremely high price to claim this land for Jesus, and to bring Jesus to the savages here. There was so much blood shed, not only to colonize the land, but to evangelize the land, the rivers and streams ran red from the Martyrs. We're told that the Indians in North America, the area of Canada and the Upper United States, were the most savage and most violent.

They were either completely amoral, or lived by a moral standard completely foreign to anything we have ever known. This civilization is what the new evangelists of the North were walking into.

Spurred on by the heroic accounts of conversions which had taken place in Central America, a new group of religious entered into the Mission field, the followers of Ignatius Loyola. They were officially named the **Company of Jesus**, but are better known as Jesuits. They had only been formed in 1540, and so their devotion was extremely strong. They were brand new zealots for the Lord. They wanted to bring the light of Jesus to the whole world, so the Mission field was the perfect place for them to devote their lives. Amazingly enough, it was not the Jesuits from Spain, where they had been founded, who made such an impression evangelizing the New World, but the French Jesuits who evangelized the northern United States and Canada.

Their first expedition into the mission field of Canada and northern United States began at the request of a group called Franciscan Recollects, who had tried their best to evangelize the natives, but due to a lack of funds and support, had to leave. They turned their mission over to the Jesuits, who sent over the first of what have been termed *The Jesuit Martyrs of North America, all of whom were canonized in 1930.* They were:

St. John de Brébuf	**St. Charles Garnier**
St. Isaac Jogues	**St. Noel Chabanel**
St. Antony Daniel	**St. René Goupil**
St. Gabriel Lalemant	**St. John Lalande**

†

St. John de Brébuf

John de Brébuf was born in Bayeux, in the Normandy section of France. His birthplace was in the same diocese as St. Thérèse of Lisieux, although he was born in 1593, almost two hundred years before the Little Flower. He entered the Jesuit order in Rouen, France, at age 24. John was very humble. He had no grand illusions about his abilities. He wanted to be a brother, not believing himself worthy enough to become a Priest. He was tall and rugged when he went into the mission field, but he was also tubercular, and unable to devote himself to any one task for a great length of time, due to a lack of strength. He was not at all what anyone would have considered to be good material for the rough life of the missions in the New World.

However, his superiors saw qualities in John which he didn't see, qualities which were just what was needed in the Lord's new garden of Evangelization, New France (Canada and Upper New York State). He was encouraged to study for the Priesthood, and in 1612, he was ordained.

It is inconceivable that this same man would become a bull for Jesus, able to put up with every form of anguish and torture possible. He became a role model for the new missionaries; he was called the Giant Apostle of the Hurons. He was one of the first to go to Quebec, at the request of the Franciscans. He came from France in 1625 to Quebec, with Charles Lalemant, who was also destined to be a Martyr. John's transformation from the sickly invalid to the Jesuit Superman was nothing short of miraculous.

He was immediately thrown into the field, which was the conversion of the Huron Indians. He didn't gain the trust of the Hurons right off, so he spent his first winter with the Algonquins, learning the language and customs of the natives. John learned some very important messages on that first trip, which would stay with him all the days of his life. In a secular vein, he had to condition himself to accept the ways of the natives, such as sleeping on the hard ground, working until he was ready to drop, and for a Frenchman, the most difficult condition to accept had to be eating tasteless food. The hard spiritual lessons he had to learn were that the Indians were deceitful and arrogant, extremely superstitious, totally non-trusting, spiteful and unmerciful.

They never trusted him, his predecessors or successors, not any of the Missionaries. Everything was always conditional with the Natives. If things went well, they were all right *for now*. But if anything disastrous happened, like drought, or torrential rains, or blighted crops, or plagues, or whatever, they always blamed the Missionaries. A perfect example occurred when a drought scorched the land. The local medicine men worked themselves into a frenzy, but to no avail. They instinctively blamed the red Cross, which hung outside the quarters of the Jesuits. The chiefs ordered John to take down the Cross. He refused. But then John de Brébuf told them to pray a novena. Our Lady came to his aid. At the end of the novena, torrents of rain fell. But even then, there were those who remained suspicious.

He finally went to the Huron country, 600 miles away from Quebec. They were to be his converts. They didn't want to take him; he was too big. They were sure he would tip the canoe. But they weakened to the god of bribery, gifts and glitter, and took the young Jesuit. His journey to his first assignment was like something out of a high adventure story. He had to drag his canoe 35 different times, and his luggage at the same time. Shortly after he arrived at his post, his traveling companions, a Franciscan and Jesuit, were recalled, and he found himself alone among the Indians.

John de Brébuf's first voyage was not very long. A skirmish between the French and the English forced the Missionaries to return to France. But as soon as things settled down, in 1633, he returned to Quebec. He prepared himself well. He mastered the Huron language, studied their customs and beliefs, and wrote a grammar book. He was invited to a Huron camp. But at the last minute, the enemy of fear and suspicion reared its ugly head, and he had to wait a year to go to the Indian Settlement. Antony Daniel, another of the Martyrs, went with him, and became his companion for a good deal of his time in the mission field. There were no adult converts, save some deathbed conversions. They turned to the children; there was the opening for the Lord. Together, the Missionaries concentrated their teaching as much as possible on the little people of the village. They were receptive to the message of Our Lord Jesus, His mother Mary, and all the Angels and Saints. They had not become contaminated by the elders at this point in their lives, but without the work of the evangelists, it would be just a matter of time.   Vice was rampant in the Huron settlements.

†

We have to take a moment here to marvel at the faith, and unbelievable patience these inspired men of God had. They lived in the worst conditions possible, in an environment so completely foreign to them.   Add to that the extremely poor results they were experiencing.[5]   In the first year, they counted twelve Baptisms, four dying infants, and eight dying adults.   Even after they were established, the numbers never reached any great heights.   Two years later, they registered eighty, followed by an additional sixty.   Fr. De Brébuf wrote his superiors in 1641 that they baptized two hundred that year.

With the exception of an outbreak of smallpox, which took the lives of over a thousand natives in a short period of time, all of whom were baptized, in the eyes of the world, their mission would have been considered a failure.

And yet, after they had gone to the Father, all those who had been instrumental in their Martyrdom, came to accept the faith.   In a relatively short period of time, Christianity became the major force in the New World. These people give such a tribute to Our Lord Jesus.   They gave up everything, mother, father, brother, sister, husband, wife, children, everything for the Kingdom.   We really have to think twice about what *we are doing* to glorify God.   No one's asking us to live a life of utter poverty, and give up our

---

[5]A Priest once said to us, "The downfall of any Ministry is the ongoing search for results.   We Americans are a can-do society.   We measure success by the immediate results, that which we can see, or touch or count." He directed us to Hebrews 11:1-13, which begins with *"Faith is confident assurance concerning what we hope for, and conviction about things we do not see."* and ends with a comment on Abraham, Isaac, Moses, and others. *"All of these died in faith.   They did not obtain what had been promised but saw and saluted it from afar."*

lives for the Kingdom. We're just being asked to hold onto those values for which *somebody else* was willing to give up his life.

†

De Brébuf and Antony Daniel separated, when Antony went to begin an Indian Seminary in Quebec. He took some of the children with him, who would be his first students. De Brébuf was left alone again with the Indians. He was given a first hand demonstration of their savagery. An Iroquois was captured and executed by the Hurons. John de Brébuf wrote, "*Their mockery of their victim was fiendish. The more they burned his flesh and crushed his bones, the more they flattered and even caressed him. It was an all-night tragedy.*"

These Missionaries didn't mind suffering all sorts of deprivation. Many of them had asked Our Lord for the gift of Martyrdom for the sake of the Kingdom. We have to believe their worst frustrations and fears were the constant mistrust and suspicion. They never seemed to overcome it. One day the Missionaries were their best friends; the next day the natives were ready to kill them. As an example, an epidemic in the village put all the Missionaries out of commission, as well as most of the villagers. But as soon as the Jesuits were better, they spent grueling shifts of 20 hour days ministering to the sick of the village. When the scourge ended, the chiefs began looking at the Priests again with suspicion.

In spite of this, John de Brébuf felt the confidence in their progress. He wrote his superiors, "*We are gladly heard, we have baptized more than 200 this year, and there is hardly a village that has not invited us to go to it. Besides, the result of this pestilence and of these reports has been to make us better known to this people; and at last it is understood from our whole conduct that we have not come hither to buy skins or to carry on any traffic, but solely to teach them, and to procure for them their souls' health and in the end happiness which will last forever."[6]*

Now, with that kind of letter, and that kind of reception, you would think that the Missionaries had finally overcome the satan of suspicion. Right? *Wrong!* Shortly after having made this statement, a council of Indians held a meeting, and it was determined that De Brébuf and his companions should die. Their logic is beyond belief. But that didn't phase John De Brébuf. He arranged a farewell feast. He invited the Indians who were going to kill him. Throughout the dinner, he emphasized the theology of life after death with them so much, that they wound up adopting him. The companions were not killed either.

Progress among the Hurons went well. The Jesuits advanced in their evangelization for the better part of five years. They were not able to make a dent in the Iroquois, who not only wanted to destroy the Hurons, but the Missionaries as well. They kept attacking the settlements. Finally, in March of 1649, they invaded the village where De Brébuf was stationed. He was with Fr.Gabriel Lalemant.

†

Fr. Gabriel Lalemant was the last of the Jesuit Martyrs to arrive in Canada. He had had two uncles who were Missionaries. He took his vows to the Jesuit Community in Paris, on the Feast of the Annunciation, March 25, 1632, but added one to the three of Poverty, Chastity and Obedience. *His fourth was to sacrifice his life for the conversion of the Indians.* He was to keep that vow. But it was not to be in his timetable. All his requests to go to the missions in North America were denied. The reasons were simple. His health was not strong enough to hold up under the conditions in the missions. His superiors felt he could do more for the Jesuits in France than in the wilderness.

---

[6]Butler's Lives of the Saints, Volume III, Pg. 648

However, Fr. Lalemant pulled a few strings with his uncles, one of whom was superior of the Huron Mission, and in 1646, he found himself sailing across the ocean to begin his greatest adventure, to be a part of the conversion of the Indians to Christianity. He spent his first two years at Sillery, familiarizing himself with the people, the language and the customs. Then in 1649, he was assigned to be with Fr. de Brébuf in Huronia. It was during their weekly tour of the Huron camps that the Iroquois invaded the village where they were staying.

These two Jesuits were captured. We're told that the torture inflicted on these two men was as bad, if not worse than anything that has ever been recorded in the history of the American Martyrs, or for that matter, *any war in which the United States has taken part.* The torture actually defies description! Fr. Lalemant's suffering may have been even worse than Fr. De Brébuf's in that the former had to watch the torture and execution of his friend and mentor. After Fr. De Brébuf was finished, they began on Fr. Lalemant. In addition, the Indians tortured him just short of killing him, so that they could have more fun with him the following day. He lay in unbelievably excruciating pain overnight, until they resumed their savage torture on him the next day.

We're going to quote from **Butler's Lives of the Saints**. The language is graphic. It may offend your sensibilities. We apologize for this. But it's akin to showing an aborted baby. *If you don't see it, you'll never believe it.* The same applies to this situation, to the price these Martyrs paid for the rights which we're throwing away, or are allowing to be taken away from us. We think it's important to put it down on paper. You'll never know the price our Church paid for the religious freedom of this country if you don't read what happened.

"The torture of these two Missionaries was as atrocious as anything recorded in history. Even after they had been stripped naked and beaten with sticks on every part of their bodies, Brébuf continued to exhort and encourage the Christians who were around him. One of the fathers had his hands cut off, and to both were applied under the armpits and beside the loins hatchets heated in the fire, as well as necklaces of red-hot lance blades round their necks. Their tormentors then proceeded to girdle them with belts of bark steeped in pitch and resin, to which they set fire. At the height of these torments, Father Lalemant raised his eyes to Heaven, and with sighs, invoked God's aid, whilst Father de Brébuf set his face like a rock as though insensible to the pain. Then, like one recovering consciousness, he preached to his persecutors and to the Christian captives until the savages gagged his mouth, cut off his nose, tore off his lips, and then, in derision of baptism, deluged him and his companion Martyrs with boiling water. Finally, large pieces of flesh were cut out of the bodies of both the Priests and roasted by the Indians, who tore out their hearts before their death by means of an opening above the breast, feasting on them and on their blood, which they drank while it was still warm." Butler's Lives of the Saints, Vol III, Pg. 650-651

✝

St. Isaac Jogues
St. René Goupil
St. John Lalande

Isaac Jogues, a native of Orlean, France, joined the Jesuit community at Rouen at age seventeen. After ordination, he was sent to New France. He had a great desire to share in the Passion of Christ through suffering and even Martyrdom in the missions. It had become a great badge of courage among these new followers of Ignatius Loyola to contemplate death in the field of conversion. At one time, when Isaac was praying to the Lord to allow him to undergo any afflictions, even Martyrdom for the sake of evangelizing the savages in Canada, he heard the words spoken to him, *"Be it done to you as you asked. Be comforted! Be of strong heart!"*[7]

His mission, as was that of all of the Jesuits in New France, (Canada & Upper New York), was to the Huron Indians. Things got very bleak for that tribe in 1642. Supplies were desperately needed if they were to survive that winter. The only place they could be gotten was in Quebec. Jogues was chosen to lead the journey. All went well on the trip there. They got enough provisions to save the Hurons from extinction that year. But on the way back, they were waylaid by the Iroquois, whom we told you hated the Hurons with a passion, and therefore, these Missionaries who were ministering to the Hurons. They tortured St. Isaac Jogues and his companion, **St. René Goupil.**

During their captivity, they were beaten unceasingly with sticks; their hair, beards and nails were ripped off their bodies, and their fingers were bitten through. Also, during this captivity, René Goupil was caught making the Sign of the Cross on the forehead of one of the Indian children. He was tomahawked on September 29, 1642.

Stream where Isaac Jogues hid the body of Rene Goupil

---

[7]Jesuit Saints and Martyrs Pg 371

St. René Goupil was the first of the Jesuit Martyrs, even though he was not officially a Jesuit. He had wanted to be a Jesuit. He had entered the novitiate, but poor health prevented him from living the strict rule. He left the Seminary, and went into medicine. He became a surgeon, and enjoyed a successful practice. But he always felt the gnawing in his heart to be a Jesuit, and to be in the mission field. In 1639, at age 37, he offered his services to the Jesuits as a lay assistant, called a *donné*, and went to Canada where he joined up with the Jesuit mission. He worked for two years in the hospital in Quebec, caring for the French settlers and the Algonquin Indians in Sillery. It made a lot of sense. His expertise was in medicine; they desperately needed qualified medical help, so they did what was best for them.

He was obedient; he worked in the hospital. But his love was always the missions, converting Indians to Christianity. He was happier with what he was doing, than if he'd have stayed in France. But he really wanted to be in the field, converting the savages. His opportunity came when Fr. Jogues came to Quebec in September 1642, looking for volunteers to be assistants in the Huron Missions. René immediately volunteered, and Fr. Jogues snapped him up. His thinking was the same as the hospital's. He needed someone trained in medical skills to help him in his work.

Their *first day out,* they were captured by Mohawk Indians. They were taken by canoe to the village of Ossernenon[8], which is called today, Auriesville, N.Y. During this trip by canoe, René asked Fr. Jogues, seeing as how their situation was tenuous at best, if he could make his Jesuit vows, and thereby be accepted as a Jesuit. Fr. Jogues granted his request, and accepted him into the community as a Jesuit. René made his vows, and recited the words of

---

[8]Ossernenon, the birthplace of Blessed Kateri Tekawitha, born ten years after St. Isaac Jogues was murdered.

commitment he had memorized when he was in the Seminary. His two lifelong dreams were about to come true; one that he be a Jesuit; and two, that he die for the Faith in the Missions in the New World.

Once they arrived at the camp, they were made to run the gauntlet[9]. When they were finished, René's face was so swollen and disfigured, he was unrecognizable, save for the whites of his eyes. Then their fingers were chewed off by Indians. They were put on exhibit in front of the whole village as animals. Braves beat and stabbed them. A woman of the camp cut Fr. Jogues' left thumb off with a scraggy shell. They were tied up to stakes, where young children played by dropping hot coals on their bodies. Then they were given as slaves to the head of the village, who used them as you would a horse or a mule. The inhumanity was outrageous.

It was during this time that René made the Sign of the Cross on the head of a child. The child's grandfather saw this, and ran over, grabbing the child, and beating René. Fr. Jogues and René knew this was serious. They went out to the forest to pray, and prepare for death. Then the young Indian's uncle came with some other braves. They walked Fr. Jogues and René back to the village. Fr. Jogues walked ahead of René. He turned, looking for his friend, just as the Indian welded his tomahawk, and crushed René's skull. Fr. Jogues went down on his knees to pray for his newfound friend and brother. They grabbed him, and made him get up. They threw the body of René into a ravine. The next day Fr. Jogues went out to where the body had been thrown. He covered it with rocks, intending to return again in a day

---

[9]A savage sport, in which Indians line up on a hill in rows, leaving a path in the middle. The prisoners are stripped naked, and made to run up the hill. They are beaten on the head, neck and shoulders by the Indians until they drop. Most of the Jesuit Martyrs had to go through this treatment.

to give his friend a decent burial. When he returned the following day, the body had disappeared. He assumed it had been caught up in the stream, or that wild animals had devoured it. Some months later, native children said they were playing with it, and then, when they were tired of their game, let it go downstream. Fr. Jogues traveled downstream, until he found some bones and a skull which had been bashed in. He assumed this to be the body of René Goupil, the first American Jesuit Martyr. Fr. Jogues buried the remains of the future saint, and marked the spot.

When Fr. Jogues wrote his superior some time later about René's death, he recommended him for the name Martyr. *"He deserves the name of Martyr not only because he has been murdered by the enemies of God and His Church while laboring in ardent charity for his neighbor, but most of all because he was killed for being at prayer and notably for making the Sign of the Cross."*

†

Jogues remained as a prisoner of the Indians for over a year. Then they tired of torturing him, and so they decided to kill him. In September 1643, he went with a group of Indians to the Dutch settlement at Albany, New York. If not for the governors of two of the provinces, who had heard of the brutal condition he and his companions were subjected to, he would surely have died then. They convinced him to stay with them until they could safely get him out of the area. He hesitated to leave, because there were Huron converts being held prisoner at the camp. He was the only Priest they had. But the Dutch persuaded him that theirs was the better plan. They hid him from the violent Indians until the riot died down. Then they sent him to New York, which was still called New Amsterdam at that time. He went by way of England, across the English Channel to Brittany, France. He arrived on Christmas day, 1643.

He was a great hero there. Everybody knew[10] about the atrocities he and his fellow Jesuits had suffered in their effort to bring the savages to the altar of Jesus. He had a major problem; he couldn't celebrate Mass, because of his missing thumb and forefinger on his left hand, and the mangled thumb and forefinger on his right hand. But his superiors obtained special dispensation from Pope Urban VIII, who said the following: *"It would be shameful that a Martyr of Christ be not allowed to drink the Blood of Christ."*

Isaac Jogues felt like a fish out of water in France. He didn't belong in his native land anymore. The Lord had spoiled him. He knew where his life was, where his heart was, where his work was, and no matter what the cost, he longed to go back. He was a non-person in France, a statue, a monument. They didn't know what to do with him. Finally, his wish was granted. In May 1644, he was on his way back to his beloved savages in New France.

Because of his physical condition, he was kept in Quebec, working with the local Indians. He wanted to get back to the Huron settlements, which were his love, but he was obedient to his superiors. With his physical handicap, he was not really able to function as he had in the past. Besides, it was becoming more and more difficult to get to the Huron settlements, because they were constantly being attacked by the Iroquois, who blocked anyone trying to get

---

[10]The greatest source of documentation on all that we have been bestowed on the lives of the Jesuit Martyrs comes from a brilliant concept, called the "Jesuit Relations". Fr. Le Jeune, one of the earliest Jesuit Missionaries conceived the plan of keeping all of France informed of the actual conditions in New France by a series of graphic descriptions, letters and writings of the various missionaries, giving their impressions of life in the New World, as well as reports on what was going on there. They continued to pass from New to Old France, almost without interruption. These "Relations" found their way all over Europe, thus the reason for the great knowledge of what was happening, and so much interest in the people involved.

to them. But surprisingly enough, in July, 1644, the Iroquois sent a peace party to ask for peace with the French. A meeting took place, at which Fr. Jogues was active. Finally, a pact was considered, but Jogues, who was present at the meeting, noticed that no one had come from the main Mohawk village, Ossernenon. Jogues was selected to go as a representative to the chiefs at Ossernenon.

The chiefs at the village were amazed to find their former slave, whom they wanted to kill, now coming to them, not as a blackrobe (Jesuit), but as a representative of the French Government to talk terms of peace. He was not dressed as a Priest, but as a French gentleman. He was successful at having a pact confirmed with the Mohawks, but he made an understandable mistake. After hearing confessions of the Huron prisoners he had been prisoner with over a year before, he left a box of religious articles, vestments, lectionary and sacramentary in the village, because he fully intended to return to evangelize the Mohawks. To be honest, unless they could be converted, the Huron nations didn't stand a chance of survival against them.

Well, the Natives, being as superstitious and suspicious as they were, began blaming that box for every bad thing that happened to them. They were convinced that Jogues was sent to destroy their nation. So when they heard he was coming back, they ambushed him and his companion, **St. John Lalande**, another layman working for the Jesuits. They beat him and Lalande, and brought them back to the camp. They began slicing strips of flesh from their necks and arms. They were ready to kill the two.

But there were factions in the camp who were tolerant of the Jesuits, and wanted peace with the French. Somehow, the friendly clan got Fr. Jogues and John Lalande, and put them under protection in their hovel. The chiefs wouldn't hear of Jogues being killed by the unfriendly faction in the camp. As long as the two Jesuits stayed inside this lodging, they were safe. So the enemy set a trap. They invited St. Isaac Jogues for dinner. He had to go, or risk antagonizing the chief of that group, even though they had never been his friends. They behaved predictably. The moment he set foot in their tent, they tomahawked him. They decapitated him, and stuck his head on a pole in the camp, to let everyone know that this enemy of the Mohawks was at last dead. Ironically, that label, *enemy of the Indians* never stuck. As a matter of fact, to this day, St. Isaac Jogues is considered the Apostle to the Indians.

†

St. John Lalande

Not very much is known about John Lalande, because he did not come from the Jesuit community. He was a native of Dieppe, France, who came to the New World as a settler about 1642. His major skills were that he was a woodsman, which was needed in the New France expedition. He was also known for his intelligence and bravery.

He wasn't in the Quebec province very long when he felt the call of the Lord to work in the Missions. It wasn't that he could see all that much progress. As a matter of fact, it was an uphill fight all the way. But he could not help but admire those brave men who were giving up everything for the call to conversion, and he wanted more than anything to be part of that great mission.

He was accepted as a *donné*, which was a lay assistant. He worked at whatever task he was given, and joyfully. He devoted his life to the work of the Lord in the land of the missions.   When Fr. Jogues asked for a volunteer to accompany him to the Mohawk village at Ossernenon, John jumped at the opportunity.   Fr. Jogues' reputation had preceded him. He was considered a legend, a living saint.

But this time, Fr. Jogues, remembering the fate of his friend, René Goupil, sat John down, and explained graphically, what could possibly happen. He held nothing back, but no matter what he said, the young man was filled with the Holy Spirit, and could not be talked out of it. Very possibly, Fr. Jogues' negative explanation about the work ahead only made the young man want to join him more than ever. Finally, John took the older man's mangled hands into his own. He kissed them, and vowed his allegiance to him. He would stay by Fr. Jogues' side, for the sake of the Gospel, even if it meant his own death. This turned out to be somewhat of a prophecy.

As we read above, they were caught, and went through terrible torture and indignation. Fr. Jogues walked into a trap, and was killed. When John heard the news that Fr. Jogues was dead, he was warned not to leave his quarters. He was safe from harm as long as he didn't go outside. The bloodthirsty contingency of the camp wanted more than anything to kill John Lalande as well. The Indians tried to lure him out of his sanctuary, but to no avail. John kept thinking about Fr. Jogues. It was impossible for him to believe that he was dead. And yet death was such a common occurrence in this land.

John wondered what had been done with Fr. Jogues' body. He wanted to get any memento he had left in his pockets. He thought if he waited until it was dark, late at night, he might be able to sneak past the Indians posted outside his shelter, and find the body of Fr. Jogues. Whatever he had on his person would be considered relics. If John were ever released, and he was fully certain, he would be, he could go to the Jesuits in Quebec, and give them the mementos of Fr. Jogues.

What he didn't know was just how badly the Indians wanted to get him. They had posted a 24 hour watch on his quarters. The moment John left the shelter, he was tomahawked by a waiting Indian. He died the day after Fr. Jogues. Both bodies of Fr. Jogues and John Lalande were thrown into the Mohawk river, while their heads were put on display at the Mohawk village.

†

St. Antony Daniel

Fr. Daniel was from Dieppe, France. He heard the call to the Priesthood in the ranks of the Jesuits. He had been studying to be a lawyer when he felt the strong urging of his vocation. While teaching at the college in Rouen, he met a young Huron

Shrine of North American Martyrs, Auriesville, NY

Indian who had been sent there to study at the college. He became completely taken with the stories of the Missions in America. He was ordained in Paris, and sent to teach at a college in Eu, in France. He met Fr. John De Brébuf there, who had been sent there after the English closed the Missions in Canada.

After his ordination, he came over to New France in 1633. He began his work in the missions with Fr. John de Brébuf. They worked well together, learning enough of the language of the natives that they could lead the children in the Lord's Prayer. Fr. Daniel had a good way with children. He put their prayers and the commandments to music, and taught the children in that way. He did so well with the children that he was chosen to begin a Seminary in Quebec for Indian children. However, the suspicious nature of the

Hurons clicked in. He could never get more than five students, and so the school was closed. He returned to Huronia.

The conversion of the Hurons was becoming so successful that the mission had twenty four Missionaries working there. Fr. Daniel was a very charismatic figure among the other Missionaries. But the dreaded Iroquois continued their campaign to destroy anything that had to do with the Hurons. On July 4, 1648, they raided the little village where Fr. Daniel had just finished celebrating Mass. He could see that a massacre was in the making. He tried to baptize as many of the catechumens as he could put his hands on. He ran feverishly all over the settlement, not considering for a moment that he was running right into the line of fire. He finally just wet a handkerchief and touched it to the heads of the catechumens in order to baptize them.

He ran into the church, to find it packed with frightened Christian Hurons. He begged them to flee, scatter in as many directions as possible. He turned to meet the Iroquois head on, to distract them from going after those that had scattered. He closed the doors of the church, and blocked it with his body. He refused entry to the Iroquois. They were amazed at his courage. But there were so many of them, and just one of him. The Indians began to shoot arrows into his body, until he was completely shot through. He lie dead on the ground outside the church. They profaned his body, terribly. Then they threw him into the Church, which they proceeded to put on fire. He gave up his life for his God. There was nothing left of his body when his brother Jesuits came for him. He was forty-seven when he died.

St. Charles Garnier

Charles Garnier was a Parisian from a very well-to-do family. He joined the Jesuits in 1624 at age eighteen. He was ordained at twenty nine, in 1635. He immediately began a campaign to be sent to the missions in New France. His father was having none of it. He hadn't raised him to die at the hands of savages.

Reliquary of bones of Charles Garnier, Auriesville, NY

He put pressure on the Jesuits, and Charles' request was denied. The following year, evidence of the pressure John put on his father was obvious, because this time, his request was not challenged by the father, and John was allowed to go to the New World. His traveling companion was Isaac Jogues.

He arrived in June, and by the beginning of July, was sent to Ihonatiria in Huronia. He met Fr. John De Brébuf, who was a legend by that time. He stayed with Fr. De Brébuf for two years, learning the language and customs of the people. In 1639, he and Fr. Jogues went to evangelize another tribe of Indians, the Petuns, who turned out to be very unfriendly to the Jesuits. They left, but Fr. Garnier knew in his heart, they could be converted. He went back in 1640. He founded a mission in 1641, which he had worked successfully. This time the natives were much friendlier and more open to the work of the Jesuits. He returned to St. Ignace from 1644 to 1646, and then returned yet another time to the camp of the Petuns. The Jesuits had two stations there in 1649. Word got out that the Iroquois were on the warpath, trying to destroy everything in their way. They wanted to flatten everything that had been built. Reports of the Martyrdom of Priests in the area of Huronia came in every day. Fr. Garnier knew they should be leaving, but they were just starting to get really good results. So they waited. He made his newly-arrived assistant, Fr. Noel Chabanel, return to Sainte-Marie. But Fr. Garnier had baptized many Indians. He couldn't take it upon himself to leave. Fr. Chabanel left on December 7. Two days later, a warning went through the camp that the Iroquois were attacking. The villagers went out to fight them, but the Iroquois came by the rear of the village, and surprised the defenseless people who were there.

Fr. Garnier was the only Priest on the mission. He ran all over, giving absolution where he could, baptizing who he could, giving last rights. He was like a wild man, charging all over the mission. An Iroquois shot him with a musket, once in the chest, and once in the abdomen, but he didn't go down. He kept going, trying to reach an old man he felt he could help, but finally collapsed. A tomahawk pierced his brain, and he was dead. The Priest from a neighboring mission came the next day, and buried his friend. He was buried on the very spot where he was killed, in the missions to which he had dedicated his life.

†

St. Noel Chabanel

Fr. Chabanel was from the south of France. He entered the Jesuit community in Toulouse, at the age of seventeen. After his ordination to the Priesthood, he taught in the Jesuit college in Toulouse. He may have been caught up with the romance and adventure of life in the mission field, and the possibility of Martyrdom. Or he may just have been caught up in what everyone else expressed a desire for. He wanted to go to New France, that is, until he got there.

He arrived in August 1643, and began studying the language and customs of the people, because at that time, it was too dangerous to go out to Huronia, the Huron settlement. The Iroquois were on the warpath. His teacher was Fr. John De Brébuf, who was a veteran in the mission field. We're not sure if he was as impressed with Fr. John as everyone else was, or if he was a victim of peer pressure. Whatever the case, he went with Fr. John De Brébuf and some others to Huronia in 1644.

Everything about his new life revolted him. He never really picked up the language; it was just too different from French. For him, it was too guttural; it was vulgar, as was the entire way of living of the Huron Indians. To his way of thinking, they lived in filth and squalor. He found himself on the brink of vomiting every time he had to eat their food. Although he tried his hardest to cover his feelings, he loathed the people whom he had been sent to convert, and they had to sense it.

Fr. Chabanel suffered his entire time in New France, which was six years. His superiors were very aware of his feelings, and offered to send him back to France. He refused. He had made a commitment, and he would stick to it. In June of 1647, he made a vow to God, *"I vow perpetual stability in this Huron Mission."* That done, he continued with his job, but never enjoyed it. He spent six years of the dark night of the soul in the mission field.

Fr. Chabanel stayed with Fr. De Brébuf until 1649, when he was sent to be with Fr. Charles Garnier among the Petun Indians. Before he left, he confided to a comrade, *"This time I hope to give myself to God once and for all and to belong entirely to him."* So it was obvious that although he was trying desperately to keep his commitment to the Lord, he was having a very difficult time with it.

Fr. Chabanel only stayed with Fr. Garnier for about two weeks, when word came about the Iroquois threatening to destroy all the Petun Indian camps. Fr. Garnier sent Fr. Chabanel back to Sainte-Marie. Along the way, one night he and his companions heard a group of Iroquois walking along the road. They were singing songs of victory. Fr. Chabanel could hear the cries of captives, who were in terrible pain from having been tortured. He woke his Huron companions. There was an error in communications. The Hurons decided to go to the nearest camp, which was St. Matthias. Fr. Chabanel headed towards Sainte-Marie, which were his instructions. He was all alone. He came to a very deep river, which he couldn't wade across. He sat there, waiting for help. He was given help across a deep river by a Huron in his canoe. This Huron turned out to be an apostate, and hated Christianity. He killed Fr. Chabanel and threw his body into the river. He boasted about the crime two years later. And so this unhappy soul, who tried with all his might, and never did believe he fit in, finally joined with his fellow Martyrs as having been warriors of the Lord. His shortcomings turned out to be his virtues. They were what brought him into the Kingdom. Fr. Noel Chabanel was the last of the Jesuit Martyrs of North America.

†

We want to comment on how these Martyrs held up under the most inhuman conditions in which they found themselves, how violent and savage the Indians were, those to whom they had ministered, and how they were able to function under these conditions. Just think, every night when they put their head down to sleep, they never knew if they might not be victims of a tomahawk. Consider how tenuous their existence was. When we say they never knew if they were going to wake up in the morning with a tomahawk in their head, we're understating the fact. Anything that went wrong, hurricanes, tornadoes, frost, snow, heat, pestilence, you name it, was blamed on the blackrobes (Jesuits). The degree of danger ranged from a demand to remove the cross from their quarters, to exile, to torture and execution. Every day, they might go from one end of the spectrum to the other. But they stuck it out. It's amazing; these dear men were not only able to do this, but actually embraced this way of life. At one time or another, during their ministry in our country, most of them were sent back to France for one reason or another. They didn't have to come back; they were heroes back home. But they returned, to be Martyred for the faith.

We'd like to believe, the blood of these Martyrs brought about immediate conversion. That's not what happened! The taste of blood led the savage Iroquois indians on a rampage. They vented their anger on every mission, they could find. What the blood of the Martyrs did accomplish in the New World was to create a series of role models which gave evangelists to follow, such a zeal and desire to save souls for Christ, that the enemy didn't stand a chance. There was such a fervor pumping wildly through the veins of the Missionaries, nothing was strong enough to stop them.

Our Protestant brothers and sisters in Christ, who have researched the work of the Martyrs in the founding of our country, have praised the selfless sacrifices, brothers and sisters of long ago made, so that we might be a free people. There was a love there, for God's people. There was no division drawn between one race and another, one nationality and another, one denomination and another. We were all on a great mission, to bring Jesus to this world.

There's only one thing that can put out the light, extinguish the fire, kill the dream, and that's apathy, not caring. The enemy can settle in nicely, snug and warm in an apathetic, bored people, insensitive, or desensitized to the cares and problems of their brothers and sisters. Apathy is a strong satan, a virus, which if left unchecked, can infect and destroy the world. *Look what it's done to our country, this land founded in the name of Jesus.* If it could happen here, it could happen anywhere. And it will; it is happening. Which of the Martyrs will you imitate? What will you do so that your country, your family is not swallowed up by the enemy, the savagery of our generation?

The Maryknoll Martyrs

It is so beautiful how the Lord works. We have just shared with you how our brothers and sisters from Europe, most especially France and Spain, answered the Lord's call, and selflessly evangelized the New World, what we call today, North America, or more specifically, the United States. There was no thought given to personal comfort or safety. The focus was the salvation of souls, and spreading the Good News of Jesus to the whole world. That's all they cared about.

Now He turns the tables. He takes the people from the United States, those who were converted and evangelized to by the European brothers and sisters, to evangelize the pagans, the savages of our time, the Twentieth Century. A perfect example of this was The Maryknoll Missioners. They were founded as a home-grown, American group of Missionaries, begun in this century, devoted to put back in the pot, so to speak, to go to foreign lands, as did our forefathers, to bring the word of Jesus, in thanksgiving for the brothers and sisters who made our country a nation under God.

Although the Maryknollers were only founded in the early years of the Twentieth Century, it seems like we've grown up with them. From the time we were children, we knew about the Maryknoll Fathers, Brothers and Sisters. We used to get this little magazine every month. In it were awesome tales of American men and women who devoted their lives to the Foreign Missions, bringing the Word of Jesus to the Pagans. There were always adventurous stories about far-off places like China, Korea, far eastern countries.

We came back to the Church in 1975, and became *churchaholics*. Anything that had to do with Church, we were there. Sometimes we'd go to Mass twice a day if there was a St. Jude's Devotion on Wednesday night after the Mass. God can work through that. It was because of that

desire to embrace anything that had to do with Church that
we attended the first Mass celebrated by the first member of
our Parish to be ordained. His name was Fr. John Harper;
he was ordained into the Maryknoll Order. His family had
lived in our village. Fr. John lived there too, until he went
off to the Seminary. We never really got to know Fr. John
very well. We'd see him when he came home to visit his
family. Then, he'd celebrate Mass at our Church, St. Jude.
We got to talk to Fr. John. He shared a little about his life at
Maryknoll. He was stationed in New York State, but was
anticipating being sent to the foreign missions, because that
is what Maryknollers do. Every now and then, when we'd
receive our copy of the Maryknoll Magazine, we'd see Fr.
John's picture, and a little blurb about him.

We lost touch with Maryknoll, and all the gifts, the Lord
has given us through them. We began writing our book on
Saints and Other Powerful Men in the Church in 1990. As we
researched the life of Archbishop Fulton J. Sheen, we
discovered a Maryknoll Martyr, **Bishop Francis Xavier Ford**.
Penny did the chapter on Archbishop Sheen, and she wrote
a short biography about Bishop Ford. When we began
working on this book, especially this section on American
Martyrs, we came across Bishop Ford again, plus many other
Maryknoll Martyrs. They run the gamut from China to
Japan to Korea, and on and on. We can't possibly cover
them all in this chapter, but we'd like to pick out a few that
have touched our hearts, and about whom we have some
information. These Martyrs are important to us as
Christians; they're important to us as Americans; they're
important to us as Church!

Bishop Francis Xavier Ford - 1952

Francis Xavier Ford was born of good Irish stock in Brooklyn, New York on January 11, 1892. His father, Austin Ford, was the publisher of the *Irish World*, a reactionary newspaper, promoting Irish independence, and the rights of the Irish people. We know there are no coincidences with the Lord. We have to wonder how Francis was given the name of one of the greatest Missionaries in the history of our Church, St. Francis Xavier. Which came first, the name or the vocation?

Whatever the Lord's plan was, it became very obvious to everyone, early on, that Francis would be following in the footsteps of his namesake, rather than in his father's. Austin wanted his son to take over the family business; the Lord had other plans for Francis. He zeroed in on being a Priest. That was going according to the *Lord's* plan. There's a story that Archbishop Fulton J. Sheen told about Bishop Ford. It seems that when he was about twelve years of age, an Italian missionary came into the neighborhood church, making an appeal for the lepers. At the end of the talk, Francis put a nickel into the collection, which at that time, could very well have been his allowance for a whole week. Young Francis never forgot the last words of the missionary, "*My one ambeesh is to die a Martyr.*"

When Francis met **Fr. James Walsh**, co-founder of Maryknoll, in the Seminary, his mission in life was also sealed. Francis became the first seminarian in the newly formed organization, the Maryknoll Missioners. He was ordained in 1917, and left for the foreign missions in September of 1918. He was part of the Maryknollers. His destination was China.

In the early days of the missionary work in China, the Maryknollers were under the jurisdiction of the *Paris Foreign Missioners*. Then they were assigned their own territory, where a classmate of his, and another Walsh, James *Edward* Walsh, became the first Bishop of the Maryknoll Missionaries. Fr. Ford was to write the following in those early days:

"Grant us, Lord, to be the doorstep by which the multitudes may come to worship Thee. And if, in the saving of their souls, we are ground underfoot and spat upon and worn out, at least we shall have served Thee in some small way in helping pagan souls and we shall have become the King's Highway in Pathless China."[11]

In 1925, the Maryknoll Missioners were given another area, the Kwangtung province, and Fr. Ford was put in charge. Almost immediately, he opened a Seminary, followed by a community of sisters, all of whom were native. His reasoning was brilliant. *"A country without a native clergy is always in danger of being stranded for lack of a pilot. In time of persecution, the first to be wiped out or driven out is the*

---

[11]American Martyrs, Fr. Albert J. Nevins, MM - Page 139

foreigner." He had learned well in the seven years he had been in China.

It was about this time that the Communists began their war for control of China. They were very active in the Kwangtung province. There were reports of outrageous behavior on the part of the Communists. Also, during this time, in 1929, the territory was made into a *Prefecture Apostolic*, and Fr. Ford was named as the first Prefect. The mission blossomed; seminaries, novitiates for sisters, newspapers, schools, student hotels, all these things began to come about. On the other side of the coin, Priests were being killed in neighboring provinces, held hostage, brothers were being sent home, total chaos reigned.

The Boxer Rebellion had taken place in 1910, overthrowing the dynasty form of government which had held up for over a thousand years. The result was very unsettling. Anarchy became the favored form of running the country. Everyone tried their hand at running the government. No one knew quite how to do it. The Japanese had captured much of China, and were intent on taking the entire country captive, thus making all Chinese slaves of the Japanese empire. Discord and disorder reigned. The people were looking for something to hold onto, and the lure of Communism was very attractive to them. Little did they know, they were becoming victims to a lie, the same lie their brothers and sisters in Russia had bought into. They were sold a bill of goods about a better world which didn't exist. They sold their God and their souls for that world, which never came into being. Instead of being slaves of the Japanese, they became slaves of totalitarian governments.

But the Missionaries' lives became more difficult than had been previously. China was never really open to Christianity. It was an uphill battle all the way. With the introduction of Communism, a deadly enemy of Christianity, the situation became even worse. But these brave followers of Mary were willing to give their lives to bring just one person into the Kingdom. There were stories of Priests from other communities in China being killed by the Communists. One, of now Monsignor Ford's own Priests, was held captive for a time.

But in spite of all that, his mission prospered. Rome was so pleased with the progress of the area that it was changed again, this time into a Vicariate[12], and Msgr. Ford was raised to the station of Bishop, the first Bishop of the new Vicariate. He went back to his roots, to Maryknoll in New York State to be ordained Bishop. It was a time of great joy and pride for the brothers at Maryknoll. Their work was being respected, by this honor given to one of their own. The newly ordained Bishop Francis Xavier Ford took, as his episcopal motto, the Latin word *Condolere - "To Suffer With."* How could he have known how prophetic this motto was? Had he already had a special relationship with the Lord, wherein he knew in advance the type of persecution and death he would have to endure for the people he ministered to?

We've said many times that the Saints and Powerful Men and Women, the Lord chooses to work in His vineyard, are given special graces, have special relationships with Jesus, Mary, the Angels and their other brothers and sisters, the Saints. That's not to say we can't all have that relationship. We are all called; those who say *Yes* are chosen. But God allows us to make the decision. Francis Xavier Ford gave the Lord a big *Yes*.

The Second World War came. The Chinese were on the side of the Allies, against the Japanese. Bishop Ford opened a Major Seminary in his Vicariate. He couldn't take a chance on sending his young men out; they may never return. It turned out to be a move of great wisdom. He set

[12]A district administered by a Vicar - the office or authority of a vicar

up a relief effort to care for the refugees of the war. He motivated his people to work together with the community to feed and shelter those who were in need. It really cemented relations between the Missionaries and the children whom they were evangelizing. It sounded good on paper. It even seemed like the Communists were working with the forces of Chiaing Kai Shek to drive the Japanese out.

But no sooner was the war over than the civil war started up again. For the Chinese, the war never ended. Only the players changed. The war dragged on for four years. The Soviet Union poured men, troops and money into Mao Tse Tung and his army. In 1950, Chiaing Kai-shek and his army fled to Formosa. The Communists were in charge. All hell broke loose.

They came into the Mission and turned it into a prison. All the *foreign* Priests were exiled. The native Priests were jailed and the sisters sent home with instructions to marry. They put Bishop Ford under house arrest just before Christmas of 1950. The interrogations began. Bishop Ford was sure it was just harassment. The questions were foolish. But what he was counting on was logic. There was no logic, there. They made up stories, called him and his people American spies. They kept pounding that in, not only to Bishop Ford and his Sisters who were left, but to all the local people whom the Maryknollers had helped so much. Now *they* believed the lies, the Communists were spreading; or did they want to believe, to survive?

On April 14, 1951, Bishop Ford called in a Nun and told her, he was worried they would confiscate his property. He said, "*Here is the key to the Tabernacle. I want you to remove the Blessed Sacrament before It is desecrated.*" She took the key and a loaf of bread to the Bishop's Chapel on the second floor of his home, removed the Blessed Sacrament and hid It in the loaf of bread. As she closed the Chapel door, a

Communist Colonel, known all over China for his cruelty, said he was taking over possession of the Chapel. As he tried to unlock the door, it wouldn't open. He demanded the Nun open the door. She replied, she could not as she had her hands filled with the loaf of bread. He demanded she give him the bread. She passed the bread to him and, she later recalled, he looked down at it as if it were an infant. The Nun brought the Blessed Sacrament (hidden within the bread) to safety and was later imprisoned.

The Bishop's Chinese cook who had served him many years, and whom Bishop Ford regarded as a good friend and Christian, was the man who delivered him over to the Communist authorities and falsely accused him. This he did, knowing the tremendous love and compassion, the Bishop had for the people, always consoling the sick and burying the dead. And the reward he received for delivering his Bishop and friend over to the Communists? He was made chief of police of the village.

That day, Bishop Ford and the Maryknoll Sister, Sister Joan Marie, were dragged through the streets of the village. They were tied up. Bishop Ford's hands were bound behind his back and fastened to a rope which was tied around his neck; so that when he tried to lower his hands, he pulled his head back in excruciating pain. It was a terrible way to treat someone who had been so loving to these people. The soldiers ran ahead of the two prisoners, inciting the people; so that when the two religious passed, they threw stones at them, pummeled them with sticks and garbage. There was no relief for them in their cell, at night. Lines of people filed by, committing the same outrages which had been heaped on the two, during the day.

After weeks, days, hours and minutes of inconceivable suffering, they finally arrived at the federal prison in Canton, where the Priest and the Sister were separated. She could only see him on rare occasions when he was paraded in front of the people. So, like Our Lord Jesus Who came only to love His Children and bring them everlasting life: "*He will be handed over to the gentiles where He will be mocked and spat upon.*"(Luke 18:30), they tortured Bishop Ford, abusing him physically and mentally calling him all sorts of names. It was another "*Do away with Him! We choose Barabbas!*" They had forgotten all that the missionaries had taught them, all the good they had done. They had chosen life on earth.

Just as the people in Jesus' time they turned on him, angrily. As with Jesus, it was almost as if they wanted to forget what he had said, forget the world he had shown them of love and compassion. *What they did not know would not hurt them*! Now they knew and they wanted to wipe out that memory of how good it had been and would never be again. They wanted to wipe him out of their thoughts. They spit at him, and threw all sorts of garbage at him, calling him all kinds of vile names. It was more torture for Bishop Ford, seeing his innocent lambs losing their souls than the physical pain he was suffering. Bishop Ford, as with many of the other Martyrs who shed their blood for the Faith, walked the Way of the Cross right up to Calvary. That is the price that has been paid for our Church, you who would choose this *temporary* world over Life Eternal!

The day finally arrived for Bishop Ford to process in the *death march*. The Communists would never kill anyone; they would just let him die. The Communist Colonel who had taken over the Chapel, tied a sack, weighing over twenty pounds, and placed it around the Bishop's neck. The Nun who had been with him at the Chapel, seeing what he had done to the Bishop, broke out of the death march! Standing behind the Bishop, she shouted at the colonel, "*Look at the man.*" It was as if he could see the pain carved in the Bishop's face for the *first* time. A look came over his face. Was he remembering when humanity reigned, for a short time, over insanity? He soon recovered his Communist composure and ordered the Nun back in line.

The Sister watched, as the death march weaved in and out, her eyes never leaving the Bishop. Barely able to walk, he was being supported by two Chinese men on either side of him, but *the sack was not around his neck*! Years later, when Bishop Sheen asked the Nun why she believed the colonel removed the sack, she replied, **"Because he once carried the Blessed Sacrament."** The power of the Eucharist to change men's hearts! The colonel was placed into prison and the Nun never heard of him again.

Bishop Ford lived to see the prophecy: *my ambeesh is to die a martyr* fulfilled. He died a *"dry Martyr"* in February of 1952; they didn't execute him; they just let him die. The former cook who had been made sheriff of the village, was ousted in a new purge that took place fairly regularly. He went back to the Chapel, where he had betrayed his good friend, threw a rope over a rafter and committed suicide.

Bishop Patrick J. Byrne - 1950

Whereas Bishop Ford was the first seminarian in the Maryknoll Fathers, Patrick Byrne was the first Priest in the Maryknoll community. He was ordained a Priest before there was a Maryknoll Missioners. He wanted to work in the foreign missions, and had received permission to do so. He joined the Catholic Foreign Mission Society, which was then  incorporated into the Maryknollers. But he didn't go overseas for quite a few years. He taught in a prep school, or Junior Seminary until 1922, when the Maryknoll Missioners were given a territory in Korea, and Fr. Byrne was chosen to be the Superior. Although he had no experience working in the missions, he relished the possibility, and jumped at the chance.

Fr. Byrne was a good-humored Irishman. He let a lot roll off his shoulders before he got his Irish up. So he was really perfect for the job. Those without the gumption of Fr. Byrne would have hesitated to jump into the frying pan, so to speak. But in those days, there was an excitement about these young men who had committed themselves to the service of the Lord. They were eager to bring in converts. Nothing could stop them. They had God on their side; they had Our Lady and the Angels to protect them. And so in 1922, Fr. Byrne barreled through, and headed to Korea, on the border of Manchuria.

He did very well, there. His superiors could see he was a man who got things done, so when the Holy See gave Maryknoll yet another territory to evangelize near Kyoto in Japan, they immediately chose Fr. Patrick Byrne to do the job. He went there in 1935. Again, the Lord was smiling on the work of Patrick Byrne. He must have been so proud of this special son. Two years later, the progress had been so great, the mission was upgraded to a Prefecture, and Fr. Byrne was also advanced. He became Monsignor Patrick Byrne.

Kyoto began to struggle. The Missionaries were not attracting enough potential converts. Whereas in Korea, they were overwhelmed with converts, in Kyoto, it was very difficult. Monsignor Byrne was a very aggressive evangelist. He was not about to let anything stand in the way of bringing them into the Church. It was decided that they would build a hospital for Tuberculosis. It was in need, as there was a prevalence of the disease in Kyoto. But there was an ulterior motive. It would make the Maryknollers more visible, and give the local people reason to come in contact with them. It seemed to have the desired results. But we must remember our time clock here. By the time the hospital was completed, we were fast approaching 1940, and enmity between the United States and Japan.

Monsignor Byrne was a man with vision, and without ego. He adapted Bishop Ford's philosophy about native Priests. When the situation became dark, he asked the Holy See to accept his resignation as administrator of the hospital. They understood his thinking, and went along with his decision. A Japanese administrator was appointed, and the work continued. The war broke out, as we all know, on December 8, 1941, Feast of the Immaculate Conception. By this time, a Japanese administrator was well in place. Monsignor Byrne was allowed to stay in Kyoto, in his own home, because of all his good work for the people. You see how the Lord works. If Monsignor Byrne would have stayed at his post in the hospital, he could have been considered a threat. Chances are, he would have been accused of being an American Spy, jailed, and either exiled or executed. As it was, he was looked upon more as a philanthropist who just happened to be American.

Msgr. Byrne helped the Japanese tremendously during the war years, taking care of the sick and homeless. At war's end, the Japanese asked him to speak to the people on national radio, and assure them there would be no craziness, as had happened in Germany. There would be no "*Scorched Earth Policy*", ala Hitler. He was a great help in the transition of power from the Emperor to General Douglas Mac Arthur.

Monsignor Byrne was given a mixed blessing. He was made the Papal Nuncio for South Korea. He was elevated to the honor of Bishop. This took place on June 14, 1949. That was the good part. Then there is the other side of the coin, unfortunately. On June 25, 1950, just a year later, the

North Koreans began pouring into South Korea. The Korean war had begun. If it had been in 1922, the early days of his missionary work in Korea, he wouldn't have had a problem leaving. There was nothing there to worry about. But now, he had built a large Catholic community of Priests as well as lay people. He was their Bishop. They most likely would have understood perfectly, and not complained a bit if he had sought safety in Rome, or back in the United States. After all, he was sixty-two years old. But he never even asked the question. It was just his natural assumption that he would stay with his children.

Four days later, on June 29, the North Koreans reached Seoul, and raided his delegation. They took anything worth anything. They arrested Bishop Byrne and his secretary, Fr. William Booth. They moved them north to Pengyang, which is where it had all begun twenty eight years before. His captors proved to be ruthless, not caring at all for his position or age. Dear Bishop Byrne never made it through the cold winter of 1950. When MacArthur launched an offensive, he and other prisoners were brought up into the mountains where it was extremely cold. He was not dressed for this kind of weather. Anyone who could not make the march into the mountains was shot, and left where they died. They put Bishop Byrne into a hut crammed with other prisoners. They were mostly American prisoners. They tried to help Bishop Byrne, but he had contracted Pneumonia. He said to his fellow prisoners at this time, "*I consider it the greatest privilege of my life to have suffered for Christ with you.*"[13]

Because of his condition, he and another Priest, who was dying from Tuberculosis, were put in a hut separated from the other prisoners. There were no windows, and only a straw covering for the door. There was also some straw on

---

[13]American Martyrs - Albert Nevins, MM

the floor. He was placed on the straw. Did it remind Patrick Byrne of his Savior's birth on a bed of straw in the wintertime, in a land far from His home? He lay like this, on the floor, for four days. He virtually froze to death. As the end was approaching, his fellow prisoner gave him absolution. On November 25, 1950, Bishop Patrick Byrne, strong stock of Ireland, missionary and evangelist to the brothers and sisters in Korea, ended his pilgrimage on earth, and returned to his Home in Heaven.

†

These two men represent the tip of the iceberg of Americans who have left their country to go to foreign lands to bring the Word of Jesus, and die in the process. They've planted a thorn in our hearts and we will never be the same. We believe them to be Martyrs, even though they did not die in the true sense of the word, or in the tradition of *Wet Martyrs*. These two Maryknollers fall into the category of what Archbishop Sheen referred to as "*Dry Martyrs*".

The missions, and the *Martyrs* of the missions, were very precious to him. Because of the unequaled suffering of the Missionaries under Communist rule, he wrote there should be a new type of Saint proclaimed in the Communion of Saints, *the Dry Martyrs*. Those who shed their blood for the Faith are called "*Wet Martyrs*". Bishop Sheen wrote, "*since the enemies of Christ do not always kill, but instead torture, the dry Martyrs suffered over a period of years pain that far exceeded that of the brief interval of the Wet Martyrs.*" He cited that each day, hour, and minute of their lives was a Profession of Faith. He said the Church, in the last *seventy years* has had more Martyrs, "Wet and dry" than in the first three hundred of her existence. In this Honor Roll of God's faithful, he included reverently the victims of Auschwitz, Dachau and other camps of cruelty, those Jews whose only crime was they believed they were the chosen people of God and were faithful to that belief.

Seeking more information on Bishops Ford and Byrne, we looked for Maryknoll in the *Official Catholic Directory*. That's when we realized the scope of their activities all over the world. As of 1991, they had 571 religious and associates working as Missionaries in 26 countries. At the same time that we were marveling about the number of American men and women who have gone overseas, to Foreign Missions to Evangelize to those who do not know Jesus, we saw how many other missions we have overseas. There are close to 4,000 American Missionaries serving in 109 countries.

It's only been forty years since Bishops Ford and Byrne were Martyred for our Faith. The Cause for the Beatification has not been opened, *as yet.* . We don't know if anyone is trying to have their cause considered, or if there *even is* a cause for them. The general attitude of many religious orders is *"But there are so many!"* And they're right. We have no idea how many people died bringing the Faith to *our* country. We have no idea how many Americans have died, putting back in the pot, bringing the Faith to *other* countries. The cost in lives has been staggering.

We see our young men and women going to foreign countries to give up their lives to bring the Word of Jesus to pagans, to make the world a better place. And in our country, we've thrown God out of our public schools. We won't allow Him in any of our public buildings or parks, or allow His Name to be mentioned. Our currency reads *"In God we trust"*, and yet we don't do anything of the kind.

What we do know is their lives should not have been wasted; they should not have died in vain. The only way we can be assured that that will not happen is for us to protect our Faith and our Country for which they lived and died. We can't sit back and be polite. They weren't; the people who killed them weren't. They fought for what they believed in. They've done their job; we have to do ours. It won't happen without us. Jesus is counting on us.

The Martyrs of Mexico

I believe the best way to describe the Mexican Martyrs, the Martyrs of Poland and Ireland is with the spanish word for Martyr which is *mártir*. When you pronounce *mártir* in spanish you hear the word *tear*. The Catholic Church in Mexico has been bought with blood and *tears*.

The Mexican people we know and love

Who are the Mexican people and why do we love them so very much? How did we, two kids born in *New York*, come to know the Mexican people? I believe it started with God sending our family to Southern California. But it wasn't until we went on our individual Cursillos that we really met any Mexicans. Although it was an English-speaking retreat, most of the retreatants were Mexican-Americans. On that weekend, when I got the Lord's message to find Him in the people around me, I balked: *How could I find Him in a personal way from brothers and sisters who spoke predominantly Spanish, most of whom also came from the poorest barrios* (Mexican ghettos)? And so, God was preparing us for this time and this walk with our Mexican cousins from the South; but because of my bull-headedness, I had to wait to know them and ultimately love them.

In 1983, a beautiful Mexican Priest asked to join our Pilgrimage, with his Mexican-American pilgrims. When we began our Pilgrimage, Bob and I agreed to switch back and forth from the pilgrims on the English-speaking bus to those on the Spanish-speaking bus. We felt it would be difficult for one of us to remain *full time* with the Mexican-Americans who spoke little and understood less English. After the first day, I asked to remain with the bus of Mexican-Americans.

We were supposed to be leading this Pilgrimage; *I* was assigned to teach *them*. Instead, without the help of a common language or background (cultural or economic), with no great education in the Catholic Faith, *they* were teaching *me*. Whenever I became upset with the bus driver, who was determined to get us lost and separated from Bob and the other bus, they would start singing the most beautiful hymns of praise and worship. Suddenly a peace would enter the bus. Without understanding what was going on, they would come up to me and console me, telling me with their eyes, they loved me and most importantly, Jesus and Mary loved me. What they may have lacked in *worldly* knowledge, they excelled in *Spiritually* infused wisdom. They listened with the gut and responded with the heart.

On this Pilgrimage an English-speaking young blonde-haired boy, with blue eyes, opted to remain on the Spanish-speaking bus, and became a Mexican. [That boy is our grandson.] He and the maroon-haired, brown-eyed, olive-skinned youth on our bus became inseparable. The other pilgrims lovingly called them "*the Sweet Peas*." They sang together. They laughed together. They learned from each other. They became family. And one of this group, Luz Elena *truly* became our grandson's spiritual sister.

What is a Mexican and what makes them capable of Martyrdom? One of the things that so endeared us to Luz Elena was the love, she had for our Lord and His Mother. She, so like her Mexican brothers and sisters, has a very simple faith. When we first got to know her on Pilgrimage, we found ourselves drawn to this young girl who adored her Lord so deeply. She would get lost in contemplation as she knelt at the different Shrines, as if she was far off in another land, in another time. She would apologize when she realized the rest of the pilgrims had walked ahead and I was waiting for her. As I watched her day after day, I discovered a part of what makes up these people we now love.

How was a young girl, now living in California, able to remain faithful to her heritage and her Church? From the time Luz Elena was a little girl, her grandmother brought her to Mass *daily*. Her life revolved around Church. They would go to Church several times a day. She prayed the Rosary with the ladies and the other children, and recited the Angelus at twelve noon. On different Feast Days, she and the other children dressed up as their ancestors before them, at times giving honor to their Lord and other times to their Heavenly Mother. They wore white dresses and carried baskets of flowers, and dressed as Indians when they were commemorating our Lady's coming to Juan Diego. They can't tell you now how these customs began. They just observed. They just obeyed. And you won't find a happier people. Luz has never felt the necessity to explain *why* she believes. She does and that's it! And that's Mexican.

The Mexican people have always fought to maintain their strong cultural roots. But, as with other immigrants who come to our beautiful United States, in an effort to become *Americans*, many sacrifice all the treasures they brought to this nation of the great melting pot of the world. They cast aside their language and their heritage. They become Americans! But not Luz Elena's family. The first day she was going to come to work for our Ministry, her parents refused to give her their blessing. Being the strong-willed Mexican we will talk about, she told them she could kneel at their feet for as long as it took, but she would not leave for work, without their blessing. [This is a beautiful tradition of the Mexican people that many maintain till today.] Although the young Luz Elena did not understand their reasoning (after all, she complained they did not know us) we told her, we did. They did not want to happen to her what hundreds of years of Martyrdom could not accomplish, that she lose the treasure that is Mexican: their strong Catholic roots. We are happy to report that not only did they give their blessing, but we, over the years, have become *family!*

The Mexican people we encountered in Mexico

Who are the Mexican people, we encountered in Mexico, and what makes up the faith of these wonderful people? When we visit Our Lady of Guadalupe on her Feast Day each year, we learn more and more what makes up this beautifully woven fabric that is Mexican. It is in the faces of those who have travelled by foot hundreds of miles, a knapsack on their shoulders with a bed-roll and very few provisions. Reminiscent of the early Disciples, isn't it? They dot the roadsides carrying banners of their Mother, *Guadalupita* and her Son on a Cross. They sing and walk, almost dancing, with a contradictory *spring* to their step. They look like children anticipating the joy of a party. They know their Mother has prepared a *Fiesta* for them. They have left everything they own in the world, behind them. For you see, to the Mexican, his real treasure is Christ the King, and his Mother, Our Lady of Guadalupe.

We see it in the very young and the very old. Their eyes blind you. They have come, not out of curiosity but out of devotion to their Mother, the one their parents introduced to them right after they were born. And they come, speaking many forms of the Indian language, as well as Spanish. But they have a link, these people of many faces and many colors: they have one Mother and therefore they are one family; they are Catholic. As we pilgrimage through the small towns and visit the local parish Churches, we encounter the same kind of devotion you see in the Basilica of *Our Lady of Guadalupe*, the faithful of all walks of life going up on their knees to the Altar in petition and thanksgiving to their Lord through His Mother.

What makes up a Mexican? A Mexican Priest comes to our hearts, as we write this. He has to be one of the most spiritual Priests, we have ever met. He is always filled with the joy and peace only his Savior can give him. Even when his own community of Priests persecute him, he remains among them exchanging love for rejection. When his superiors give him orders contrary to where he believes the Lord may be calling him, when they tell him he must leave the youth he so dearly loves, he obeys, trusting the Lord will work through his obedience. *And the Lord does!* What gives this Priest the strength to believe and live out that belief? We pray the following pages will give you a hint to not only the spirit of this Priest, but to the Mexican people our own holy Pope John Paul II so dearly loves.

How it all began

When Our Lady of Guadalupe came to Mexico, to an Indian named Juan Diego, she formed a family of two of the most powerful and *determined* cultures: that of Spain and Mexico. She not only blended artfully a beautiful people, brown with white, she united Spaniards who were groomed for battle, and Indian braves who had never been defeated. Only she could have brought about peace and reconciliation, ultimately making them brothers.

Before we can speak of Cortes, the *conquistadores* and the missionaries, we have to speak of Spain of the 15th Century. What makes up the Spaniards who ventured into this strange new land? They were a proud people who had been enslaved for almost 800 years. The Moors invaded Spain in the year 711. Their captors killed not only all those who professed Christ, but closed the Churches in an effort to kill Christ, Himself. The plan was to wipe Jesus Christ off the face of the earth. The name of Christ was forbidden in this country that had always been predominantly Catholic.

The Moors thought they had dealt a death blow to Spain. But the spirit that is Catholic in Spain would not die. The Lord sent King Ferdinand and his Queen Isabella. After they freed Spain from the Moors, they were determined Christ would never be exiled from Spain, again. They saw the destruction of the Faith under the Moors.

There had been no compromising; you followed Allah or no one. Because of this, they gave the Moors an opportunity to convert to Catholicism or leave the land. Those who pretended to convert began to preach heresies (some were even Bishops). This brought about the Inquisition. Maybe to those of us who have lived under our Constitutional rights to practice our *own* religion freely, the Inquisition may seem harsh. And we pray *we* will never see our Religion outlawed in our land of the free. But, we believe, when we are seeing people arrested because they are being faithful to the 5th Commandment "*Thou shall not kill!*", as they try to defend the unborn, the *Holy Innocents* of our time, we may be closer to that persecution than we realize.

Spain had been bankrupted by the Moors. When Christopher Columbus was sent to find a route to the Indies, he was financed primarily from the personal wealth of *the Catholic Queen*, as Isabella was called. There are different viewpoints on *why* she financed Columbus' journey. And again, according to their own agendas there are varied pictures painted of Columbus, as well. I wonder if all the Columbus bashing isn't a desire to bash the Catholic Church.

The Crown of Spain was committed to bringing the Catholic Faith to the people of the land they had discovered. Queen Isabella knew that the success of the return of Spain to the Spanish was only through the Grace of God. In thanksgiving, for having delivered them from the almost 800 years of domination by the Moors (Muslims), she would bring the Light of Jesus to the darkness of the pagan world. She also believed, any work absent of God would ultimately fail. When it is His Will, it will ultimately *triumph*. Although the Church may appear defeated, she will rise again stronger than ever, because the *Church* is the work of God and God cannot be defeated.

The blonde god returns to his people

When Cortes landed in Mexico with the Franciscans, the Indians greeted them with open arms. Cortes reminded them of the blonde god *Quetzacoatl*, the one their ancestors had spoken of for almost seven hundred years. They remembered how they had been told of this fair, blonde god with his great beard who had suddenly emerged from out of the sea, one day; and how one day, he then disappeared into the same sea from which he had appeared.

There is a theory that St. Brendan of Ireland went to Mexico and evangelized the Indians, and that he might have been the one they mistakenly gave the title, Quetzacoatl. Some historians write that this *god* taught them it was wrong to sacrifice. With the passage of time and no one to keep his teachings alive, had they reverted to their paganistic gods? One of the Indian rituals was that of sacrificing certain *chosen* children to the blood-thirsty god Quetzacoatl. The people believed that calamities, such as pestilence and earthquakes, were because their god was angry, and that when these innocents were sacrificed, their god would be appeased. They also looked upon themselves as *"people of the sun"*. They thought, by feeding their god with human blood, he would continue to shine upon them.

When the missionaries arrived with the *conquistadores*, they began to teach the Indians of the One God Who was sacrificed once and for all, so that no more spotless lambs were sacrificed. Although some Indians adopted the religion of the Spaniards, many continued practicing their pagan rituals. The Spaniards were afraid of these Indians who performed such barbaric sacrifices that were totally abhorrent to them. They looked upon them as *ignorant* savages. The Spaniards did not understand that the Indians' customs, very often, were part of *their* religious worship. Not understanding, they did not know how to bring about change. They were frightened; would the Indians turn on them and sacrifice them? There were those tribes, especially those who worshiped the war god *Huitzilopochtli*, who conquered neighboring tribes for the express purpose of sacrificing their prisoners of war to their gods. The Aztec *Emperor Auitzotl* built a temple in 1487, and 20,000 warriors were sacrificed on its altar to commemorate its inauguration. Whatever the motivations or the origins, this pagan practice was what greeted the *conquistadores*. And so, the Spaniards, some out of fear, and others out of greed for more gold, annihilated whole tribes of Indians.

Our Lady comes to Mexico

The Indians were planning a holocaust; they were going to wipe out every European in Mexico (including much of the southwestern United States, which was part of Mexico). *That's when the Mother of God, Our Lady of Guadalupe*[1] *came.* Had she been sad, along with her Son Jesus, over the 6,000,000 innocent faithful in Europe, subtly led away from His Church by the Protestant Reformation? When she came to an Indian convert Juan Diego, she was not only to make up for the number lost in Europe, but to be instrumental in the conversion of *8,000,000* Indians in less than seven years.

When word got out, Indians came to see the Mother of God (in the miraculous tilma). We are told by the Archpriest in the *Basilica of Our Lady of Guadalupe* in Mexico City that conversion began with the story-telling of a simple Indian *Blessed Juan Diego*[2]. Many Indians had heard about this special Lady coming. Maybe initially they came to Tepeyac Hill because they thought she was a goddess. But then, they encountered a humble Indian caring for the small chapel that had been built at Our Lady's request. Juan Diego spent his final years telling the story of our Lady's appearance to an *Indian*. After he finished telling the story,

[1]Bob and Penny Lord's book: "*The Many Faces of Mary*, a love story."
[2]Juan Diego was beatified with Junipero Serra, in 1990.

the Indians would go to the Priests who would finish the conversion process. And this Lady, their Mother from the very beginning, is what has kept the Mexican people faithful to the Church through centuries of blood and tears.

Were Jesus and Mother Mary's hearts breaking at the merciless inhumane sacrifice of innocent children? Did she come that the wrath of God would not fall upon the Indians? Did she come that they would accept the teachings of the Roman Catholic Church and stop sacrificing the innocent? Is not Mother Mary coming to us today? Are we listening to what she is saying to us? Is she not coming to us, as a Mother, (*Our Lady of Guadalupe*) as she did on Tepeyac Hill?

[Author's note: Last week, when we were giving a talk at one of our Churches here in the United States, beside us was the pilgrim image of Our Lady of Guadalupe that is travelling from town to town, reaching out to the faithful of our country. A thought came to us: What was happening when our Lady appeared to Juan Diego? Over 20,000 innocents were being sacrificed each year, on an altar to a false god. Are we not sacrificing our innocent, our very own flesh and blood, our 2,000,000 unborn, each year, on the altars of false gods of greed (use of aborted babies for scientific research), of permissiveness (do what you want and if it is not convenient to carry the baby to full term, kill it; rather than take responsibility for your actions)? So rather than sacrifice our conveniences, our self-gratification, we justify. We claim that our bodies, a gift to us from God in the first place, are our own, and if the baby happens to be attached to that body, we have the right to do with it what we will, not what God wills. And so we dispose of what God has so carefully fashioned and molded, our own flesh and blood. I don't believe even the so-called savages did that!

It was on the eve of holocaust, of total annihilation. Read the papers; watch the news on television; witness the wiping out of Christ's Name from this country founded under God.   Could we be on the eve of holocaust?   Has our annihilation begun?   Starting in the 60's, we lost, each year, more young men and women to overdoses of drugs than died in the entire Vietnamese war.   And many who did not mercifully die, became mindless walking dead.

Beginning in the 70's, we have annihilated, through abortion, over 30,000,000 Americans.   We have killed our future presidents, congressmen, senators, supreme court justices, scientists, men of God, doctors and nurses, mothers and fathers.   We are erasing ourselves from the face of the earth, just as the Indians were doing, only more so, when our Lady came.

Is this why, after hundreds of years Our Lady of Guadalupe has come to the United States?]

The Martyrdom begins - New Sacrifices

Our Lady's sons, the missionaries taught the Indians how to build and trained them in the crafts they produce till today.   Most of the magnificent Cathedrals and Churches were constructed by the Indians.   The beautiful artworks within their walls, equal to those of any country in the world, were done by Indians.   As the Missionaries developed their talents, the Indians became aware more and more of the One God Who loved them.   And so, as is the tradition in our Church, they learned through art what words could not begin to express; they *personalized* God and His Mother.   And through this personalization, they became a new creation, just like their new art.   The Church, under the helm of the missionaries, taught the Indians to be fishermen, rather than feeding them a fish.   Through these loyal sons of the Church and their dedicated teaching and training of the Indians, Mexico (or New Spain) became a highly cultural center of learning.

Above:
This Shrine marks the place of the Martyrdom of Cristobal

Above:
*Franciscan convent in the town where
Antonio and Juan were martyred*

The Three Martyrs of Tlaxcala

There was a price to be paid, and the price was the blood of Martyrs. *"Amen, amen, I say to you, unless a grain of wheat falls to the ground and dies, it remains just a grain of wheat; but if it dies, it produces much fruit."* (John 12:24)

There is always a sadness, when we hear of children suffering, dying. They are so innocent, so full of life. For many of them, the world, with its lies, has not had a chance to take hold and drown out God's Love and Plan for them. They are still filled with the thoughts, the Lord has given them, before their souls left Him to come to earth. Sometimes, we look into a baby's eyes and see wisdom beyond a baby's years. We wonder: *"Little one, what did our Lord tell you?"* When the baby smiles back at us, we think this is not a gas bubble, as the world tells us, but feelings words cannot describe if the baby *could* talk.

With Hernan Cortes came missionaries, sent by the Church, to bring the Word of God to this new land. They were followed by other missionaries. In 1524, three short years after Cortes landed with the *first* missionaries, twelve more were sent by the Franciscan Order.

Although Cortes *conquered* the tribes of Tlaxcala, they for the most part became *friends*. Their senators were the first to be baptized. This was an important sign to the other members of the tribes, and they soon followed suit. The baptismal font is still there in the Cathedral of Tlaxcala, as witness to what transpired, as is the pulpit from which the first Gospel was preached in the New World.

In the beginning, the Word of God was preached from four Franciscan convents located in the states of Mexico,[3] Texcoco, Huejotzingo, and *Tlaxcala*. Tlaxcala had a history of being a very religious area. What the missionaries found was a profoundly religious people worshiping *many* gods.

[3]In the 16th century, Mexico was called New Spain.

The three martyrs of Mexico
Cristobal, Antonio, and Juan

Not only did they believe in multiple gods, but in multiple wives. Especially among those of the higher class, who felt themselves superior, this practice was wide spread. As in many cultures, the sign of a man's wealth and position was reflected by how many wives he had.

God speaks in many ways. Man has an agenda; but if his heart is with God, He will use it for His Will. *"Man proposes and God disposes."* The Tribes' Chiefs sent their sons, along with sons of their braves, to the Mission Schools. They wanted their children to be taught the language of the Spaniards, so that they could communicate more fully with them. In addition, they were very pleased with all the other skills the children were learning. *Now, this was man's plan.* But, the Mission Schools would not have been *authentically* Franciscan, without teaching the youth about Jesus. The *greatest* teaching was the missionaries *living out* of the Gospel, each day. If they had not uttered a word about Jesus and His Church, this sign was enough that there was a a God Who loved them, unconditionally!

Blessed Cristobal - First of the Young Martyrs of Tlaxcala

And so, the children listened! They could feel a *fire* blazing inside their hearts. It was not that which had been instilled in them, one of war and hate, but of peace and love. *Acxotecatl*, chief of a large tribe of Tlaxcala, sent three of his sons to the Mission School, but not *Cristobal*. He was not only his favorite son, but the one who would inherit the tribe from his father. *Acxotecatl* wanted to be the only one influencing his son's philosophy. But you know when you begin to be filled with knowledge of Jesus and His Church, you find yourself overflowing; you cannot withhold it. And so, it was with Cristobal's brothers. They started to share the teachings of the Franciscans with him. And then, seeing his openness and reception of the Word, they turned him over to the Franciscans. Upon hearing of Cristobal and his yearnings to learn, to know more, *they* converged on him with all the ammunition they had. Before you know it, this young man who was destined to lead a tribe, was being instructed to lead many more by his *crown*, his choice of the Lord.

Cristobal was like a sponge absorbing the Truth. He was like a new born baby tasting his mother's milk for the first time. Having made tremendous strides in learning the Faith, the Franciscans agreed to Baptize him. Now that he knew the Truth, he had the deep desire to convert his people. You see, his father knew well the leadership and the caring heart of this son, when he chose him to inherit the tribe. It was this quality, the father admired, that would cause friction between them. Cristobal listened attentively, as the Franciscans preached; then went home and imparted the Gospel to his father and the servants. He urged them to throw out their idols and alcohol. He told them, God was not pleased with them worshiping false gods. He tried to reason with them, telling them that drunkenness was a sin against the One True God, and they must stop! I am sure, he probably tried to sway his father into giving up his life of *polygamy*, admonishing him that the Lord only permitted *one* wife.

At first, his father thought, this too shall pass. *Acxotecatl* kind of laughed it off. The Franciscans had made this Jesus sound romantic. He would fix him up with a young wife and his mind would turn to more important things. But when the hounds of Heaven are after you, you cannot stop or think of other things; you are in love with the Lover and all else is so much nothingness. When Cristobal saw that all his reasoning with his father and the servants was falling on deaf ears, he decided to take matters into his own hands. He removed all the alcohol from the house, and ripped the idols from the walls smashing them into tiny pieces. His father still hoped his son would let go of this madness. After all, he was his son!

As the father and the servants brought *back* the liquor and the idols, Cristobal threw them out and destroyed them. They persisted in their pursuits and Cristobal in his. This went on and on, until *Acxotecatl* sadly realized his son would not stop. As he was going against the gods, his father was probably afraid there would be some calamity if Cristobal was not stopped. He would have to die. Of course, this was not without encouragement from *Xochipapalotzin*, one of his wives who was not happy with the ideas, Cristobal was preaching, especially that of *monogamy*.[4] Furthermore, if Cristobal died, her son Bernardino would inherit the tribe.

Acxotecatl summoned his sons home from the Franciscan Mission School. He said, he was calling a feast for the family. When the boys arrived, the father sent all away but Cristobal. When they were alone, he grabbed Cristobal by the hair and flung him to the ground. As his boy lay at his feet, he kicked him unsparingly, his anger taking over any reason, he might have had. He struck him with a huge oak club, over and over again, until his arms and legs were crushed, bleeding stumps. Cristobal's once young rugged body was now hanging flesh covered with blood.

When Cristobal's mother heard what was happening, she broke into the room and flung herself between her husband and their son. Her husband took his rage out on her, dealing out to her what he had to their son. He then ordered his servants to throw her out of the house. We don't know if this was by *his* design alone, or by the helpful instigation of his other wife Xochipapalotzin, but a few days later, *Acxotecatl* had Cristobal's mother killed. He had to *silence* her. He could not take the chance she would report him. What he did to his son was against the law of the

---

[4]practice of only one wife

Spaniards and if he was discovered, the chief feared they would kill *him!* The servants *dumped* Cristobal's mother's body in a place called *Quimichucan*. A famous historian of Tlaxcala, *Diego Muñóz Camargo*, has written, both mother and son are Martyrs. We would have to agree. Even if she had not been beaten and killed, the pain she suffered because of the merciless Martyrdom of her son would have been enough to declare her a Martyr. There is no testimony that she ever tried to dissuade her son. As Mother Mary before her, she saw and said nothing, knowing the possible risk he was taking for the Faith, he believed in.

[It's so sad. Herod's wife had him kill St. John the Baptist because they could not bear what he was saying, and now we have another ruler doing the same. Did they not know that the Light of the Truth will always cut through the darkness?]

As his father was torturing him, Cristobal turned to his Savior:

"My God, have mercy on me, and if You wish that I shall die so be it; but if You wish me to live, free me from my father's cruelty."

His father, seeing that all his inhuman beating and torture was not about to kill Cristobal, he thrust his son's poor body into a raging fire. Cristobal did not die! All the while he was suffering, he called upon the Lord and his Mother Mary to intercede for him. The following day, near death, Cristobal called for his father. His last words were:

"Father, do not think that I am angry. I am very happy, and I know that you have done me a greater honor than all the dignities you might have given me."

And with those words, he gave up his spirit to God.

[We can just see Our Lady of Guadalupe enveloping him in her arms, leading him to the Throne of God.]

Acxotecatl, afraid of being detected, buried his son's body in one of the rooms of his home. But the crime had not gone undetected; Cristobal's brother Luis witnessed the whole thing from his window.[5]   He revealed what had happened to the missionaries.   One year later, *Father Andres de Cordoba* (one of the first Franciscans to evangelize the Tlaxcala Indians) solemnly processed Cristobal with an entourage of Indians, following.   When they uncovered the body, they discovered it had not decomposed.   After one year's time, without any form of preservation, the Martyr's body was *incorrupt*. His love for Jesus and His Church was never corrupted by the world with its threats and promises. Our Lord was saying that now Cristobal's *body* was the visible sign for all the world to see.

Blessed Cristobal was all of twelve years old!

Antonio and Juan - Two of the First Martyrs of New Spain

As we walk through the lives of the three Martyrs, covered in this chapter, we need to pause and reflect on how the Lord always chooses who *He* chooses, not those who choose Him.

When our Church was in great need, a boy was born to a wealthy merchant. His father had great worldly aspirations for him.   But the Lord had other ideas.   One day, he spoke to Francis, the young cavalier, and asked him to rebuild His Church.   Francis was never the same.   It is said that Francis exemplified Jesus more than any other man who ever walked the face of the earth. A young man was chosen; he said yes and the sinner Francis became the Saint Francis.   Not so much by what he said, but by his every day living out of the Gospel, sons and daughters of the aristocracy and nobility of Assisi joined him; and today the Order he founded has more followers than any other.   These followers Jesus would use to call forth Saints and Martyrs for His Church which was once again in great need, in another time and place.   The Lord's Church had lost

---

[5]Luis testified to Friar Toribio de Benavente who was lovingly and respectfully referred to, by the Indians, as "Motolinia".

6,000,000 children in Europe. He desired His Promise, that hell would not prevail against His Church, would be fulfilled in New Spain.

Again, as with Cristobal, we encounter a son of a *royal* family. *Antonio* was born in Tizatlan, Tlaxcala, around the year 1516 or 1517. His grandfather was the chief Lord. Antonio was to inherit the tribe and all it encompassed.

Juan, our other Martyr was Antonio's servant. He came from a *humble* background. As with all the Indians of that day, both master and servant, the high and the mighty and the small and simple, went to school[6] together.

Father Martin de Valencia was Provincial of the Franciscans in Tlaxcala and guardian of the Franciscan School where the boys attended classes. His main focus was the *youth* of his parish and their schooling. The children were an important part of his mission. Their zeal and blinding love for the Lord and His Church, opened more doors than his eloquence could ever accomplish. Father had grown especially fond of three: Antonio, his servant Juan and his friend Diego. They were outstanding pupils. They soon knew and spoke Spanish like someone born into a Spanish family. With their knowledge of Spanish and teaching Father the Indian dialects of the region, Father had been able to evangelize the tribes. He was proud of these young lay evangelists. He loved them.

It was 1529. The Dominicans join the Franciscans to evangelize the Indians. We find *Father Bernardino Minaya*, with another Dominican missionary, travelling through Tlaxcala to Oaxaca. They would begin there to convert those tribes who had not as yet accepted Christianity. The Dominicans stopped at the Franciscan School in Tlaxcala, and requested some children to join them on their mission. They explained that, as Father Martin had himself

---

[6]Franciscan Mission School

experienced, lack of knowledge of the many different dialects of the Indians was a stumbling block. With the students acting as translators, they would be able to communicate the Word and bring about conversions.

Did Father Bernardino try to convince Father Martin by quoting Jesus and the high regard He had for children: *"...the Field is the world. And the good seed are the children of the Kingdom."?*[7]

Were *these* children to be the *seed* that would lead many to the Kingdom? Jesus spoke of the smallest seed, the mustard seed:

"The kingdom of Heaven is like a grain of mustard seed which a man took and sowed in his field.

"Which is the least of all seeds, but when it is grown up, it is greater than all herbs, and becometh a tree, so that the birds of the air come, and dwell in the branches thereof."[8]

Father Bernardino did argue that the greatest evangelists are children who have converted to the Faith. Was he prophesying, without knowing it, that God the Sower of seeds, would use these young *seeds*, through their Martyrdom, to be His instruments to bring many souls to *dwell* in the tree of the Roman Catholic Church?

No amount of persuasion would sway Father Martin. He tried to dissuade his students. He did not want any harm to come to them. He tried to warn them of the tremendous risks they would be taking. He pleaded:

"Look my children, you know you will be leaving your own country and you will come among people who do not yet know God, and you will experience hard times. There may not be enough food." But he said that he wished that hunger, thirst, bitter cold and illness were the worst they might face. *"You may even be killed. Think well on it."*[9]

---

[7]Matt 13:38 - Douay-Rheims
[8]Matt 13:31 - Douay-Rheims
[9]from Carmelite Digest Vol. 7, No. 4 - Autumn, 1992

Father Martin went on. He reminded them that there were those Indians who did not want to know our Lord. They *enjoyed* the sacrifice of sometimes 100,000 Indians each year to their gods. The evangelization they were embarking on could enrage these tribes who had so little regard for human life. They sacrificed their *own children* when they ran out of captives from other tribes. He pleaded, they were placing themselves in danger beyond their wildest dreams.

Antonio and Juan both looked at one another and then they spoke with one mind and one heart. Were they remembering all the stories the Franciscans had told them, of the Martyrs? They turned to their beloved teacher:

"Father, isn't that why you taught us all about the True Faith? We are ready to go with the Fathers and to accept willingly whatever hardship that comes with the work for God, even to give our lives for Him. Wasn't St. Peter crucified, St. Paul beheaded, and St. Bartholomew scourged to death for God?"[10]

He reminded them of their responsibility to their tribes. After all, they would be inheriting these souls, when they became Chief Lords. Who would take care of them, if something happened to Antonio and Diego? Would their braves have Chiefs who would love the Lord and bring *Him* to their people?

Father Martin looked into those eyes, burning already with the fire of Martyrdom, and he knew he had failed. The three young evangelists assured the good Father that they were aware of the barbarity of the tribes, they would be reaching out to. They knew the dangers. They thanked him for the teachings, he had given to them of the One True God. Could they refuse to bring it to those who had never heard the Good News? Were they not their brothers' keepers? They knelt before him, pleading for his blessing,

---

[10]from Carmelite Digest Vol. 7, No. 4 - Autumn, 1992

and permission to go with Father Bernardino. Their final words to Father Martin echoes the words of Martyrs and Saints before them: "*We are doing it all for God. If we should die for Him, would He withhold His Mercy?*"

Father Martin reluctantly agreed to send Antonio and his friend Diego, if they would take Juan, as well. Father reasoned that having one more along would give the youth one more to help them, in time of trouble. He held back the tears as he saw them take off. Somehow he knew in his heart, he would never see them again. God had chosen three of his top students, no, children whom he had come to love as if they were his own flesh and blood. He felt as if a part of his heart was being ripped away. Antonio, Juan and Diego joined hands and looked back only once.

The young men set out with Father Bernardino, and his companion, to evangelize Indians who had not accepted Jesus. They arrived at Tepeaca, but since there was no monastery there, they pushed on to Huejotzingo. Although there was an established Franciscan Mission there, the Franciscans had not been able to convert the many pagans who clandestinely worshiped idols and sacrificed to their false deities. The Spaniards had issued orders prohibiting such activities. But we know, and the missionaries knew, that Man can change laws, but if you do not change men's hearts, *lasting change* will not come about.

The Dominicans knew that the only way they would be able to bring the One True God to the Indians, was to find and destroy the idols they worshiped. As long as they were immersed in diabolic reveries and practices which included violence and debauchery, they would be deaf and blind to the Word of God. Who would best know how and where to find these idols? The boys! Antonio, Diego and Juan found altar after altar with pagan idols. They brought the idols back to the Missionaries who in turn destroyed them.

They went on to the town of Orduña. The Indians stealthily watched the threesome as they removed the idols. They did not touch them, but their fates were sealed that day. They must die! Not aware they had been observed, Antonio and Juan went on to the next village. They were sure to find many idols in Cuauhtinchan! Upon arriving there, Antonio spotted a house that had a young *boy* standing guard. He had a feeling, there was an altar inside. Little did he suspect anything was wrong, as he left his servant friend Juan to guard the door. As soon as Antonio entered the house, two Indians appeared, as if out of nowhere, and began striking Juan savagely with huge clubs. Upon hearing Juan's cries, Antonio rushed out and tried to stop them. He pleaded:

"Don't harm my friend. He is not in charge. He is my servant. If you want to hurt someone, strike me, as it is I who am destroying your idols. You have been worshiping what you have believed to be gods. They are not gods, but devils. And for them, you would take the life of an innocent child? Well, if you insist on revering these demons, then here take your god! Let my companion go!"

With that, Antonio threw the idol to the ground. But not even giving back their idol would satisfy their anger. Two grown men beat the defenseless Juan until he was mercifully dead, and then brutally finished their handiwork on Antonio. As he was a *Chief's grandson*, you would think fear of reprisal from Antonio's tribe would have stopped them. Not even execution by the Spaniards stopped them. Maybe, they thought that their crime would go undetected. They threw the broken, bloody bodies of the once very alive young boys into a ravine. If by some slim chance the young evangelists were found, the blame would go to someone else.

When Antonio and Juan failed to return, the Dominicans organized a search party. They found the bodies and processed with them to a small chapel where a solemn Mass was celebrated. They were immediately looked upon as Martyrs. The braves who had committed the barbaric crime were apprehended. They were sentenced to die by hanging. Before they were hanged, they confessed *voluntarily* to the crime. They described, to the last detail, what had transpired. They begged forgiveness for the taking of innocent lives. And if that does not sound miraculous enough, they asked to be Baptized.

Two holy and zealous lay evangelists could no longer hunt idols and destroy them. All they had planned to do, in the eyes of the foolish, was over. They were dead! But with this act of remorse by the murderers, and the bravery of these young boys, who chose to die for the One True God, more conversions came about than all the preaching and smashing of idols could have done in a *hundred* lifetimes.

Father Martin never forgot the price, his beloved students paid for the Faith. He would not allow any more young braves to go out and smash idols. He spent the next ten years hunting down pagan idols and destroying them. The Indians knew who was doing it, but they never touched the old Priest. Unlike Antonio and Juan, his Martyrdom was not to be of blood, but the ongoing agony of missing those two young boys who had touched his life.

Mother Church raises three young Martyrs to Blessed

Since the sixteenth century, *Cristobal, Antonio* and *Juan* have been considered Martyrs by historians. But more importantly, from the very beginning, the *faithful* of Tlaxcala have revered them as Martyrs. Because three young boys, from their number, chose *eternal life* over the world, Mexico has had a stubborn people who have followed Jesus and His Church for the last four hundred years. No amount of threats, torture and deprivation could take away the gift that their *own* paid for, in blood and tears. When Mexicans remember and recant the story of these three Martyrs, they see themselves as they can be, and a look comes in their eyes. *And Cristobal lives! And Antonio lives! And Juan lives!*

When the Bishop of Tlaxcala, *Luis Munive Escobar* requested the opening of the cause for Canonization of the three Martyrs, he introduced them as "*young models of the laity*". We are sometimes asked *why* we do not write of the heroes who came from the laity. Actually many of the Saints and Martyrs that we have written about came from our ranks. When you think about it all the Popes, Bishops, Priests, and Religious who lived and died for the Faith came from the laity. We are the Bishop, the Priest and the Religious makers. Think about it!

May 6, 1990, *Pope John Paul II* declared Cristobal, Antonio, and Juan *Blessed.* He called them *heroic models of faith and Christian courage.*[11] Through our Pope, Mother Church *officially* pronounced what the faithful of Tlaxcala have believed from the 16th century. As Spanish-speaking people from all parts of the world (but most especially the faithful of Mexico), congregated in the Basilica of Our Lady of Guadalupe, to hear *their* Pope proclaim these words, there could not have been a dry eye in their midst. Just imagining our Pope, as he addressed these people he loves so very much, his gentle blue eyes filled with tears of joy and hope, brings tears to our eyes. As we research more and more on the faithful of Poland and Mexico, we can see why the Pope and the people of Mexico claim him as Mexican.

Our Pope has been pleading for a birthday present for Jesus in the year 2000. He wants to present converts to the Baby Jesus Who was born to die for us. He wants to stand beneath the Cross with the Lady He loves, and say to Jesus Crucified, "*Here are those You died for. Lord, we remember!*"

The Pope wants us to turn around the imbalance in the world of those who know Jesus (2 billion) and those who

---

[11]from Carmelite Digest Vol. 7, No. 4 - Autumn, 1992

do not (4 billion). And he is asking you and me to be part of the Church's Evangelization. Does that seem overpowering? What can you do? You're not evangelists, you say. But by your Baptism, you are. Three young braves [what a beautiful word-brave] just said yes! They could not keep to themselves, the treasure they received. And because of their yes, millions of Mexicans down through the centuries converted to, and remained faithful to the Church, they so passionately loved. Cut a Mexican and he will bleed the Catholic Church, the blood of Martyrs.

These young men came from the New World, our world. We have an example to follow. They died trying to destroy the false idols which Indians, who had not been enlightened, worshiped. What are we doing to keep *our* innocent children, brothers and sisters from worshiping false idols? What is your answer, today? Will you live for Christ? They died for Him!

The beginning of the end - The Mexican Revolution

To look upon Mexico, and the Mexicans, as backward and different from us, is to make a major mistake and to learn nothing. The Mexico that rose from the ashes of the Mexican Revolution of 1810 was not the Mexico who was for 150 years, after Our Lady of Guadalupe came, one of the greatest nations in the world.

Ironically, the actions of a *Priest*, Miguel Hidalgo, who might have been well-meaning initially, brought about *revolution*. He began only wanting some *equity* for the Indians. The Priest was about social *justice*; what he accomplished was social *uprising*, against the wealthy landowners, and (possibly not part of his plan, in the beginning) against the Church. As we have said, over and over again: Social justice without Jesus in the center, is Judas revisited. We end up selling out our Lord, once more. This

Priest may have had good intentions, but without God in charge, he had to turn against Him.

The people followed this Priest, believing he was speaking the Church. Farmers and peasants, without weapons other than pitchforks, knives and the like, rallied round Hidalgo, and marched on the towns and villages of Mexico. The force swelled to over a hundred thousand, at which point, Hidalgo lost control of his followers completely; it became a bloodbath. Hidalgo was not a military man; he became the dupe for ambitious men, who would use him for their own ends. Finally, he was killed, a year after his ill-begun revolution. And from that poor beginning, revolution upon revolution has *continued*. The Spanish regained control of the *towns* after Hidalgo was killed, but they never quite controlled the *country* again.

So not all Priests represent Jesus? It was *Father* Hidalgo who issued the *first orders* which instituted the Revolution's ongoing, brutal attacks on both God *and* His Church. And when God is taken out of a movement, then the world with its lies and promises, pollutes and destroys. So, for almost two hundred years, Mexico plummeted downward from a highly respected, advanced civilization to a country and a people looked down upon as backward and ignorant. Since the infamy of the Revolution, that which was to be for the good of *all the people* ended up just changing hands from one landowner to another (most often the general in charge of the coup).

Ten years after Hidalgo was killed, a shrewd upstart took control of the country, and proclaimed himself its Emperor. His empire lasted less than two years, but accomplished two things. Spain *was banished* from Mexico, including its soldiers and governors, but also its money. The Emperor bled the country of what remained of its treasury, setting the stage for many to continue doing, down through the years. The bloodsuckers remained; only now they were home-grown Mexican opportunists, rather than the Spanish Overlords. In a period of fifty five years, from 1821 to 1876, Mexico was ruled by *forty* presidents, *two* emperors, and a few provisional governments. Everyone took their best shot at raping the people. It was also during this time that Mexico lost a good deal of her territory to the United States in the Mexican War of 1846: Texas, California, Nevada and Utah, in addition to parts of New Mexico, Arizona, Colorado and Wyoming.[12]

The country had been looted of all its treasury *systematically* by Santa Anna, who had been in some degree of power for almost twenty five years. While he was exiled from the country *three times*, he was also asked to come back *twice*. Each time he returned, he wiped out the treasury again. Finally, in 1854, the people had had enough of him, and he was exiled his third and last time.

Juarez - "the Thomas Jefferson of Mexico"

The country had been ruled for many years by *military* men, who kept increasing and increasing their own personal fortunes. The people looked with hope to a strong non-military man, a full-blooded Indian, *Benito Juarez*. He was the only one who seemed to care about the people. During his eighteen years in power, he brought his country to financial ruin; not because he was crooked, he just didn't know how to run a country. Juarez, who has been called the *"Thomas Jefferson of Mexico"*, because of his reforms, was also most instrumental in *persecuting the Church* in Mexico. This seems strange for a man who was taken off the streets as a young boy and given his education through the generosity of a Priest.

As soon as Juarez had attained even a small degree of power in the Mexican government, he passed a bill,

---

[12]this section on Miguel Hidalgo was taken from Bob and Penny Lord's book: *Saints and Other Powerful Men in the Church*

forbidding the Church to buy property. He followed this with another law, called the Reform Laws, which *confiscated* all church property, *broke up* monastic orders, *dismantled* convents, and *prohibited* seminaries. Religious were not allowed to wear *clerical vestments* on the streets. The Reform laws of Benito Juarez, and his focus, that of crushing the Church in Mexico, have existed in one form or another until this day. Once begun, the persecution never ended. Sadly enough, this man would not have remained in power, if it were not for the support, he received from the United States.

Mexico stopped growing

Mexican turned against Mexican. All building ceased until Porfirio Diaz began the construction of public buildings. The once beautiful religious art, the Spaniards taught the Indians, was replaced by the Bolshevist-inspired propagandist work of Diego Rivera. [Sadly, when you are touring Mexico City, under the direction of many city guides, one of the main highlights will be the huge mural by Diego Rivera defacing the outer wall of the National Palace. Diagonally across from this desecration of our Lord and defamation of His Church, looms the true spirit of Mexico - The Cathedral, reaching up toward Heaven. The hammer and sickle that adorns this work of man (Diego Rivera) has crumbled and will long be forgotten. But the test of time, the evidence of a people's faith and faithfulness will never die. What will live until our Lord returns is what the Mexican Government announced in 1935, it fears above all else, **...the Catholic Church**:

"*...one thing which above all else it fears, more than the foreign exploiters of oil and metals, more than the Gringo Government in Washington, is the same Catholic Church.*"[13]

---

[13] from chapter Dilemma P.4-Mexican Martyrdom by Father Wilfrid Parsons, S.J.

Mexico - Land anointed by the blood of Martyrs

As we have seen, down through the centuries, the Church will always rise from the ashes of Martyrs. And that is what this book is about.

The Revolution, purportedly for the freedom of the working class, was anything but that. It was just a changing of the guard: the few still had too much, and the many still had too little. The faces of the few had changed, but not that of the many. Only now, *all* were to be robbed of what treasure they had: the Catholic Church and their *Salvador Jesús*. The Revolution, although started under the guise of equality for all, was to continue as a subtle and then outright *"life and death struggle with the Church"*.[14] But the Revolution and its instigators did not reckon with the faithfulness and *Holy Stubbornness* of the many who refused to give homage to man. This ancient people, who survived pagan atrocities and Spanish betrayals, knew *Who* their King was and no one was going to depose Him.

Priests were rounded up, and expelled from many of the states of Mexico. But not even threats of imprisonment and death could deter these representatives of Christ. They returned (disguised as laity) and returned, and returned until they were, *yes*, imprisoned and executed. Their only crime was, they celebrated Holy Mass. You see, services were no longer allowed in Church. The government even closed the Churches down, in an effort to keep people from silently praying within the holy walls.

Unable to celebrate in a Church, the faithful with their loyal Priests went *underground*. They would pick a house that would not arouse suspicion, and they would come together. There were as many as seventy at a time. They crowded in as many as they could. You may have heard the

---

[14] from chapter Dilemma P.7-Mexican Martyrdom by Father Wilfrid Parsons, S.J.

expression: "*They were so close there was no room for the Holy Spirit*", well the Lord had no problem here. He reigned! They may not have had spacious quarters for their Lord to be born again in the Holy Eucharist, but their grand hearts adored Him, just as His Mother, St. Joseph, the Angels, and the shepherds did *that* time, long ago, when the world changed in Bethlehem.

They went to confession and then Mass. Several of their number would unobtrusively stand guard outside the home. They all knew the price, but they would not allow their Lord to die. If they were caught, the home, where the Mass and services were held, would be confiscated with all its contents,[15] or burned. That was the least of the punishment, they would suffer. Many men were separated from their families, and never seen again. The women had their children taken from them, never to see them again. And then, there were those who were made an example and shot after they were mutilated before their families and friends. And still, the people worshiped their Lord.

There were Communion stations set up around the cities and villages where the faithful would go, and after hearing the Word of God extolled, would take Communion themselves. The Pope gave them dispensation to do so. As with Jesus his Founder, the Pope knew that the Church without the Eucharist would not last. The Blessed Sacrament was hidden inside radios, medicine cabinets, behind books in a bookcase, in some of the most unlikely places in order to avert the Lord falling into the wrong hands.[16]

They knew Who their Lord was; they did not take Him for granted. [*A Priest in the United States, grieving over the lack of respect and reverence shown to our Lord and Savior in*

---

[15]Usually it went to the governor or a captain of the army. Sometimes as a reward to the informer.

[16]"The Pope gave the privilege on December 23, 1927," - P.9 Mexican Martyrdom by Father Wilfrid Parsons, S.J

the Blessed Sacrament, said he wished that all the Churches would be closed for 90 days. Then, he said we'd see how we all felt about our Lord.] Do we take Him for granted? Do we assume we will always have a Mass and a Priest to administer the Sacraments? So did the Mexican people. We were once told that we were too fat, in the United States, that we would only have vocations after we were made lean like Poland, Ireland and *Mexico*! We were told we would become a catacomb Church in the United States. We felt as if someone had thrust a sword in our hearts. But, did we believe it? Can it happen here? Can we be the next Mexico?

We could like to share the story of Saint Tarcisius here, because there have been many like him in Mexico.

St. Tarcisius was an acolyte, in the Early Church, who brought the Eucharist to Christians in prison. The guards never suspected the amiable young boy of his appointed task, as he pretended to bring them news from the outside or some other subterfuge. One day, as he was hurrying to the prison, carrying a Treasure, the Eucharist in a pyx, he was accosted by some rowdies. They could see that he was holding something precious in his hands. They insisted he turn It over to them. He refused. When they realized, they could not wrench the Prize from him, they beat him to death. Try as they may, they still could not pry his hands open. Only the Priest, upon arriving on the scene was able to retrieve our Lord. When the Priest touched St. Tarcisius' hands, they opened freely. He is celebrated as one of our early Christian Martyrs who died for the Faith. You will know them by their fruits.

Mexico, in the *twentieth* century, from 1927-1929, had its jails crowded with Catholics whose only crime was, they refused to deny Christ and His Church. One of the prisoners had a beautiful son who was *six* years old. As with St. Tarcisius, he was so lovable, even the jailers loved him. Little did they suspect his true mission, as he danced and sang. He was entertaining not only his father and the other prisoners, but he was truly delighting the jailers. What they did not know was that on certain visits, he left the captives the only lasting Joy, our Lord in the Eucharist. How precious and important was the Lord that a father would allow his son to face torture and execution if he was caught.

[Author's Note: Last year, a lawyer came to visit one of the pro-life prisoners. His client was a Catholic who had been arrested for demonstrating outside of an abortion clinic. The lawyer was bringing consecrated Hosts to the prisoners when he was stopped, searched and ordered to hand Them over. When he refused he was arrested for smuggling in contraband! He was brought before a judge who sentenced him to a suspended sentence and warned if he were arrested on any future charge he would have to serve time for this crime! No, this is not Mexico, but the United States! Could it happen here? It did.]

Father Gonzalo de Tapia, a Mexican Martyr who was killed by pagan Indians in 1594, came from Pátzcuaro. The Martyrdom which faced the people of Mexico and this village did not begin in the 1900s but in 1520 when Dominican friars, Franciscans, Augustinian Monks and later Jesuits set out, without the protection of soldiers, to evangelize to the Red Indians. Almost in retribution for having taken away their bloody sacrifices to their gods and their exhilaration at the spectacle, tribes demanded blood for blood. When they captured these men of God they exchanged their blood for the blood of the tens of thousands of children they were robbed of sacrificing each year.

The blood of the Martyrs flowed over the darkness of what had been *pagan Mexico* and the land sprouted a people nourished by the Body and Blood of their Savior, the unbloody Sacrifice, they would never deny. The cup of agony, suffering, sacrifice and death, the Martyrs drank from, has never been blotted out from the memory of the Mexican faithful. Is this what the faithful of Pátzcuaro saw, as they marched unafraid, braver than the bravest soldier, to Mass on Sunday?

One Sunday, two Priests arrived in *Pátzcuaro*. They *thought*, disguised in lay clothing, they would be able to move about undetected. But, as they passed by, Indians donned their hats respectfully, and bowed before them. They witnessed to churches filled with the faithful from early morning to late night. What did these Priests find here? Holy Clusters! They saw Holy Clusters of Holy People *on Holy Ground*, sanctified by those Martyrs who went before them and who *would be* of their number. And they knew it! Is this why the forces of hell has never been able to prevail against the Catholic Church?

The more the faithful defied the President of Mexico, *General Plutarco Elias Calles*, the angrier he became and the more vindictive. He would break their spirit, once and for all. Get rid of their Priests! He ordered all the Priests to leave their parishes and report to Mexico City. It has been reported that not one Priest obeyed this order. They all remembered, their obedience was first and foremost to their Lord and Church.

[The separation of Church and State had been instituted by the Early Church because of the insistence of the emperors to control the people by controlling the Church. Many lived and died that the Church would never be under the tyranny and authority of the State.]

To disobey meant that all the Priests became fugitives, under the law. The search began: *Find the Priests, at all costs.* Bribe, and if that fails, threaten and torture, and then kill. But the Priests must be found and done away with. The sad truth about this Calles, was that everyone, including the United States had had high hopes for Mexico under the tutelage of this man.

Go after the Children

Can't get the older generation to submit, go after the children. But what Hitler was successful in doing, the Government could not do in Mexico. There are some interesting and uplifting stories, sometimes comical, as the Mexican can always laugh and joke even when he is crying inside. But if we pause to reflect, they become also tragically alarming, a foretaste or prophecy of what may be to come, or what has already begun in our country.

In one school, a teacher ordered the children to chant *"Uno, dos, uno, dos, no hay Dios. Uno, dos, uno, dos, no hay Dios* - One two, one two, there is no God; one two, one two, there is no God." Instead the children chanted *"Hay Dios. Hay Dios.* -There is God. There is God."[17] The teacher finally had to give in. The children, who were supposed to be brain-washed, would not succumb. Instead, it was the teacher who capitulated, exhausted. One for our team. But not for long. Satan never gives up. Although we foolishly take this Church of ours for granted and become apathetic, Satan never sleeps!

This would not be the only instance when the people stood up for their Faith, and their children. There was reported, in an American newspaper, that a young man was hanged by villagers because he had rounded up their children for the express purpose of teaching them there was no God. A *"March of Time"* reel covered it in the movie theaters in the United States. The people of Mexico were giving notice: *"We will lose our lives rather than lose our souls; and if need be, take the lives of those who would try to take our souls from us."*

All right, the government could not break their will, and their belief in the One True God. Teach the children about

---

[17] from chapter Dilemma P.8-Mexican Martyrdom by Father Wilfrid Parsons, S.J

the gods who appeal to the lower senses; *teach them Sex Education!* In another state of Mexico, one of the children came home and told her mother that the teacher had the children do things, under the pretext of Sex Education, which we cannot print in this book. The mother, crazed by the thought of the debase acts her child was forced to do, took a gun, went to school and shot the teacher. *She* would no longer steer children to sin. When she stood before our dear Lord, I wonder what the teacher said to Him, as He gazed into her eyes? Did His words suddenly come to life:

"Whoever causes one of these little ones who believe in Me to sin, it would be better for him to have a great millstone hung around his neck and to be drowned in the depths of the sea."(Matt 18:6)

Children were lead to stock yards, under the pretense of *Science.* They were graphically explained *human* reproduction, as they were instructed to watch animals mating. The teachers, as part of their school curriculum, also brought children to maternity wards where they could view a woman giving birth. As if this was not enough, in the classroom, teachers instructed children to remove all their clothes, and then she explained how two people went about the act of intercourse.

To give the instructors the benefit of the doubt, they may have been deluded into believing they were teaching the children about sex, rather than have them learn erroneously from one another in the streets. This is how they may have begun, but as more and more permissive direction came down *authoritatively* from the government, they soon found themselves involved in something hideously resembling perversion. There were school dances held where both girls and boys were told to disrobe and perform acts, our resource writes are too profane to include here. And this, all in the name of enlightenment and education.

Did the parents of hundreds of years of *Our Lady of Guadalupe* and *Christ the King* just sit back and do nothing?

In one village, a young girl refused to return to school the next day. When her mother questioned her, she began to cry. She told her that the teacher had forced *all* the children, boys and girls, to remove all their clothes in class, in front of one another. When the mother told her husband (who was the mayor of the town), he loaded a gun and rushed to the school. He called the teacher to come out of the classroom. First, he told her, his daughter only undresses in front of her mother. *"What you have done"*, he said, *"was to bring disgrace on her and her family"*. He went on that since this is the new education of the government, and she sincerely believed she was doing what was right, then she should be willing to participate in the same exercise she had instructed the children to do. He pointed the gun at her, and ordered her to remove *her* clothes. He told her, he would join her and remove *his* clothes. This proved to be too much for the teacher. She screamed and then fainted. The whole incident was so traumatic, she snapped and suffered a nervous breakdown. Imagine, this had so shocked her that she, a grown woman, collapsed. What had the new modern form of *education* (as it was called), and the experiences she had imposed on these innocent children, done to them?

The Mexican people were up in arms. A vote was called by the people. The results were *80,000 against* any form of sex education and *75 for*. [These percentages never changed.] The people sent out protests to over 3000 schools and institutions, demanding these practices be terminated. When that failed, the people took to the streets with peaceful demonstrations. But when the police used force to break up their gatherings, they fought back. They turned to the legal system to save their children. But when *all* failed, half crazed with helplessness, seeing their children corrupted, they often took matters into their own hands. And this is how vigilantes are dangerously begun. When a government ceases to represent the people, they will represent themselves and solve problems on their own. And most often, chaos results.

How to get the children? The government went after the Catholic schools. They knew, the people would accept this new teaching from the *Church*. The Church refused, as did the Catholic schools. When they were given the ultimatum: "*Either teach this new form of socialism*" (members of the government had brought these teachings back from the Soviet Union), "*or close down*". They closed down! They taught in the homes, setting up *home schools*. Former teachers of Catholic schools held classes in the parents' homes, in the back of stores. And when they burned down homes and stores or confiscated them from their owners, they taught in the town squares.

The government would use *many* as examples of what happens to those who will not bend. They lined up teachers and students and threatened them! "*Deny Jesus Christ! Say there is no God.*" When they would not deny Christ, they cut out their tongues. There were several young men rounded up, one day. They were lined up against the school wall to be shot. When one of the youngest, a teen-ager fifteen years old, began to cry, one of the others said: "*Die as the Martyrs before you, bravely.*" To keep him quiet, the soldiers cut off his tongue, as he was proclaiming: "Long live Christ the King! - *Viva Cristo Rey!*" What praise, his voice could no longer exclaim, he offered with his heart. They could not look into his eyes, gleaming with love and forgiveness. These young Martyrs, more boys than men, went to their deaths, their arms outstretched in imitation of their Savior on the Cross, proclaiming "*Viva Cristo Rey!*" They had commended their spirit to their Father in Heaven, as the Martyrs before them. Their rosaries clutched in one hand and a Crucifix in the other, their eyes heavenward, they went Home.

Go after the Bishops, Priests, Religious and the Church

In the United States, in the year 1929, all the godliness and promiscuity of the 20's would come crashing down on that crazed generation. As the Stock Market plummeted downward, those who had traded the One True God for the pagan gods of sex, power and money threw themselves out 30 story windows. They had betrayed their Lord for 30 pieces of silver and now *they* were betrayed. The whole world was going mad.

Two years earlier in February, 1927, the president of Mexico, *Plutarco Elias Calles* issued an order for all Priests throughout Mexico to leave their parishes and report to Mexico City. As this would place them under the supervision of the State, robbing them of their allegiance to Rome and the Pope, they refused. They stood on their Constitutional *rights* which insured clear separation of Church and State. All the Priests, Bishops and Religious were in *communion*, rejecting the State's authority over the Church. They knew the outcome. They chose to become fugitives rather than deny the Faith. As the early Church Martyrs before them, they would not swear allegiance to Caesar (the head of state); for to do so would be to declare him God. They became hunted, and when caught, arrested, mercilessly tortured, and very often executed. And while this was going on, the United States was giving credit to Mexico in the sums of *tens of millions*!

Close down the Church completely! The Constitution, instituted in 1917, declared the Church illegal. They made Priests and Religious bloody examples of what happens to those who defy the government. Instead of the faithful being intimidated, their fervor for their Church grew stronger. The people would not give up.

The Church was no longer allowed to have private schools. The government closed them down. There would be no place where children could go to hear God's Word taught. The government then reopened the schools with a total philosophy of Atheism. If the future citizens were to be educated at all, it would be with this Marxist ideology that had been brought back from the Soviet Union. That's what the government thought! The instructors, who had taught in the Catholic schools, *refused* to teach the new curriculum. They would not lead innocent children against the Church and God. They went underground! *The Church became a catacomb Church, and the Catholic schools along with her!*

The Church was no longer allowed to own property. Therefore, the government plundered all the magnificent tributes of praise and homage to their God, the faithful had built and paid for. With one fell swoop, the *new* despots, who had promised the people of Mexico a new, fairer world, tried to rob them of a dream they had cherished for close to 400 years. The government took the beautiful churches, schools, convents and etc. and used them as office buildings, museums, and often stables. But this was the brick and mortar that was the Church. The faithful met in homes, in back of stores, in squares. The Church would not lie down and die! *The Church was alive!*

They closed down the seminaries. No seminaries, no seminarians, no Priests, no Mass, no Church. That would be the end of vocations to the Priesthood in Mexico. As if this was not enough, the government used the constitution to deport all foreign missionaries, and forbid any from entering Mexico. The idea was to rob the people of all Catholic instruction. Without the Priests to pass on the Faith, it would surely die. If only godliness was taught, without any teaching of Christ and His Church, these modern day Pilates would kill Christ once and for all. So, they thought!

Each state was given the power to determine how many Priests would be permitted to serve the needs of the citizens of their locale. The constitution made the Priesthood a profession not unlike those requiring licenses from the government to practice; such as doctors, lawyers, engineers and etc. By this act, the government was declaring the Church a part of the State. This would mean that the State would determine how, when and what the Church would teach. In other words the Roman Catholic Church in Mexico, under obedience to the Vatican and the Holy See, would no longer exist. It would become the Mexican *State* Church.

This was not an original idea. When the mad revolutionaries of France went on their blood-seeking rampage, they vented their hostile anger on innocent Priests and Nuns because the Crown of France had been Catholic. As we know hate knows no boundaries, neither does revenge. Blood once poured out is like an elixir to the mad; their thirst can never be satisfied. Those clergy, whom they did not kill by the guillotine, the French revolutionists demanded they take an oath swearing sole allegiance to the government. Unlike the Priests and Bishops of Mexico, some did take an oath.

Russia was going to give the riches of the few to the many, but the pattern is always the same: One totalitarian for another. Russia followed France by setting up its own *Living Church*. This new government that was to stand for liberty and equality for all, like Mexico and its other counterpart France, destroyed any semblance of the Church in their country before the Revolution. All this is not new. Satan has always known that the Church, as the Instrument of God will always have the love and faithfulness of the people. Oh, they may stray temporarily but they will always come back home to Mother Church. Emperor Constantine knew it. Rulers since have known and tried.

Hitler started his own religion, calling the German people to pride in being an Aryan[18] race. Whereas they had formerly hailed Jesus and Mary, they were now made to hail the *new* god, Hitler. The hate of Church became so intense that the day before the Nazis capitulated to the Americans, SS men rounded up a local Priest and six men, lined them up before a firing squad and killed them. *[We heard about them from the local Priest, when we filmed a documentary in Altotting, a Marian Shrine where Catholics have venerated the Mother Of God and worshiped Jesus since 700 A.D.]* How do these monsters, the Stalins, the Hitlers, the Mussolinis and the Calles of the world take over a majority of the faithful and rob them of Jesus?

The men of Mexico went to the hills, and their wives and sisters stayed behind to defend their homes and children from the enemy, their own countrymen. Many women saw their children sacrificed because they would not tell the whereabouts of a Priest or Religious who some Judas had reported to the government. These people of Mexico whom the world does not know, believed that the Catholic Faith was more precious than life on earth.

Many young men and women gave their lives crying out *Viva Cristo Rey*, but this was not only a fight for freedom of religion. When one freedom is taken away, you can be assured, others will follow. They lost freedom of the press, the right to assemble in public, the right to associate with whom they wished. A government, which underwent a revolution for supposed equality for all, was now denying freedom to all. *All* that is, but the favored few who were in charge of the government. It is said that Abraham, Moses and the other prophets never saw the dream. Those who died never saw their country free, but did they die in vain?

---

[18]Descendants of prehistoric people who spoke that language. It has no ethnological value, although Hitler claimed it to mean a *Caucasian of non-Jewish descent*. This, however, was not true.

The Martyrs never saw the Promised Land in this world but they all did in the Next.

The government hunted down Priests, accusing them of leading the rebellion. That was totally untrue. Their crime was that they stuck to their God-appointed vocations of tending the souls of the faithful. With the exception of three, no Priest took up arms or incited the people to revolt. Nevertheless, it was reported to an American newsman that over 100 Priests had been executed for treason against the State.

One incident, we would like to share with you is typical of what went on. When the order had been given for all Priests to leave their parishes, *Father Elias Nieves*[19] chose to stay behind with his people. Warned that soldiers were looking for him, he fled to another village. It would appear, he was safe. Then someone sold his soul for a promise that would probably never be kept. When the soldiers arrived, a traitor told them the Priest's whereabouts. They looked all over the village where the Priest was hiding. Everyone was silent; but when they frightened a poor old lady with descriptions of the horrible tortures she would undergo, she pointed out the house. They dragged out Father Nieves. Two men who were trying to defend him, were taken and placed in prison, as well.

Some people offered money for the release of the three captives. The sum was high and this usually worked. Not this time! The captain wanted blood, not money; but not of the two men; he offered *them* their freedom. It was the Priest, he wanted. They insisted they would go with their Priest, to their death. The captain shrugged his shoulders: *Oh well, what's two more lives*, he thought.

---

[19]from chapter on Defiance p.29 Mexican Martyrdom by Father Wilfrid Parsons, S.J.

The sun rose. The villagers were held at gunpoint, as their Priest and two villagers were led out to be executed. The two men knelt down before Father Nieves, confessed their sins. After he gave them absolution they stepped forward. Together they said: *"We are ready!"*. Then, with the Signal Grace of the Martyrs before them they stood there, without blindfolds, never flinching, as the explosion of bullets struck them down one by one. Men and women cried, their hands clamping their mouths to stifle their screams.

It was time for the Priest. He walked toward the bullet-riddled corpses of the two brave men who had preceded him. He told the firing squad he was ready; but then asked for a moment to pray. Then he turned to the soldiers: *"Kneel down. So that I may bless you."* They obeyed and knelt. Was this an instinctive response dating back to the time they were Catholics and not soldiers? Were they remembering their childhood and the love and respect they'd had for their Priests? Did they remember the many times the Priests had come to their home to be with members of their families, as they lay dying? In imitation of the Savior Who asked the Father to forgive those who were crucifying *Him*, Father Nieves laid his hands on their heads and pardoned the soldiers for what they were about to do. He blessed them all with the Sign of the Cross, the one He chose to die for.

As he turned to bless the Captain, his forgiveness was met with a bullet. The Captain raised his gun and shot the Priest, without a moment's hesitation. To make sure, his dirty work was done, the Captain coldly aimed his revolver at Father Nieve's head and blew his brains out. I wonder if, some day, he will be pleading for Father Nieve's intercession, as he faces his death and final judgment?

All the villagers were no longer frightened of the soldiers. The next day, they processed with the three bodies and lay them to rest. It was a day of rejoicing, of resurrection. It was a day of hope. It was plain, these three had conquered death. By their Martyrdom, they were with the Father in the Kingdom. For every villager who betrayed his Church and Priest, whether it was because of fear or greed, there was hundreds who chose death rather than betrayal.

One of the greatest hurts, and unbearable pains suffered by the people, was they could no longer have Mass said for them. But this was not for *all* the people. Those who could *bribe* the soldiers and police were able to hide a Priest and celebrate Mass in their home. Poor women, shawls hugging their heads were followed, as they went to Mass. They were killed, along with the other worshipers and the Priest, while the privileged *few* had the benefits of the Sacraments. If those *few* were aware of the plight of their less fortunate brothers and sisters, I wonder what all the earthly consolations will mean when they beg of their Lazarus', in Heaven, some water for their fevered and parched lips?

The murdering of Priests knew no boundaries. There was no longer sanctuary in the Church, or on the Altar for that matter. One day *Father Francisco Vera* was celebrating Mass in Jalisco. The soldiers stormed into the Church. The Captain took a picture of the Priest in his vestments, before and after he shot him. He proudly sent it to President Calles who was so pleased, he sent it to the papers for all to see and be forewarned. There are hundreds of stories like this and worse. They did not stop at Priests celebrating Mass. An American correspondent was shocked, as local authorities bragged that forty old men and women, caught attending Mass, were brought to the cemetery and shot. Their crime against the State was worshiping God.

They were not satisfied with robbing property from Mother Church. They then began to confiscate homes and lands belonging to Catholics. For rewards, for envy, for spite, Judases began reporting that people were praying in

their homes.   This warranted the eviction of the rightful
owners of the haciendas and the turning over of the property
to an official of the government or another dishonest despot.
Then, it became a crime to have anything of a religious
nature in your home.   Some of the haciendas had *objets des
arts* which had a religious motif, like for example a
Michelangelo or a Da Vinci.   The art and the home were
seized; and if they were lucky the owners were allowed to
escape with their lives and the clothes on their backs.
Sometimes, that was not the case.

As with the Irish Martyrs, the Mexican Martyrs held
their starving children in their arms, as they stood helplessly
by and saw food being carted out of their villages.   A
correspondent from the United States, Mr. Beals, seeing the
atrocities and the suffering of the people cried out[20] that he
did not understand "*how Christ the King, the Prince of Peace
was served by the slaughter of innocent men, women and
children.*" Yet he did concede that it was not the Catholics
who were responsible, but the military and unprincipled
bandits. What did Mr. Beals want? Did *he* know their Lord
Jesus? Did he not *understand* they could not deny this Lord
and His Church, for that would be true slavery? They would
rather live forever in His Arms than a poor lifetime in man's.
But, how do you explain the love one has for Jesus and His
Church? You have to live it, to know it. As you walk with
Him, and talk with Him, you find yourself filled with an
ecstasy so sublime, life is pale by comparison.

A young father, *Anacleto González Flores*, was tortured
because he would not reveal the whereabouts of the
Archbishop of Guadalajara. "*I die, but God does not die!*"
He cried out these words, as they lined him and the men
with him who had refused to save their lives by exposing the
Archbishop. Anacleto's young widow brought their young

---

[20] from Mexican Martyrdom by Father Wilfrid Parsons, S.J.

son to the spot where his father lay. She took his picture standing beside his father's lifeless body. She wanted to insure he would never forget his father and the price he paid for the right to be Catholic.

As we get to know Guadalajarans, and see them set their jaws stubbornly when someone tells them there is no God, when they turn off some intellectual who tells them they have been taught a lot of superstition that the Church has drummed up to control them, then we know that they too have not forgotten. Is this what makes up the God's people who would not allow Him to die or fade away as a Memory? What do you think? So, you see. Mr. Beals, wherever you are, and the others who think like you, we believe the message is that the ecstasy is worth the agony.

Miguel Pro
a Clown who became a Priest,
who became a Martyr,
who became a Saint.

On September 25, 1988, a fairly large group of Mexicans, led by a Priest, walked to the National Lottery building, located on a busy thoroughfare in Mexico City, and celebrated Mass there. The crowd was large enough to attract the attention of the police, and we believe they *did notice.*

But the faithful were not stopped, or hindered in any way. We were very surprised to hear of this, until we were told of a little bronze plaque on the wall of that building. It reads very simply, "This is the spot where Padre Miguel Pro was executed on November 23, 1927." The day Mass was celebrated was the day Miguel Pro was *beatified* by Pope John Paul II, at St. Peter's Basilica in Rome.[21]

In 1927, The execution of Miguel Pro, and the publicizing of that execution, was a huge mistake on the part of the Mexican government, which they have never been able to live down or sweep under the carpet. It highlighted the persecution of the Church by the government. Padre Miguel Pro just refused to go away, and based on his recent beatification, he never will.

Who is Padre Miguel Pro?

Miguel Agustín Pro, God's *clown*, was born on January 13, 1891. Miguel was of the upper class, but he never thought of himself that way. His greatest love, as a child, was to be with the workers. To Miguel, this was the best way to spend his life. He delighted in bringing some sunshine into their overworked hearts.

One talent Miguel acquired early in life, which would be extremely important to him later on, was as a *caricaturist*. He was able to capture, in exaggerated form, the peculiarities in people's faces. He would embellish noses, thick bushy eyebrows, long chins, funny eyes, buck teeth. This ability to disguise himself was to prove *crucial* in later years.

From 1872 to 1913, tensions between the Church and the state had cooled, somewhat. The fact that Miguel Pro attended a *Jesuit seminary* in Mexico, is proof of this. But the fire between Church and State was never put out. In the years to come, it would rekindle into a roaring blaze. As it was developing, the attitude of many people was, the country had been under some form of revolution since before their birth; they had survived thus far; they would continue to survive. But we always say, how many dead bodies would be

---

[21]All the information and quotes, on Miguel Pro, are taken from chapter on Blessed Miguel Pro in Bob and Penny Lord's book: *Saints and Other Powerful Men in the Church*

left to lay in the wake of this new revolution. The *common man* would see the balance of power affect him in a devastating way. Miguel's father had to flee from his home, as did his mother, and his younger brothers and sisters. Financially, they had lost everything. The Revolution of 1910 would cause suffering that equaled or surpassed the holocaust of the past.

Miguel put all his trust in the Lord. He had made a commitment to become a Priest, and he was going to live by it. While he was able to keep in focus with his mind, his body began to give way. He contracted an agonizing illness which would be with him, the rest of his life. But being who he was, he never let on that he was ill. He was the jester of the seminary. Very few knew what lay behind his cheerful exterior. Although on the surface, he was a clown, he was very firm on his observance of the Rule, and his studies.

The Persecution intensified

Conditions in the country were approaching *disaster* proportions. Law was virtually *non-existent*. The military ruled by intimidating landowners, confiscating their possessions, and then *shooting* them. Miguel spent much of his spare time at the outer edges of the seminary, listening to stories from passersby of how bad things were going in the rest of the country. In addition, it became very obvious that a new wave of persecution was being aimed at the Church. Pope Pius XI termed this period in Mexico as *"exceeding the most bloody persecutions of the Roman emperors."*

War stories of *Religious* being beaten, and strung up to die, found their way back to the seminary. The possibility of becoming a Martyr for the Faith, became very real to Miguel, for the first time. A fellow student testified that Miguel expressed *"that ardent wish, which he felt, to suffer persecution for justice' sake."*

A heavy blanket of tension covered the Seminary, towards the end of the school year. The superiors were aware of the atrocities that were going on all around them; but were not saying anything to the students, in order not to frighten them. The students, for their part, were aware of the problems; but said nothing to their superiors, in order not to alarm *them*. A band of guerrillas attacked the neighboring town. They did not stop at pillaging and destroying. As they barraged the innocents of the village, with violence upon violence, the general[22] in charge of the guerrillas killed the head of the village. Finally, what the seminary feared, most, came about. One night, these pistol-shooting, drunken, vicious men found their way into the seminary. They broke down doors, chopped up furniture, shot up the building, and generally terrorized the superiors. No one was beaten, or hung, or shot; but the seminarians, and their superiors knew, their days were numbered. They didn't have to wait long; shortly after, wholesale persecution of all religious orders went into full force, *once again*. The superiors determined, it was best they all abandon the seminary and flee for their lives. All were given civilian clothing to wear.

On the Feast of the Assumption, they left the seminary. The Priests and novices went by twos, sporadically, in different directions, to avoid attracting attention. Miguel went to the nearest town, Zamora. The plan was for all of them to *mix* with the local population, and stay undercover until they could regroup as a community. For some reason, everyone in Zamora knew that Miguel and his companion were Priests, or about to become Priests. This didn't present a problem until a few days later, when the Churches were closed; and everyone who had anything to do with the

---

[22]General - a very loose term given to any bully who could gather enough of a gang to terrorize and intimidate. It diminished the integrity of some really brilliant military men, by giving all the same title.

Church, from a sacristan to a Bishop, had to appear before the head of the town. Miguel and his friend didn't go. All who *did* were thrown into jail, manhandled and tortured.

But for Miguel, a very important chapter of his life began. He knew that he had to fool the soldiers and police. In order to do this, he began to practice his art of elaborate *disguise*. This was to be his salvation during his active ministry; no one could identify him. One evening, he disguised himself as a *peon*, dressed in cotton pants, wrapped in a serape, with a large sombrero on his head. He walked casually through the town, past all the armed revolutionaries, who were on the lookout for *religious*. According to the plan set by his superiors, he made his way to Guadalajara, to meet up with the rest of the community. There, he found his mother and his brothers and sisters, living in the poorest of conditions. But they were *alive*; that was all that mattered. Word came to him that his father was definitely alive and safe, though they didn't know where.

Risk-taking became a way of life for religious in Mexico. At one point, the Bishop met with a group of five hundred faithful on private property, and celebrated Mass. During the service, the house was surrounded by *armed* revolutionaries, and all were placed under arrest. However, their plans were foiled by a huge group of people who surrounded *them*, and demanded, they free the Bishop. The revolutionaries backed down, in the face of such a mob.

It was becoming more and more difficult to function, under the suppressed circumstances. Finally, word came by *code* for Miguel and the other seminarians to leave Guadalajara for Los Gatos, in California; there they were to continue their studies. It was very a heart-breaking experience for Miguel at the Guadalajara railroad station. His mother and brothers and sisters saw him off. He knew he was leaving them in an impossible situation, but he had to continue in his commitment to the Lord. He knew, as he bid his mother good-by, that he would never see her again on this earth. *He never did.*

Miguel in exile

Miguel and sixteen other companions, from the Jesuit seminary in El Llano, traveled together through Mexico, which was now enemy territory for them, across the border at Nogales, Mexico, and up through California to Los Gatos, some fifty miles south of San Francisco. Although he had never visited this country before, he knew that at one time, it had belonged to his beloved Mexico, and now, he was a *foreigner* here. But he was an *outcast* in his own country, an *outlaw*, a *deserter* from the cause, whatever that cause might be at any given time. Still, it *was* his country; his mother and father, his sisters and brothers, were still there. The people, the Lord had commissioned him to minister to, were there.

The Jesuits at Los Gatos were extremely hospitable. Though they were filled to capacity, they found room for their sixteen Mexican brothers. Language, however, was a major problem. The Americans didn't speak Spanish; the Mexicans couldn't speak English. They had complete access to the library, although there was only one book in Spanish, which they could use. They felt out of place. It was extremely difficult for them to study. In addition, bad news from home was followed by worse news, always leveled at the Church. Carranza had written the devastating Constitution of Querétaro in 1917. In it, no foreigner was allowed to possess *anything in Mexico*. Religious vows were forbidden. All ecclesiastical property was to belong to the State. Priests could not practice their ministry. They had absolutely no rights, at all. Hundreds of Priests, a number of Bishops and Nuns were *expelled* from the country. Two thousand Catholic schools were closed.

The situation in Los Gatos was not working out for the Mexican students. They decided to send the Mexican students to Spain to finish their studies. After all, Spain was the home of the Jesuits. And so, the sixteen packed up again, made the long trip to New York by way of El Paso and Miami, and boarded a ship for Spain. They arrived in Granada, in July of that year.

Miguel spent five years in Granada, Spain. While he was very sad inside, to be so far from his home and family, and while his internal illness gave him fits of agonizing pain, he maintained a great, cheery exterior. He became the ringleader of most of the students of his group, but definitely all the Mexicans.

Miguel was sent to Nicaragua, to teach at a Jesuit boy's school. He threw himself into the work, teaching the younger students drawing. He thought that the next stop would be Mexico. But after two years, he was sent back across the ocean *again*, to attend Theology school in *Barcelona*.

It was 1921; Miguel was thirty years old. He studied very seriously in Barcelona until 1924. Then he was sent to Enghien, Belgium. He didn't speak French at all, and the French spoke Latin differently from the Spanish. In spite of the language barrier, he charmed all the Europeans at that college. He became the clown again, the joker of Jesus. Everybody loved him.

But this was also a time of intense reflection for Miguel. He focused on what his apostolate would be. He would work with the people, the commoners. He didn't know if he would ever be allowed to return to his beloved Mexico; things just kept getting worse. But that could not stop him from working for the Lord! To this end, he studied the Encyclicals of Pope Leo XIII on the working man. He delved into anything of a sociological nature that might help him in his quest to do the Lord's work. It was in Enghien that he was *ordained* on August 31, 1925. At long last, after fourteen years of preparation, he was given the gift he hungered for, bringing Jesus to the people through the ministry of the Priesthood.

Padre Miguel returns to Mexico, at long last.

He was given orders to return to Mexico! He couldn't believe that was possible, considering conditions there. With Calles' takeover as president, the reign of terror against the Church became the worst yet. All the persecution that had preceded him was like child's play, compared to what Calles was determined to do to the Church. But Miguel was relieved that it was finally settled. His ministry was in Mexico, and that's where he was going, no matter what.

On the way home, he went to Lourdes. His words:

"I have been, therefore, to Lourdes. And if I did not visit Calvary, nor see the river banks, nor the outward shape of the Basilica nor what it contains? All the same I went to Lourdes! That is, going there for me, was meeting my Mother in Heaven; it was to talk, to pray to her. And I met her; I talked and prayed to her. At 8:30 (next morning) I was back in Paris and at nine said Mass in the house. I could not sleep even for an hour. Tomorrow morning at 8:30 I leave, and arrive at St. Nazaire at 5:30 in the afternoon. The liner leaves at midnight.

"My crossing will not be as hard as I thought, since Our Lady told me so. Ay, Padre, it was very painful to my wretched natural self to return to Mexico without health, without finishing my studies,[23] to find my poor country ruined by its government, not to find there any mother, that saint to whom I owe my life and for whose death, I still weep. . . But my journey to Lourdes has given me courage, and this journey I owe to the charity and delicacy of you and your family."

Miguel sailed for Mexico on the feast of John the Baptist, June 24, 1926. What happened there with Mary, that day that he knelt before her at the Grotto? We know that Miguel Pro is a Saint. Did she say things that he had to

---

[23]He had not finished his theological studies in Enghien, Belgium

hear, in order to give him the strength he would need for the days ahead? Was it the same as when she appeared to James the Apostle in Zaragoza, Spain,[24] and told him to go back to Jerusalem to be Martyred? Did Mary tell Miguel Pro to go back to Mexico to be Martyred? We do know that she was his last contact in Europe, and he returned to Mexico, with courage and joy.

Mexico Clandestinamente (Mexico underground)

What was Miguel Pro coming back to? Wholesale massacre was the order of the day. The aim of the terrorists was the weak: Priests, old people, young boys, girls and women. The clergy, the young people, the old men and women, decided it was time to fight back. And so they did. The Bishop closed all the Churches in Mexico. There was an *uproar* from the people against the government. An underground youth group was formed, which became the force behind the people of the country. A boycott was begun, in protest against the persecution of the Church. People just stopped buying. Banks *failed*, and closed down.

Underground printing presses churned out anti-government propaganda. Balloons were sent into the air; thousands of pamphlets, filled with propaganda material attacking the government, cascaded to earth. President Calles countered with his *iron fist*. That was all he knew. He had not an iota of an idea how to put his country back together. So, like his predecessors, he ruled with force, and piled up as much money as he could, in anticipation of the day, he would be forced to flee the country.

This vast city was to be Padre Miguel Pro's parish; these catacomb Christians were to be his parishioners. Miguel ministered to his hundreds of thousands of parishioners, in

---

[24]More about our Lady going to Zaragoza came be found in the chapter: *Our Lady of Pilar and the Angels* in Bob and Penny Lord's book: "*Heavenly Army of Angels*"

Right:
Miguel Pro holds a retreat , underground, dressed as a mechanic

Left:
Father Miguel Pro blesses the food and feeds the poor of Mexico

secret, in constant hiding, running from the police. He began his ministry, the day after he arrived in the capital. First, he found his father and brothers and sisters. Then, he went to work! Every trick he'd ever learned, every disguise, was put into use. He organized *Communion Stations* all over the city. They were houses where the faithful would come to receive the Lord. He never distributed less than 300 Communions. On First Fridays, the figure swelled to *1,200*, and all under the noses of the police!

Masses were celebrated all over the city, before dawn. There were private homes, different ones all the time, with watch-dogs looking out for police, passwords, being changed constantly. The rich and the poor gathered together, in these small rooms, to adore their Lord, and receive the *Nourishment* they could only get at the hands of their Priests. Those who wanted to confess, had to arrive at the appointed places earlier than the Mass, sometimes at 5:30 in the morning. It was truly a *catacomb* Church.

A crack underground organization had been put into effect. The police tried to smash it. They found out who a given set of leaders might be, arrested them, tortured them and killed them. They were no sooner arrested than they were replaced by those under them. The movement never slowed down for a minute. Calles bore down *harder*, hoping this might stop the nightmare which he had caused. Every now and then, the police found the printing presses, and smashed them to pieces. New printing operations would start up almost immediately, so smoothly, so secretly, none of the spies that Calles had employed, could keep up with them.

The Mexican Catholics, who had been apathetic about their Church, now stood up for it. The Bishops and Priests could see them joining as "*one*", becoming stronger and stronger, against this attack by the government. One Bishop was arrested for this statement, said during his homily, at Mass:

"*Let Catholics repair their sins of omission, affirm their civic rights; let them courageously resist the destroyers of the laws of humanity....Let all, old and especially the young, sacrifice pleasure and fight the fight of God, never retreating until all confiscated liberties are reconquered.*" The people rose to action.

It was this excitement, this drive to stand up for their beliefs, under pain of death that brought about the balloon incident, we mentioned before. On December 4, 1926, *six hundred balloons*, about three yards in diameter, were sent floating over the city, at about noon. Each balloon carried the symbol of the youth organization, and the word *Boycott* on it, both of which made president Calles' blood boil. This was followed by thousands of multi-colored pamphlets, falling from the buildings, with strong anti-government comments. The people ran all over, trying to catch the pamphlets. The police, in turn, ran all over, trying to catch the people. Wholesale arrests took place. Although Padre Pro was not known by the police, his brother Humberto was, and so one evening, the police arrested Humberto, Miguel, his other brother Roberto, and a host of young men.

Finally Miguel and his brothers were released from prison. But it was too close for comfort. His superiors caught wind of what had happened, and suggested he lay low for awhile. He bravely shrugged off their suggestion, until twenty five days later, the police burst into his apartment again, and wanted to arrest everyone. He begged, pleaded, and finally bribed the officer in charge. But he knew he and all his relatives had to leave the apartment and not come back. When his superiors heard about this, they changed their suggestion to an *order* to stay out of sight for awhile.

Miguel managed to keep himself under cover for two months. He wrote a heart-rending plea to his provincial, which could not possibly have been turned down:

"...folks have such need of spiritual help; every day, I hear people have died without the Sacraments; there are no more Priests to defy danger; from obedience or fear, they stay home. If I gave my little contribution of a grain of sand, as before, it would be to expose myself; but to do it with discretion and measure does not seem to me rash...Between rashness and fear there is a middle course; and between excess of prudence and audaciousness, there is a middle course. They (his provincials) fear for my life! My life?...But what is that? Would it not be saving it to lose it for my brethren?

"Certainly one must not expose one's self idiotically. But the sons of Loyola!..."

He got them with that one. He put himself right back in the middle of the battlefield. He went into prisons, disguised, *"for they are brimful of Catholics,"* and laughed at how he got away with it. He walked around with a cane as a cripple, with a police dog; and went on his appointed tasks on a bicycle. His mastery of facial contortions made him the man of many faces.

On Good Friday of 1927, Miguel was giving a retreat to a large group of people in the capital. A young man, Manuel Bonilla, aged twenty three, had been arrested for being a member of the youth group. Because he was a typographer, they judged him guilty of working with the underground printing press. On this Good Friday, to put across a point, they took him and hung him from a tree, arms and legs attached, in the form of a cross. This was done right near Mexico City. They kept him like that from noon to three o'clock, at which time, he was taken down from the "cross", and shot to death. He, like Our Lord Jesus, had been sold out for money by a farmer with whom he had had dinner. The parallels are incredible.

Padre Pro wrote many letters, chronicling his activities in his country, during this terrible time. But he wrote as he lived, joyful, cheerful, always the joker. Very often, we don't really get a true picture of the outrages that took place. We want to share just a few actual experiences.

A young girl led a revolt in a small town, *Ciudad Victoria*. She and some other brave women had been able to run off a small group of soldiers. A regiment was sent back to the town to deal with her. They arrested her, insisting she shout "Long live Calles." She refused. They asked where the Priests were. She remained silent. They began to beat her with a whip. Before they were through with her, they ripped each of her fingers off her hand, then cut her arms off in pieces. As she went through this torture, and even up to her death, she kept up the cry, "Viva Cristo Rey", *Long live Christ the King.*

But not all the soldiers were animals. One Priest was being led to his death. He couldn't walk too well, so an officer offered to let him ride on his horse. The Priest refused. The officer said, "I cannot shoot an innocent man." The Priest replied, "*My poor friend, you will only expose your own life if you do not.*" The officer refused to shoot the Priest. He was shot *alongside* the Priest.

A young lawyer in Guadalajara, *Luis Padilla*, was arrested and tortured for six hours. He was hung up by his thumbs, and stabbed with bayonets. He watched his companions shot before his eyes. His teeth were crushed. By the time he was taken down, he was a mass of bleeding, hanging meat. The soldiers then shot him in front of his young wife. When his body was brought to the cemetery, three workmen there praised the young man for his courage. They were arrested and shot.

These are just a few of the thousands of atrocities committed by brother against brother, in the name of God knows what.

Miguel feeds the poor

The economic state of Mexico was deplorable. Unemployment was high; poverty was a way of life. Many of the people Miguel ministered to, belonged to the poverty class. He began finding ways to feed and clothe them, and put a roof over their heads. Because his ministry was so diverse, rich as well as poor, he was able to appeal to the *rich* to help the *poor*.

His *staff* consisted of about six good men and women, who weren't working at regular jobs.

Very often, Miguel could be seen running around the streets of Mexico City, carrying sacks of goods. He had no trouble carrying live chickens and turkeys to his clandestine destinations. People laughed at him, calling him crazy. He kept on going, at breakneck speed. But while he put up an indifferent front, he was embarrassed by *begging*. That was one of the most difficult things he did.

The Way of the Cross

Miguel Pro became very popular, very famous. At the same time, he became notorious and infamous. Calles wanted him dead. Warrants were issued for his arrest. He was always able to slip by the police. His plastic face enabled him to disguise himself in many different ways, and his flair for the theatrical gave him the inclinations to wear the most flamboyant costumes.   There is a tradition about Padre Miguel Pro that was given in testimony, at the process of his Beatification. We really believe it is so in keeping with who the man was, and how loved he was by Our Lord Jesus, we feel it important to share it with you.

"He celebrated Mass every day in secret. On the day before he was arrested for the last time, he was celebrating Mass in a home, attended by a small number of people. It is said that during the Consecration of the Mass, as he held the Consecrated Host, a brilliant light surrounded his entire body. His vestments were so bright that people had to turn their heads away. His face and hands were gleaming; he levitated.[25] He was transfigured, as Our Lord Jesus on Mount Tabor before him." We like to think of this as a *Miracle of the Eucharist* of Mexico.

A plot was hatched. We don't know if it was directed against Miguel Pro, or former president Obregón. Some think it was Calles' way of killing two birds with one stone. Obregón was motoring in the area of Chapultepec, when a car came alongside him, and bombs were thrown at his car. He escaped with minor injuries, but his guards chased the four terrorists, who ran from their car. Two escaped. One was shot dead, and the other through the temple. He was brought to the hospital. *His wife stayed with him until he died, and testified he never regained consciousness.* However,

---

[25]Levitated - to rise and float in the air

the police claimed an undercover policeman got into his hospital room, disguised his voice as the assailant's brother-in-law, and spoke to him. The assailant supposedly put the blame on Padre Pro, his brother Humberto, and Luis Segura.

Miguel and his family knew nothing about the plot. As a matter of fact, he had felt somewhat of a lull in the police's intensity to get him. He had even moved back into his father's house. The lady, at whose house Miguel had stayed, prior to moving back with his father and brothers, was arrested. Somehow, they managed to trip her up, and she told them where Miguel was. Early the next morning, before anyone was up, the police raided Pro's father's house, and arrested Miguel, Humberto, and his other brother, Roberto.

Miguel actually thought what the police was doing was *hysterical.* There was no way, he thought, the plot against Obregón could be connected to him or his brothers. They were nowhere *near* the scene of the crime when it happened. So he went about his normal routine of clowning around and joking. He made friends with the guards, gave them cigarettes. He even converted one while he was in prison.

They stayed *incommunicado* for three days. There was questioning and brow-beating; but no charges were made, and no trial was set. Miguel insisted upon a trial, to prove that he and the others were indeed innocent. Meanwhile, the head of the prison, General Cruz, issued a statement that all three had *confessed* to the crime. It read that Miguel had been one of the organizers of the plot, and Humberto and Segura had been in the car from which the bombs were thrown. *But the prisoners knew nothing of any of this!*

Article 20 of the Mexican Constitution, (which President Calles had written) states that within 48 hours, a prisoner must be able to make a declaration of his innocence or guilt. At the end of 72 hours, the judge decides whether to free the accused, free them under bond, or give a formal order of imprisonment for the accused. None of this ever happened, in the case of Miguel Pro and his companions.

On a parallel course, former president Obregón was conducting his own inquiry. Not for a minute, did he think the Priest or his friends had anything to do with the attempt on his life. He was *convinced* it was political. As he was getting mixed messages from the investigators, he sent *his* lawyer to the prison to get to the bottom of it. The report that came back to him was: There was nothing in the way of a police report, other than one made *prior* to the investigation. *"And what does the chief of police, General Cruz, think of the guilt of the prisoners?"* the lawyer asked.

The secretary replied, *"The Pro brothers have not confessed any connection to the crime, and we have no proof against them."*

But the following morning, without benefit of an examining judge, or lawyer, or anything, sentence on Miguel Pro and his three companions, was to be carried out. The guard came and told him and his brother Humberto to follow him. Miguel turned to the other prisoners in the cells, and with a bravado, said *"Good-by my sons, my brothers."*

The guard, Mazcorro, asked Miguel's forgiveness for his part in what was about to happen. *"Not only do I pardon you, but I thank you. I will pray for you."* Then he and his brother, without any handcuffs, followed the guard out onto the courtyard. Miguel went out first.

The cold, biting air of the November morning sent a chill across his face. His hair blew in the wind. The sun was shining brightly. It was a *glorious* day. Miguel surveyed the situation in the courtyard. Soldiers were lined up. It was a firing squad! All the eyewitnesses, various generals and dignitaries, as well as members of the press, came to attention, as they saw for the first time, the famous Jesuit, who had made such fools of President Calles and his entire police force for so long. Cameras began clicking photos for posterity, of this man who looked more like a student than a conspirator. Miguel walked straight as a rod into the center of the courtyard. He was asked his last request. He asked to pray. He went down on his knees, folded his arms, and closed his eyes.

Eyewitnesses report, his face was aglow, shining as if a reflection of the sun. He raised his arm to his executioners in the form of a blessing. He shouted in a loud, strong voice,

"May God have mercy on you! May God bless you! Lord, Thou knowest that I am innocent! With all my heart I forgive my enemies!"

The command was given the soldiers. "Prepare!"

From his breast pocket, Miguel took out a brass crucifix, he was given on the day of his ordination. In his other hand, he held the rosary he had gotten in Lourdes. He held both outstretched, at arms length, in the form of the Cross. He said, in a voice which was not loud, but could be heard by everyone in the assembly:

"Viva Cristo Rey!"

"Fire!"   The sound from the blast of the rifles, ricocheted against the walls of the courtyard, shattering the tense silence. Bullets ripped through Miguel's chest, pushing him backward; but he remained standing. Cameras went off like crazy, catching the image of the dead man, who wouldn't go down. Finally, he slumped into a heap on the ground. The captain came over to him, and shot him in the head, to end his torture. Miguel Pro was dead, but never forgotten.

A Martyr for Mexico

Word had rumbled through the underground of *Catholic Mexico* that the Priest was to be murdered. Peasants, business people, hundreds, thousands of people gathered outside the prison, waiting to see what would happen. When the word went through the crowd that Padre Pro had been killed, seething anger against the government filled all of them. They began shouting and screaming. The police formed a barricade. Machine guns were set up on top of the buildings.

After the other three, Miguel's brother Humberto, Luis Segura, and a young boy Tirado who had been unfortunate to be an eyewitness on the attack of General Obregón, were killed; the bodies were brought to a van outside. The crowd moved in slowly, but in short order, surrounded the van, so that it could not move. The driver started up the engine, revved it to frighten the people to move aside, but no one budged. The driver didn't know what to do. The crowd knelt in front of the van, and prayed. Finally, the van was able to move very slowly through the streets, to a hospital, where Miguel's father claimed the bodies of the two brothers. The fifth intended victim, *Roberto Pro*, was saved from execution.

The bodies were brought back to Miguel's father's house, where they lay that day, November 23, and the next. Roberto had been told he would be able to come home to venerate the bodies of his brothers. The Blessed Sacrament was brought to the house so that he could receive Communion. They put the pyx on Miguel's chest. Roberto was not released that night, so the Blessed Sacrament remained on his brother's chest.

Thousands of people filed by the bodies of the two Martyrs. They kissed the caskets, touched the brothers, as if touching saints, with linen, rosaries, and other objects. *Miracles* began to descend on the people of Mexico, while the bodies were still warm. An old woman, who had been blind for six years, had wanted to pay her last respects to Padre Pro, but couldn't leave her house, because of her blindness. A friend suggested she pray to Padre Pro, in her home, for recovery of her sight. She claimed that no sooner had she finished her prayer than her eyesight returned to her. The friend who had made the suggestion, couldn't believe what she was saying. He asked her to read a newspaper, which she was able to do without any problem.

A woman in great financial problem, had given all her papers to Miguel to try to help her. When she learned of his death, she ran to her lawyer, not knowing what to do, now that the documents were probably lost forever. She told her lawyer what she had done, and that Padre Pro had been shot. He said to her, *"That's not possible. Not ten minutes ago, he came himself and brought me your papers."* Miguel Pro was still in rare form; only now he wasn't encumbered by space and time. Miracles abounded from that time on, in the tradition of St. Thérèse, the Little Flower of Lisieux.

Tribute to a Saint

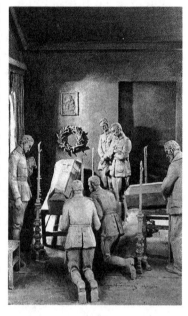

Perhaps the greatest miracle was his funeral procession. Miguel Pro, from Heaven, gave each of his followers a special gift, *courage*. The caskets were carried down to the hearses at 3:30 p.m., on November 24, for the procession to the cemetery. Miguel had a white hearse. Masses of people were on hand to follow the hearses through the city. But as the hearses progressed, more and more people followed. They got off streetcars, and joined the crowd. Five hundred cars formed walls to block crossing traffic; the crowd processed between the blockade of cars, on the busy Paseo de la Reforma. More than twenty thousand people marched down the main street of Mexico City, pushing their way past soldiers with fixed bayonets. The streets were carpeted with flowers. Balconies all along the procession route, were filled with mourners.

But the climate was not at all that of mourners. They were jubilant. As the crowd swelled, the voices, as one, began singing,

"*Viva Cristo Rey*, Long live the Martyrs! Long live the Pope! Long live our Bishops! Long live our Priests! Long live religion!"

It reached fever pitch; it never ended. After the procession got out of the main part of the city, the coffins were taken out of the hearses; men took turns carrying them the rest of the way. When the throngs in the automobiles saw this, they left their cars, and went the rest of the way on foot. The body of Miguel was interred in the Jesuit vault, while his brother Humberto, was buried nearby. All the followers deposited flowers at both grave sites. It was like two mountains of flowers. The people broke into song, and continued late into the night, until the cemetery doors were finally closed. Miguel had never witnessed such homage paid to a human being. Now he was the center of it.

God will have His way. If Miguel Pro and his fellow victims had been judged guilty of attempted murder of the ex-president Obregón,[26] they would have been put in prison for eight to twelve years. Most likely, they would have died in prison, or in any event, never be heard from again.

But President Calles had to do it his way! He executed Miguel and his companions, and *photographed* the murder. Then he made sure the photos were *plastered* all over the newspapers, as a stern warning to anyone who would dare to disobey him.

---

[26]As for Obregón, whoever wanted him killed *(Calles?)*, got their wish less than eight months after the attempt on his life, which cost Miguel Pro his life. A month after having been re-elected president, Obregón was victim of an assassination plot in July of 1928, while dining with friends at a restaurant.

What he managed to do was create a national hero, a Martyr, a role model so strong that the people of Mexico would rally behind the banner of this young Jesuit, until all brothers and sisters could enjoy religious freedom in this land of 97% Catholics and 99% Guadalupeans.

We really believe, however, it was God's plan all along to raise Miguel Pro as a *Martyr* for Mexico, a national hero, and a *Saint*, whose light blazes across the sky of his homeland. There were many Priests executed under Calles' regime. There were over five hundred lay people tortured and murdered by his home-grown Gestapo. Why was this one man, Padre Miguel Agustín Pro, singled out as Martyr, hero and saint?

We've said it from the beginning, and the Lord bears us out. In times of crisis, *God sends us Saints and Other Powerful Men and Women in our Church,*[27] *God sends us Martyrs.* God gave us Miguel Pro, not only for the Mexican people, but for God-loving people everywhere, to let us know loud and clear, *God is alive!*

There are many messages in the story of our modern-day Martyr, Miguel Pro. Perhaps the greatest lesson, the most important truth we will ever learn, is Blessed Miguel Pro's battle cry, the victory cry of Catholics everywhere, for all the world to hear, *"Viva Cristo Rey!"*

---

[27]For the lives of more Saints and Other Powerful Men and Women, read Bob and penny Lord's books: *"Saints and Other Powerful Men"* and *"Saints and Other Powerful Women".*

Archbishop Oscar Romero

Archbishop Oscar Romero shepherding his flock

The story of Oscar Romero is one of *transformation*, from one born of poverty, to one living comfortably within the system, to one determined to change the system. The story of Oscar Romero is one of conversion, of Paul on the road to Damascus, of a man who was blinded, and whose eyes were opened by the Lord, to see his brothers and sisters in agony and misery. The story of Oscar Romero is one of a man who committed his life to right wrongs to his flock, or die trying. The story of Oscar Romero is one of a Martyr for Christ. The story of Oscar Romero is an affirmation of the power and mercy of God.

A boy from the poor side of town

Oscar Arnulfo Romero y Galdamez was born on the Feast of The Assumption of Our Lady, August 15, 1917, in Barrios, a small, mountainous village high above sea level, in El Salvador, Central America. His father, Santos Romero and his mother Guadalupe de Jesus Galdamez, were not what you would call very *religious* people. The Church, and its rules were not uppermost in their minds. Proof of that is that the child Oscar wasn't even baptized until he was two years old. His father had to be given Marriage instructions before he and his fiancee could be married in the Church. And if that's not enough, the father, Santos, admitted to at least one illegitimate child, the fruit of a wild youth.

Santos Romero was a Postal worker. Little Oscar, as well as his four other brothers and one sister, used to play at the post office. They sent telegraphs, and helped deliver mail. It was a very casual village. Rules were not strictly adhered to. It sounds like a good, solid, secure job. Don't be taken in. It was a small village. There wasn't that much mail. The pay was poor. There was no security. Everything was tenuous in those days. Who knew if Santos would have a job the next day. Sounds much like the United States of the 90's. To supplement the family income, Santos grew coffee and cacao on acreage which his wife inherited from her side of the family. And still, they lived an extremely modest life. But so did everyone else in Barrios. There was no electricity, hot water or inside plumbing. The children had to sleep together in beds. Nobody had his or her own room.

From an early age, it was obvious that Oscar was cut from a unique cloth, not typical of the Romero family. His father taught him all his prayers. He seemed to sense something special in Oscar, that the other children did not possess. After Santos' death, Oscar wrote his reflections of his father. One part of their life together, in particular, touched him greatly. He wrote of that time:

"Only the memories remain, memories of childhood - how you would pace the bedroom floor as my child's understanding memorized the Our Father, the Hail Mary, the Creed, the Hail

Holy Queen, the commandments that your fatherly lips taught me.

"I still see you one night waiting for us to return with Mother from our trip to San Miguel, waiting with a toy for each of us made with your own hands."[1]

Oscar was different from his brothers and sister, more serious, more spiritual. He began his education at a local school, which went up to the third grade. Then he continued with a private instructor until he was twelve. We don't know if this was the norm for the Romero family, if all the children had educations until they were in their teens, or if it was just Oscar because he showed such a proficiency for learning.

Whatever the case, when Oscar wanted to go beyond this phase of his education, the father balked. He was against more learning, getting that much education. What good was it going to do them? He made Oscar enter into an apprenticeship as a carpenter. This had to be a great disappointment for the young Oscar, but he *obeyed* his parents. He didn't just *go* into the apprentice program, *he threw himself into it* with all he had. He still went to church every day after work, to spend time with the Lord. We can see a yearning for the religious life surfacing early in Oscar's life. The Lord had touched him, and he would never be the same.

A major event took place in 1930, when Oscar was thirteen, which sealed his vocation. Fr. Monroy, Priest from the town, returned from studies in Rome, where he had been ordained. He was coming home to celebrate his first Mass. On hand for the festive occasion was the vicar general of the Diocese. Oscar was prodded to talk to him about his vocation. It took a lot of courage for Oscar to even mention it to the vicar-general, but he was spurred on by a local man,

[1]Romero - a life - James R. Brockman - 1982, Orbis Books

the town mayor. The vicar-general suggested Oscar attend the Minor Seminary at San Miguel, the seat of the Diocese.

A small conflict arose with Oscar's father. He was opposed to his son leaving their town. The minor seminary in San Miguel was not that far away, but by horseback, it took seven hours. We have to believe that either Oscar's mother, or the Priests had a great deal of influence on Santos, because Oscar finally received permission to go to the seminary.

Seminary life was exciting for Oscar. He missed not being with his family, but it was as if he belonged at the seminary in San Miguel; it was a completely different life from what he had known in the mountain town of Barrios. It was a new world for him. He had been powerfully inspired by the Lord; the direction of his life was set. He wrote a beautiful poem while he was in the minor seminary:

"Your word is pardon and gentleness for the penitent,
Your word is holy instruction, eternal teaching;
It is light to brighten, advice to hearten;
It is voice of hope, fire that burns,
way, truth, sublime splendor,
life, eternity.
But not is the temple alone Your battlefield;
You range the world with Your sword upraised,
the redeeming cross...."

As we walk with Oscar Romero through his life, we will see that it was a willing walk on the Way of the Cross. The Cross of Jesus was his strength as a young seminarian, and became more a way of life to the very end.

He didn't withdraw himself from his family altogether. He sent his laundry home to be washed. He spent his holiday time with his folks. But by and large, he had committed himself to the Lord in the priesthood. Everything in his life from that time on was in preparation for that vocation.

The excitement grew as he was sent to the Jesuit Seminary in San Salvador in 1937. He was born to live this life. Everything was an affirmation that the Lord had chosen him for the role he would play in the history of El Salvador. The bishops had their eyes on him. He was special even in their eyes. He was sent to this seminary after only a short time in San Miguel. He only spent a year in the national Seminary in San Salvador, when he was sent to Rome to complete his studies at the Gregorian Institute. Only when one is very special, when great things are expected of him, is a seminarian sent to Rome. Oscar was that someone.

His time in San Salvador was marred by the death of his father, which took place very shortly after he arrived. His whole being was catapulted back to the land of his birth, to his young years there, his mother and especially his father, his brothers and sister. The Lord brought him back, that he should never forget where he came from. But that would be difficult, because Oscar was as far away from his roots, socially, mentally and spiritually, as he could be.

He was from the poor, born into poverty. When his opportunity came to get out of the ghettos of El Salvador, and into a little better life, he jumped at the chance. But his origins came back to haunt him, to challenge him. The influence of the Lord was apparent in so many of Romero's writings. In 1940, prior to his ordination, he wrote in the magazine of the Latin American College in Rome. Again, he paralleled his priesthood with the Cross:

"This is your heritage as a priest: the Cross. Bearer of pardon and peace, the priest approaches the bed of the dying, and a Cross in his hand is the key that opens the heavens and closes the abyss....to be, with Christ, a crucified one who redeems and to be, with Christ, a risen one who apportions resurrection and life."

Oscar Romero spent six years in Rome, during some of the most difficult times for the Church and the world. He admired Pope Pius XI, the Pope at that time. He was greatly influenced by this Pope's stand against Fascism, terrorism, Nazism, and all the totalitarian bullies of the Second World War. In later years, after he had become Archbishop of San Salvador, during a visit to Rome, he stopped at the tomb of Pope Pius XI. He called him the greatest Pope of all time, All these attitudes lay dormant in the back of the young seminarian's mind, until the Lord chose to bring them to the surface for His glory.

It was at the peak of World War II. The Latin American students were given the option to try to return home when the war situation became ominous; many took it. Oscar did not. He loved what was happening in his life at the Gregorian Institute. He wanted to be as close to Church as was possible. He wanted to soak in as much of this, what he considered his real roots, as he could. He was ordained in Rome on April 4, 1942. He continued to stay on, studying for a doctorate in Theology. But a year and a half after his ordination, his bishop called him home. He was needed in El Salvador. He left Rome in August, 1943. He had some rough times getting to his homeland, because of the security of the war. But he finally arrived in El Salvador, at Christmastime in 1943. He was given a reception in the central plaza in San Miguel. After Christmas, he went up to the little church in Barrios, where he was born and grew up, and celebrated his first Mass there. Now it was time to get to work in the vineyard where the Lord had planted him.

Fr. Romero was sent to a little mountain town, similar to Barrios. He was to be Pastor there. Remember, he was only 27 years old. But there was a shortage of priests in El Salvador, and a great harvest to be labored in. It was not unusual for young priests to become pastors of churches in the outlying areas. We don't know what Fr. Oscar's reaction was to his first assignment, but we do know that the Bishop brought him back to his home diocese, San Miguel, within a few months, to be Secretary of the Diocese. Did his Bishop send him to the remote little mountain village to test his obedience? Or could he see that this young zealot would be of greater use to the Church in the Diocesan office than in the hinterlands?

Fr. Romero was to remain at this post, Secretary of the Diocese for the next 23 years, but in addition, he had many other jobs, all of which he embraced with a passion. He took over the job of Pastor of the Cathedral Church. He was a brilliant homilist. His sermons pumped energy into the Cathedral community. At one time, his Sunday masses were broadcast by five radio stations. He undertook a major construction or reconstruction of the Cathedral, and saw it to the end. He had an image of Our Lady under a very special title, *Our Lady of Peace.* He committed himself to Mother Mary in this role, and spent his life trying to accomplish peace for his people.

He was involved in everything. He promoted the Legion of Mary, Cursillo, Alcoholics Anonymous, the Rosary Society, and Perpetual Adoration. He plunged into everything that had to do with Church. In later years, he took on the role of editor of the Diocesan Catholic newspaper, rector of the Minor Seminary, and confessor to the various religious communities. When the Bishop went away, Fr. Romero became acting Bishop, which was good practice the Lord gave him to prepare for his own time as Bishop.

Fr. Romero had become very close to Jesuit teachers while he was in Rome. He was exposed to the Spiritual exercises of St. Ignatius Loyola, founder of the Jesuits. But he never took part in the Ignatian exercises until some years later, when he went on a Jesuit retreat and adopted the Spiritual exercises of St. Ignatius Loyola, trying to apply them to his life as a Priest. He was more interested in the spiritual philosophy of the Jesuits than the corporal, or worldly. They had a great influence on his spiritual life as Priest and Bishop, not on his politics.

One of the most difficult times in the life of Fr. Romero was the Sixties and early Seventies, when abuses of Vatican II began to surface in Central America. There was one thing he always felt secure about, and that was the solidity of the Church. You could set your clock on the Church. It had survived 2,000 years of trial and turmoil. It was a rock, as solid as St. Peter's Basilica. Fr. Romero embraced that Church. He was a very conservative Priest, a fact he was proud of. Many of the younger Priests had always considered him too strict. But with the relaxed stance, the younger Priests were taking with the liberties of Vatican II, he found himself more at odds with them than before. For their part, they accused Fr. Romero of blocking the spirit of Vatican II. This would not have been too much of a problem for them, except that Fr. Romero was one of the most powerful Priests, if not *the* most powerful Priest in San Miguel. Consider, he was the pastor of the Cathedral, editor of the extremely influential Diocesan newspaper, and rector of the Seminary. Prior to Vatican II, ill feelings would have been manifested by rumbling under the breath. But now, the liberties afforded by Vatican II allowed those against Romero to become extremely vocal. They wanted him out of his position in San Miguel.

Couple this with a new Bishop coming into the area, who didn't like the idea at all of anyone having as much power as Fr. Romero, now Monsignor Romero. We don't know if there was any friction between Oscar Romero and his new Bishop, but a year after the Bishop came into power, 1967, the year of Fr. Romero's 25th Anniversary, he was "*promoted*" to the position of Secretary-General of the National Bishops' Conference, which, very conveniently, took him out of San Miguel to San Salvador. Naturally, he lost all his power in San Miguel, but worse, those who had depended on him to champion the interests of the conservative Church, did not have a voice in the Diocese any more. It was bad enough that Fr. Romero was taken out of his position of strength, but Marxist philosophy was running rampant in the Priesthood, as well as the Bishops of Central America. Members of the ruling class were openly calling the Priests *communists*.

Archbishop Oscar Romero celebrating Mass

A Bishops' conference was called in 1968 to implement the teachings of Vatican II, with particular emphasis on Central America. It took place in Medellín, Colombia, South America. At this meeting, the Bishops unanimously condemned the horrible living conditions for the nearly 300 million inhabitants of Central America. As one, they proclaimed that the Church could no longer stand by and watch the people being tortured in this way. *"Injustice is not God's will"* became a battle cry.

It was the beginning of Liberation Theology in Central America, which split the Church right down the middle.

Broad, liberal interpretations of Vatican II had started the young Priests on the road towards political activism within the countries; the Medellín Conference pushed them even farther towards open confrontation with the governments accused of mistreating the people. Those who were pro-Medellín formed an elite group, which had no sympathy or patience with anyone who didn't agree with their new theology. They alienated conservatives within the Church, and tried to subvert their efforts.

This is what Monsignor Oscar Romero walked into when, within three years of this appointment, he was ordained Auxiliary Bishop of San Salvador. He was torn whether to accept the position, because he was not sure he was capable of doing the job, and it might compromise his Priesthood.[2] He had always been a hard taskmaster, being hardest on himself. He had set down a set of rules of behavior and performance for himself as a Priest, which he never carried out to his full satisfaction. For him to take on the role of Bishop, he would now set an even more difficult set of standards for himself, which he was sure he couldn't handle. No one else was as hard on themselves as he was. But it did get in the way of his decision to accept the great honor he was being offered.

However, what he was not taking into consideration was that this was definitely the Lord's plan for him, and the country, *and the Lord would have His way*. So, through much prayer and retreat time, Oscar Romero accepted the message as being from the Lord, and gave his Fiat; he said *Yes*. Did he have any idea when he did this, that it would ultimately cost him his life? And had he known, would he have made a different decision? We have to believe he

---

[2]That may sound unusual, but a retiring Archbishop was asked by the press some years ago if he had it to do over, would he have been a Bishop. He said no. When asked if he had it to do over, would he have become a Priest, he said, "*With all my heart.*"

would have done exactly what he did. Remember, he always spoke about walking the Way of the Cross as the way to the Kingdom. We believe he was a man committed to serving the Lord and his people.

Oscar Romero was ordained Auxiliary Bishop of San Salvador on June 21, 1970. It was a glorious moment, as it would be for any Priest, to be given the confidence of his fellow Bishops and the Pope, to raise him to the level of Bishop. Oscar had wanted a very low-key ordination, for many reasons. One was that a big celebration would not fit in with his desire to be a humble Priest, on the order of St. Ignatius Loyola. Another was that it was just against his personality to be the center of massive festivities. However, his Cursillo brothers and sisters sponsored the event, and wanted to show their good friend and pastor, Fr. Romero, how much they loved him. Throngs of his followers from San Miguel came to the ordination, in addition to well-wishers from all over the country. The president of El Salvador sent representatives to the ordination. So it became a gala event.

But not everybody wanted to honor Oscar. There were those who were against him. They had voiced their disapproval of Oscar Romero as candidate for Bishop, because he was too conservative, too old school. He didn't fit in this new age of Vatican II and Medellín. They pointed out that the ordination, which was too much of a celebration for the people of the country, who were so poor, was in bad taste. Oscar Romero would have been the first person to agree with them. But nobody asked him. They just attacked him.

Bishop Romero found himself in a most difficult situation. He was committed to his beliefs in the traditions of the Church. These had been with him all his life, and especially all of his Priesthood. He could not turn his back on them now. Yes, the Church was infallible. Yes, the

Church wanted us to follow the example of Jesus, Who suffered as the people of El Salvador were suffering, Who died as the people of El Salvador were dying, and was Resurrected, as would the brothers and sisters of Bishop Romero's country. He had to distance himself physically as well as theologically from those whom, he judged, were trying to destroy the Church by becoming active revolutionaries, attacking rather than defending.

The Jesuits were a prime example of this. They had become radically socialist, liberal, and to the thinking of many in the Salvadoran community, Marxist. Bishop Romero had been very close to them. He had always used the Jesuits for his retreats, and chose a Jesuit as his confessor. He cut himself off from the Jesuits. He turned to the members of Opus Dei,[3] a strong, conservative order, faithful to the Pope and the Magisterium of the Church. In 1972, when the Jesuits were removed from the University, Bishop Romero favored that move. The Jesuits never forgot that. They took this as a sign that since becoming a Bishop, Oscar Romero had abandoned them in favor of the rich land owners, which he hadn't done at all.

You see, the changes which took place in the Church of Central America as a result of Vatican II were much more severe, much more political than in the United States. The climate in the country was volatile there. It was ruled by the landowners, who represented about 4% of the population. They had everything; the other 96% suffered unbelievable poverty, and sub-human living conditions. In addition, they were taxed heavily; those who resisted were persecuted cruelly, to the point of being slaughtered in many instances. Atrocities became a daily occurrence in El Salvador.

This was unquestionably an impossible situation. Vatican II opened the door for the Church which gave

---

[3]The founder of Opus Dei, Josemaría Escrivá, was beatified in 1992

certain members the courage to condemn the practices of the government. But the Medellín conference went way beyond condemnation. While it may not have actually encouraged civil disobedience and uprising, it implied the justification of that type of behavior by members of the clergy. Priests became guerrillas, taking part in, and condoning the use of military force against the government.

Bishop Oscar Romero could not endorse these actions on the part of the Priests of the diocese. He quoted St. Teresa of Avila, who said *"My intention was good, but the act was wrong; for to accomplish a good, however great it may be, even a small evil is not to be done."*[4] He also reminded them of Jesus' words to Peter at the Garden of Gethsemane, *"Put your sword back in its scabbard; am I not to drink the cup that the Father has given Me?"*[5] Bishop Romero's stand was in keeping with the official Church. It was also in keeping with the landowners and government, but not by his design. He was completely alienated from his fellow Priests, because he had to remain who he was, a Priest of the Catholic Church.

When it was time to pick the new Archbishop of El Salvador in 1977, a great rift was created within the brotherhood of the clergy. The greatest number of Priests wanted a liberal Bishop to replace the conservative Sanchez, one Arturo Rivera Damas. He had been greatly sympathetic with the plight of the common people, and was very vocal in his condemnation of the government and the landowners. To the government, he was a communist Priest.

The clergy believed that Oscar Romero was just a tool of the rich and the government. Rome wanted Oscar Romero to be the next Archbishop. While they drastically wanted reform in the country, they did not want it at the expense of the Church losing its ability to function within the

---

[4]Saints and Other Powerful Women in the Church Pg 165
[5]John 18:11

country. In the 2,000 year history of the Catholic Church, there have been many times when she had to keep silent and bite her tongue, to avoid losing all influence in a given country, no matter how small. They feared that the clergy had traded *prayer* for *pistols*. Rome knew the Church had never been victorious with conventional weapons. In the final analysis, prayer was the most powerful weapon we had. But it was next to impossible to get the young priests to accept this.

A voice of reason and sanity in this insane situation was needed. Oscar Romero was that voice. He was chosen Archbishop of San Salvador. At the very time he was to assume his post, it would seem that all hell broke loose in the Archdiocese. A particular riot took place, in which the police opened fire on a group of people in the square. They ran to the Church of El Rosario, and barricaded themselves inside until early in the morning. The retiring Archbishop Chavez and another Bishop were called to the scene to help restore peace. The new Archbishop Romero was not there. He had gone to his former diocese to close up his house, and move his belongings to San Salvador.

The Bishops, including Romero, drafted a protest to the government, which was to be read at all the Masses the following Sunday. In it, they indicated their distress over the events of the recent past, including, but not limited to the brutality against the peasants, the deaths, threats, and the outrageous attacks on the Church, including beating and expelling Priests, especially the Jesuits. Archbishop Romero vacillated between going with the protest, and not going with it. He met with Bishop Rivera during the week, and shared his fears as to the advisability of reading the protest from the pulpits. Rivera convinced him it was the thing to do.

On Saturday, the day before the statement would be read at all the Masses, a good friend of Archbishop Romero's, Fr. Rutilio Grande, an extremely liberal Jesuit, was heading out to a small village, El Paisnal, to celebrate Mass for the people. He was accompanied by an old man and a young boy. Romero and Grande had been friends for many years. However, Rutilio Grande was a rebel, both in words and actions. He had been editor of the Diocesan newspaper, and had to be replaced when the bulk of his articles were in praise of guerrilla Priests and proponents of the Marxist philosophy of Liberation Theology. Romero had replaced him as editor at that time. The government had long ago branded Fr. Grande a communist sympathizer.

As he and his companions were traveling along the country road, they were gunned down by high-powered rifles from a distance. They were immediately killed. This act was the catalyst which blew the lid off the already tense situation between the Church and the government. Archbishop Romero demanded an investigation by the president of the country, stating that it was believed, because of the weapons used, that the murders may have been committed by members of the military. After numerous letters and visits to the president, the new Archbishop realized that he and the Church had absolutely no influence on the government, and that the only way that any headway in human rights could be achieved was by bringing it to the people and attacking the government.

The letter of protest was read at all the Sunday Masses in San Salvador, and also outside the Archdiocese, the next day. Romero was branded a troublemaker by those in the government.

The next week, at a meeting of the clergy and Bishops, it was suggested that more of a protest had to be made by the Church against the government. The murder of Fr. Grande was just the climax of a series of attacks on Priests, including exile, torture and murder. The clergy suggested the schools be closed for three days in protest, and all Sunday Masses be canceled, with the exception of one Mass for the entire Archdiocese to be celebrated at the Cathedral. Archbishop Romero thought and prayed hard before making the decision as to what course of action to take. He realized, it was a radical move, and would alienate him from the government, and the landowners. As a matter of fact, a group representing the upper class met with this new Archbishop, who had been their friend, had baptized their children, given them First Holy Communion, Confirmation, married their children, and buried their dead. Now they wanted to impress on him their strength, and how they would use it against him, to crush him, if necessary, like a bug. They disagreed vehemently with his proposal to close the schools and limit the Masses to one.

Archbishop Oscar Romero with the poor

Oscar Romero stood up against them, admirably. But he didn't want to burn any bridges. He was hoping not to alienate himself from them at the very beginning of his ministry as Archbishop. He would need the support of these people in the future. But then another attack convinced him what he had to do. Shortly after the meeting with the landowners, but before the plan was to be put into effect, he received a summons from the Papal Nuncio to meet with him. When Archbishop Romero and a companion Priest arrived, he found his secretary, a Mexican Priest, sitting with the Papal Nuncio. It seemed to Romero that his own secretary was betraying him to the Papal Nuncio. The Nuncio proceeded to voice the same complaints, and in the same order, and almost the same words, as the rich landowners. He actually scolded Archbishop Romero. Oscar Romero was crushed. It was one thing when the government and rich, turned on him. But the Papal Nuncio was the Pope's representative in this country. He was learning who his enemies were so quickly.

The Nuncio complained that Archbishop Romero was acting irresponsibly, and jeopardizing the position of the Church, not only in San Salvador, but in the whole country. We don't know if this was the final blow, the straw that broke the camel's back, but Archbishop Romero dug his heels in. He was not backing down for anyone. He had made his decision. He would stand by it.

Archbishop Romero went through with his plan to close the schools for three days, and to have the one single Mass at the Cathedral on March 20, 1977. All the Priests of the Archdiocese attended, and concelebrated with the Archbishop. The estimated turnout of the faithful was well over 100,000. It was the largest single show of strength of the Salvadoran people, in their history. It was also a death sentence for Oscar Romero.

In a short period of time, actually just a few short weeks, Oscar Romero, loyal son of El Salvador, loyal son of the Church, found out who his friends were, and who his enemies were, and that he had more enemies than friends in high places. People who had been his friends were now his enemies. People with whom he'd had a good relationship were down his throat. And those whom he had avoided since Vatican II, and particularly, since the Medellín Congress in 1968, were his supporters.

We have to wonder what happened, and who caused it to happen, and why. The incidence of high scale riot and massacre took place within days of Oscar Romero's appointment as Archbishop. The killing of his friend, the Jesuit Priest, Fr. Rutilio Grande, was the catalyst which brought the hostility between the Church and the State to its culmination. While it had been brewing for some time, the explosion occurred before Oscar Romero ever made his first anti-government speech as Archbishop.

The government insisted, the murder of Rutilio Grande was perpetrated by anti-government forces, marxist Priests and their cohorts, to force the issue between the Church and the State over the top. There are those who insist the only way Oscar Romero would come out vehemently and vocally against the State is for something like this to take place. Fr. Rutilio Grande had been a thorn in the side of government for many years. Why was this point in time chosen to murder him, and why when he was on his way out to a poor village, populated by the very people who were the oppressed? Many people believe the words of Caiphas, the high Priest, were applied to Rutilio Grande, "...*it is better for you that one man should die instead of the people, so that the whole nation may not perish.*"[6] Was he a sacrificial lamb? Was Oscar Romero forced into the role he assumed as defender of the people?

It became very obvious, very quickly, that the government was not on the side of the people. They gave Archbishop Romero lip service at the beginning, when all his Priests were being murdered. But they never followed through, and within a short period of time, they didn't even

---

[6]John 11:50

bother with the courtesy of lip service. They ignored him completely. Then, Archbishop Romero and the Church were made the targets of attack by the government. The government used the Church for their own purposes. In the four years that Oscar Romero was Archbishop, there were various coups, in which the government was taken over by one group or another. Inevitably, they would come to Archbishop Romero to seek his support. They promised to make relations better between the Church and the State. They always betrayed the Church, and at the same time, betrayed the people. Romero was to discover that the players were always the same, only the faces changed.

Archbishop Romero and his people lived on hope being dashed by broken promises. He never gave up, however. But the situation never got any better. He was thrown in jail for trying to put down a hostage situation, and protect his Priests. One of his Priests was murdered on that particular night by the soldiers. They tortured him to death, using electric cow prods, which generate an enormous electric shock and unbearable pain, especially when they were applied to the Priest's testicles.

About a year into his ministry as Archbishop, he began receiving death threats. He never paid any attention to them until he began getting advance notice from bishops outside the country, who knew what was going on in El Salvador better than Archbishop Romero. Assassination became a real possibility for Oscar Romero, a way of life. As the years progressed, he became fairly certain he would not live his life out to its normal conclusion; he would not die of old age.

Two weeks before his death, he gave a telephone interview to a Mexican newspaper. He made the following statement: *"I have often been threatened with death. I must tell you, as a Christian, I do not believe in death without Resurrection. If I am killed, I shall arise in the Salvadoran people. I say so without boasting, with the greatest humility.*

"As a shepherd, I am obliged by Divine Mandate to give my life for those I love - for all Salvadorans, even for those who may be going to kill me. If the threats are carried out, from this moment I offer my blood to God for the redemption and for the resurrection of El Salvador.

"Martyrdom is a grace of God that I do not believe I deserve. But if God accepts the sacrifice of my life, let my blood be a seed of freedom and the sign that hope will soon be reality. Let my death, if it is accepted by God, be for my people's liberation and as a witness of hope in the future.

"You may say, if they succeed in killing me, that I pardon and bless those who do it. Would, indeed, that they might be convinced that they will waste their time. A Bishop will die, but God's Church, which is the people, will never perish."[7]

Funerals had become an everyday affair in El Salvador, and especially for the Archbishop. Every time someone was killed who was close to him, he felt it a duty as well as an honor to pay tribute to the brother or sister who had died for the liberty of the country. On Monday, March 24, 1980, Archbishop Romero was celebrating an Anniversary Mass for the mother of Jorge Pinto, whose newspaper had been bombed two weeks before. Romero chose the hospital chapel, where he lived a simple life, since he became Archbishop. It was evening. It had been a busy day for Oscar Romero.

The readings and the homily would have been considered prophetic, except for the fact that he was celebrating a funeral Mass. *"Christ is indeed raised from the dead, the first fruits of those who have fallen asleep..."*[8]

A red Volkswagen pulled up outside the open door of the Chapel. Two men sat in the darkness inside the car.

---

[7]Romero, a life - James R. Brockman - Orbis Books Pg248
[8]1Cor 15:20

"The Lord is my Shepherd...though I walk in the valley of darkness, I fear no evil."[9]

One man leaned over the steering wheel, as if to fix something, while the other sat in the back seat, looking directly into the chapel through the open door.

"Unless a grain of wheat falls to the earth and dies, it remains only a grain. But if it dies, it bears much fruit..."[10]

The man inside the car pulled out a small rifle, and aimed it towards the open door of the chapel.

Romero ended his homily as follows: *"May this Body immolated and this Blood sacrificed for humans nourish us also, so that we may give our body and blood to suffering and to pain - like Christ, not for self, but to teach justice and peace to our people. So let us join together intimately in faith and hope at this moment of prayer for Doña Sarita and ourselves."*

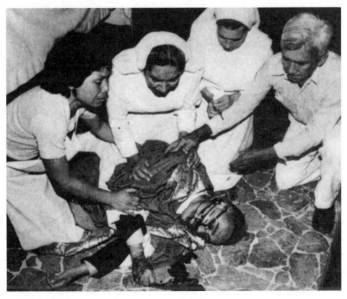

The death of Archbishop Oscar Romero

---

[9]Psalm 23
[10]John 12:24

A blast was heard outside, and a bright spark lit up the inside of the car. Oscar Romero may have been able to see the spark of light in the distance, just before he heard the cracking sound of the discharge, and felt a searing hot bullet rip through his chest, and explode inside of him. The red Volkswagen slowly drove away out of sight. Archbishop Oscar Romero lay on the floor of the chapel, in front of the altar, drowning in his own blood. He died within minutes of the assault.

Oscar Romero is a Martyr in the truest sense of the word. He died during the celebration of the Mass. He was a willing victim. *"Before He was given up to death, a death He freely accepted..."*[11]   There was an extraordinary parallel between the destiny of Our Lord Jesus and that of Oscar Romero, successor to the Apostles of Jesus. He died for his people, many of whom were yelling *"Crucify Him! Crucify Him!"*. There are those on both sides of the political coin, who believe Romero was a pawn of the other side.

There are the conservatives who believe he died because he took on the cloak and banner of the Marxist-Communist theology, under the heading of Liberation Theology, and became a militant leader of the people in their quest to free themselves from the shackles of a super-corrupt, animalistic, inhuman government, or series of governments. These conservatives believe he left himself no other option but to be gunned down somewhere along the line, because he lost his way in his ministry. He should have remained a Priest, who took care of the spiritual needs of his people, and left the physical problems, the starving, the murders, the atrocities, all of that up to the political and military men. But how can you just sit back when those dead people have faces, when they're brothers and sisters, fellow Priests?

---

[11]Beginning of Eucharistic Prayer #2

Then there are the super-liberals, who finally liked him, finally accepted him, on their terms. He died, espousing their cause, or so they think, and so he was okay. *They still don't know, twenty years later.* They talk about how he was converted, how he went from being one of *them* to one of *us.* The fact that he died in that role makes him respectable for them. They still criticize the early years, or actually most of the years of his life and his Priesthood, as being counter-productive to the movement, *(revolution?)* to Vatican II and the Medellín Conference. He died before his time, of unnatural causes at age 62, and yet he was considered an old-timer.

We believe he forgave his murderers, and those who ordered his murder, as well as the slaughter of all the innocents of El Salvador, as you would forgive a child, or a dog who had messed on the floor. They didn't have the intelligence to know what they were doing. They didn't have a conscience or a soul, because they were animals. He also forgave his fellow Priests who put him in the impossible position he was in as Archbishop. They fanned the flames of war. They were intelligent. They knew better than to become militants. They were told by their Church to stay out of politics. But they chose the way of the guerrillas. They were overpowered by Marxist philosophies, and became pawns of the powerful. They gave the government and the military the excuses they needed, if indeed they needed any excuse, to attack the people and the Church. They were frustrated at their inability to make a difference. They had forgotten the power of prayer. They traded their Bibles and Rosaries for machine guns.

It may have been a romantic, Don Quixote, Man of La Mancha approach to take to Priestly ministry, but they had to know that someone would be paying the price. Their innocent Archbishop had to take a stand. Naturally, he had to defend his Priests. He paid the price with his life.

We would like to remember Oscar Romero as a Priest, a Pastor, a shepherd, whose main goal was to love his God in the service of His people. He was a traditional Priest to the end; he loved the Church in Rome, was loyal to the Popes under whom he lived and served, and died serving his Church and people as best he could, in the only way he could. He did not want the Church to be the enemy of the government. He wanted to work with the government for the good of the people. But he was not given that gift. The gift he was given was the one he prayed for all his life; he was given the gift of the Cross, and he embraced it. If we go back to his writings while he was a seminarian in Rome, or his early homilies as a Priest in the Cathedral in San Miguel, we'll find the same Oscar Romero, we found the day his life was taken from him. The only difference was the situation. He had to be their Jesus on earth. But wasn't that the vow he took when he became a Priest, to try to be their Jesus on earth? Was it any different from the vows his fellow Priests took when they were ordained, vows that they might not have kept? Can you be Jesus on earth as a guerrilla Priest, attacking and killing the enemy for whatever reason? No matter how outraged you feel at the injustice and lack of respect for human life, can you be a Jesus on earth when you bomb buildings and cars in the name of the people? Is that the vow you took?

But have no fear, rebel Priests and godless governments. Your sins have been forgiven by the blood of the lamb, Oscar Romero. He died for your sins. Because as old fashioned as it may seem, that's who he was. *Praise Jesus!*

St. Joan of Arc

Joan of Arc is a strong contradiction in our Church and our world. She was abandoned by the country she had fought so hard to protect; she was condemned by a corrupt Bishop of the Church to which she pledged undying loyalty. After her death, that same country made her into a heroine; that same Church made her into a Saint. She is now, with St. Thérèse of Lisieux, co-patroness of France. She was the Little Flower's heroine during Thérèse's lifetime. And although Joan lived some 460 years before St. Thérèse, she was only canonized five years before the Little Flower. Little did Thérèse realize she would someday share the same title of Patron Saint of France with her role model.

Joan of Arc was illiterate. She could not read or write. Yet her story is so fascinating that great authors of the Nineteenth and Twentieth centuries, George Bernard Shaw, and Mark Twain, have both written about her. She was not stupid by any means, only unschooled. She was given the gift of being a brilliant military strategist by St. Michael.

There is such an amazing scope to this teenage saint. She was a peasant girl, daughter of a farmer. Her village of Domremy was sort of a border town. At any given time, it could be part of France, Burgundy, or the Holy Roman Empire, based on who was in charge. Burgundy had sworn allegiance to England, which confused the situation, and made things all the worse. Her country was at war with England, the Hundred Year's War, and had been since long before she was born. Consequently, her country must have been at war with Burgundy.[1]

While Joan was used to the idea of war, having lived with it all her life, she and her family had to hide out many

---

[1]Today, Burgundy is part of France, an important wine region

St. Joan of Arc - Patroness of France

times when invading soldiers came to their little village *from wherever*, to loot and pillage. These *soldiers* were not really troops for the most part. They were bandits who justified their way of life by posing as soldiers. They roamed in packs, and took advantage of any weakness they could find. [Their modern equivalent would be *terrorists*, cowards who terrorize the unarmed civilian population.] While these Fifteenth century terrorists had no courage, they had weapons, so Joan and her family found themselves running for refuge from the attacks.

Considering the conditions of her country, Joan lived a relatively normal life She was an exceptionally loving, religious, trusting girl. That may have been her great mistake, *trusting people.* But she trusted mostly in the Lord. He was in charge of her life. She spent a lot of time at Church, receiving the Sacraments whenever she could. While she was very holy, she was also the life of the party. She loved to take part in village activities. But her strongest pull was towards God and things of Heaven. She was told many stories of the Saints by her dear mother. Remember, she never learned to read or write. It wasn't really necessary for a girl of her station. She had a special secret place all her own, out in the woods, a little chapel where a statue of our Lady and the Baby Jesus presided. She spent a lot of time in that chapel, praying for her family and her country. Joan was a very patriotic girl. She loved her country and her king, even though she was not sure at any given time who he was.

Her years of joy were shortlived. At age twelve, her famous *voices* began coming to her. They were always accompanied by a brilliant flash of light, and came at the precise time the sexton rang the Church bells. At first, there was only one voice. When this voice spoke to her the third time, she knew it was *St. Michael the Archangel.* This was affirmed to her on that third visit by an apparition. She recognized St. Michael in the company of other Angels. At first, the voice just gave her instructions on how to live a good Christian life. Basically, the Angel told her to be good, go to Church often, and obey her parents. These were good instructions, but to be honest, she was already practicing these virtues.

At a given point, St. Michael advised her she would be visited by St. Margaret of Antioch, and St. Catherine of Alexandria. He told her she had to listen to their instructions, and follow them to the letter. She agreed to do this. When they came, they were beautiful. They were majestic. They wore crowns on their heads. We get the impression that all she could see of them was from their heads down to their waist. Joan grew very comfortable with her Heavenly Visitors, especially St. Michael, to whom she and much of the world of the Middle Ages had a great devotion.

But a time was to come when the messages took on a different tone. She was shocked when she was told, *"Daughter of God, you must leave your village and go to France."*[2] She replied *"But I'm only a young girl, and I cannot ride or fight."* She was told she was to save France from the English. This was all beyond her. Think about it, though. This girl was a teenager. Granted, she was much more spiritual than most adults of her time. But she was being told things that most adults would have a major problem accepting. Given the same set of circumstances, I don't know anyone who wouldn't be completely bowled over by the proposition set before this young girl by the Angel, St. Margaret of Antioch and St. Catherine.

She knew they were sincere. She *trusted*, especially in St. Michael. She knew he would not allow the evil one to deceive her. But she was very confused. As the years

---

[2]At that time, Domremy may have been part of Lorraine, the Holy Roman Empire, or Burgundy.

progressed, the messages became more specific. She would save France from defeat at the hands of the British. This continued until she was sixteen years old. Her voices would give her no peace. Then, one day in May, she was given a direct command. She was told by St. Michael to go to a Robert de Baudricourt, in a neighboring town, and tell him to provide her with troops, to escort her to the Dauphin.[3] His first reaction upon seeing this young peasant girl, wearing her worn red dress, and claiming she would save France and have the Dauphin crowned king, was to give her a swift boot. Instead, he ordered her uncle (who had brought her), to take her home. She returned to Domremy, completely crushed.

Her Angelic voices would not leave her alone! She pleaded and tried to explain how she had only been able to accomplish *humiliation* at the hands of Robert De Baudricourt; but St. Michael would have none of it. Finally, he said to her, "*It is God who commands it!*" Fortified by the courage and determination of the Angel, she set out, at the beginning of the following year, to see Robert de Baudricourt, once again. However, by this time the situation of the French was so disastrous, he was not anxious to dismiss her. He was ready to grab onto any hope. Finally, he gave in, and assigned three men to bring her to the king.

Everything she did for the next fifteen months was orchestrated by the voice of St. Michael. She could do no wrong. She was given a white suit of armor. The banner she carried into combat was that of *Jesus and Mary*. Every battle she fought, the French won by a wide margin. The English were pushed back.

The English offered a ransom for the capture of Joan of Arc, dead or alive. But no one could get close to her. She

---

[3]The only legitimate heir to the French throne, but he was in hiding for fear of being executed by the British.

was able to overcome the politics of the French court. She barreled through all the obstacles to have the Dauphin crowned King of France.

But then it was over for Joan. Her mission was completed, as far as the instructions of the Angel were concerned. What then, prompted her to continue going into battle, when she had not been instructed to do so? Whatever the reason, all her future battles were disasters for the French and for Joan. She was even allowed to be captured by her enemies, the Burgundians. They put her up for ransom. Her French king, the Dauphin, to whom she had been so loyal, whom she had placed on the throne of France, abandoned her. She was not worth putting up a franc. But, the English, who hated her, put up a sum equivalent to about $50,000, so that they could humiliate and *execute* her. They couldn't put her on trial for defeating them in battle. They could have just killed her; but that wouldn't have given them any real satisfaction. They had to disgrace and dishonor her.

They decided to try her for witchcraft. There was a great fear of witches in the Middle Ages. They had many eyewitnesses who heard Joan speaking to invisible people. But they were Angels, she cried out. They were from God. No, they insisted. They were from Satan. She was a witch. Her enemies were able to get a corrupt French Bishop, Peter Cauchon, who had ambitions to be Bishop of Rouen, to set up a mock trial. They twisted all her words. She was all alone, or so she thought. Joan was condemned as a heretic, and ultimately burned at the stake.

We have an important question to reflect on here. Why did Joan continue doing battle? As far as her voices were concerned, she should not have. Had she lost her focus? Was she now battling for God, or for herself? Was there a certain amount of self-gratification from winning all those battles? She had become the heroine of France at nineteen years old. She was a very dramatic figure. Was her head turned even a little by the adulation she was receiving? Was she looking for man's approval? Better yet, was she looking for approval from the misfit she had made king?

If *any* of the above were true, the results would have been predictable. She began working on her own agenda, not the Lord's as transmitted to her by the Angel Michael. Is that why everything she did became a catastrophe? Is that why her king abandoned her, without even attempting to rescue her from their enemies? Did St. Michael abandon her? During her last great trial, when it became obvious, she was to be the victim of a kangaroo court, did Michael come to her rescue once more, at the end? We're told that at one point, she backed off from her claims that she had truly heard Angelic voices give her instructions. She was given a period of respite. But soon after, she resumed her claim with strength and fervor, knowing she would be burned at the stake, as a *witch*.

In the account of her death, it is reported that she was allowed to have a crucifix held up so she could look at it, as the raging flames hungrily darted up the pole, mercilessly anxious and ready to devour her body. She seemed to go into an ecstasy, oblivious of the red hot flames that were closing in on her, enveloping her, attacking the young body of the former standard bearer and soldier of Jesus and Mary, and France. Everyone waited anxiously to see her react to the fire, to hear her cry out for mercy. *But she didn't. It was as if she didn't feel any pain!* Then, something unusual happened at her execution. One of the spectators, the secretary to King Henry, cried out, as Joan was dying, *"We are lost; we have burned a saint!"*

Is it possible, that although she had disobeyed him, at the end, her Angel, her Michael, came to her rescue? Could he have stretched out his massive wings and covered the body of this little girl who had trusted him so completely?

Did he protect her from the flames, so that she experienced no pain, as her body was destroyed, and her soul was lifted up to Heaven?

We believe St. Michael the Archangel, and very possibly a legion of Angels were there, to bring their sister Home, after her hard battle. We know the Lord was protecting her. But we have to trust that He was more interested in her soul than her body.

The Lord would not allow the story of Joan of Arc to end in shame. Her family fought the injustice heaped on their daughter and sister. They fought for twenty three years to have her honor restored. Finally, in 1456, Pope Callistus III renounced the charges against her, and the despicable way in which a daughter of the Church, and a daughter of France was railroaded to her death. All charges against her were rescinded. However, it wasn't until May 16, 1920 that she was raised to the Communion of Saints.

We don't understand the Lord's ways. We don't know why He allowed Joan of Arc to suffer the way she did. But we know that He loves us, that He wants nothing more than to lift all of us up into Glory. Do we hear Angelic voices the way Joan did? Do we listen to their instructions? Do we respond the way she did? Do we trust our souls to their bidding? The time may be coming, indeed it may very well be here, when the salvation of our souls will depend on how strictly we obey their directives. *Think about it!*

The Polish Martyrs

In 1945, the Nazi war machine was finally crushed and cities and countries all over Europe were being liberated by the Allied Forces. Great shouts of joy could be heard. Young girls in Rome, Paris, Amsterdam, and other cities across Europe kissed young G.I.'s and other liberating forces. Churches were filled with Masses of Thanksgiving. Prayers of gratitude were offered up by the tens of thousands to Our Lord Jesus and His Mother Mary for finally ending the hell to which these dear people had been subjected for the last six years. It was a new beginning, a new world for Europe.

But not quite all. East of Germany, and west of Russia, the little country of Poland was not liberated by anyone. It just changed tyrants. It was evacuated by the Nazi troops, and just taken over by a different monster, the Soviet Union. At the end of World War II, when Hitler knew the end was inevitably close, he had initiated his *"Scorched Earth"* policy, which, stated simply, meant, *"Burn everything to the ground. Don't leave anything for the Allies to capture."* Warsaw, the capital of Poland, was almost completely destroyed. We're told that 85% of the city burned to the ground. When Eisenhower came through some months after the war ended, he wept at the all-out devastation he witnessed. And yet, while this ruination was being inflicted on the people of Poland, the Russian Army, which was supposed to be our allies, sat on the other side of the Wisla River and just watched. Then, when it was finished, they simply marched in and took over, according to a pre-ordained agreement made by Josef Stalin, Winston Churchill and Franklin Delano Roosevelt at the Yalta Conference in February, 1945. The Communists continued the rule of tyranny over this nation for the next forty-five years. A perfect example of the way things were changed is indicated by a street in Czestochowa, a great Marian shrine. Before World War II, the street was named Mary Strasse. In 1939, when the Nazis came in, it was renamed Hitler Strasse. In 1946, it was renamed again, this time, Stalin Strasse. In 1990, it was renamed one more time, back to Mary Strasse.

When we planned this book, we didn't actually plan a section for Polish Martyrs. We planned this segment for St. Maxmilian Kolbe, and Blessed Edith Stein, Martyrs of the death Camp at Auschwitz. We honestly didn't know what else we could write about with regard to Polish martyrs. We didn't know of any other Polish Martyrs. We had such a surprise waiting for us. Thank God we went to Poland before we finished writing this book.

The Lord gave us the gift of traveling to Poland in May of 1993, to videotape shrines of Poland. We had an agenda.

Bob and Penny Lord with (starting from left)
Msgr. Peszkowski, Primate Jozef Glemp, and Fr. John Mikalajunas

We knew exactly what we were going to shoot, and for what reason. But the Lord had His own Agenda, and it far surpassed anything we had in mind. We knew we wanted to go to *Niepokolanow*, City of the Immaculata, where Maxmilian Kolbe had the largest Franciscan complex, 800 brothers and priests, in the history of the Franciscan order. We had to visit *Czestochowa*, a city of our Lady, where she has been venerated by the Polish people on about the same scale as Our Lady of Guadalupe is by the Mexicans, but we never thought we would fall so in love with our Lady at this shrine as we did, or with the Polish people who venerate her here. Sister Faustina had been beatified the month before we arrived, and so we fully planned to trace her life in Warsaw and Krakow. We also knew we had to go to Auschwitz, the death camp which made martyrs of St. Maxmilian Mary Kolbe and Blessed Edith Stein. We were not looking forward to that trip. We had been told that once someone goes to Auschwitz, they are haunted by what they see. One never wants to go back again. But they never forget Auschwitz. We knew we had to experience Auschwitz. Our chapter on Maxmilian Kolbe would never be complete until we stood in Cell Block 11, that infamous block where no one ever comes out alive, and where he died on August 14, 1941. We wept bitter tears with the Angels over the waste of human lives, Children of God. We knew we had to stand at the site of the little white cottage at Birkenau, a section of Auschwitz, where Edith Stein and her sister entered on August 9, 1942, and were immediately gassed with Cyanide. There were large white wooden Crosses and Stars of David scattered throughout the field, and human bones could still be picked up from the remains of the funeral pyres where the bodies had been burned after having been gassed. *We knew we had to do this!*

We were not prepared, however, for the ongoing suffering this people had endured for the last fifty-one years

(1939-1990) that we know of, and then some. Before the United States ever got into World War II, Poland had already been taken over, and Maxmilian Kolbe martyred. Before the Jews were ever brought to Auschwitz, it was used as a Concentration Camp for Polish prisoners, intellectuals, Catholic priests, and others labeled *dangerous.* And from the other side, the Russian side, *twenty-one thousand* Polish soldiers were massacred by Josef Stalin in a place called Katyn in 1940. The Warsaw Ghetto incident occurred, in which over 300,000 Polish Jews were rounded up from the Jewish Ghetto of Warsaw, and shipped off to Concentration Camps. The atrocities go on and on. We could really write a huge book just about the Polish martyrs and never end.

No sooner had we decided to add this martyr, or that group of martyrs than people came up with yet another martyr for us to consider. And for the most part, these are all Twentieth Century martyrs. We chose to share with you the first martyr of Poland, St. Stanislaus, mostly because he was the first Polish canonized saint, who was actually born Polish and died a Martyr. But with that exception, all the atrocities took place from 1939 on, and the most recent, Fr. Jerzy Popieluszko was martyred in 1984.

We have narrowed our choice down to three martyrs of Poland, in addition to Maxmilian Kolbe and Edith Stein. They are St. Stanislaus, the first Polish Martyr, and Patron Saint of Poland, the Eleven Nuns of the Order of the Holy Family of Nazareth, who were brutally murdered by Nazi troops in the woods of Nowogrodek on August 1, 1943, as a representative of the atrocities of the Nazi occupation, and Fr. Jerzy Popieluszko, spiritual director of Solidarity, murdered by Communists on October 19, 1984, as a symbol of the Occupation by the Soviet Union. We know that we are missing more Polish Martyrs than we're writing about, but if we were to write about all the Polish people who have been martyred, we would never stop writing, and we would never stop crying. Come with us, then, as we tell you about the people of Poland and their heroes, our brothers and sisters, the Saints.

St. Stanislaus - Bishop of Krakow - 1079

Stanislaus Szczepanoski was born in 1030. He was considered the answer to his parents' prayers, as they were advanced in age when the Lord gave him to them. They adored this child, as did everyone with whom he came in contact. His parents guided him on the path of a religious vocation. He was very learned, having been educated at the best universities in Poland. He determined to use his God-given gifts to serve the Church and people of Krakow.

His Bishop, Lampert Zula, immediately saw the spiritual as well as intellectual virtues of young Stanislaus. After the Bishop had ordained him, he made him preacher of the Cathedral of Krakow, as well as Archdeacon. His preaching was brilliant, truly inspired. A great deal of conversions, and moral reformation took place as a result of Stanislaus' preaching. He developed a large following in Krakow.

The Bishop wanted to retire, but had waited until he could find someone he could trust with the office of Bishop of Krakow. He found his man in Stanislaus. He tried to retire, and turn his office over to Stanislaus, but the young Priest refused out of humility. However, when the Bishop died, he could not refuse the post any longer. Especially when he was ordered by the Pope, Alexander II. In 1072, he was ordained Bishop, and made Bishop of Krakow.

There was a ruler in Poland at that time, Boleslaus II. He may have had some redeeming qualities, but none were very obvious. What the entire population of Poland, as well as the Church could see was that he had a great lust for women, a craving which could not easily be satisfied. He had many run-ins with Bishop Stanislaus, but because the Bishop and the church were so loved by the people, Boleslaus made believe he was repentant. It's possible he was really sincere in his efforts to change his ways, but there's nothing very definite that he really ever tried to stop running after women.

The straw that broke the camel's back, so to speak, came when Boleslaus met a woman who was extremely beautiful. She was breathtaking. She was married to a nobleman. That didn't make any difference to Boleslaus. He had to have her. He was completely crushed when she fought off his advances, but he was not discouraged. He actually kidnapped her, and took her off to his palace. This caused a tremendous outrage among the nobles, as well as the commonfolk. They called on the Bishop of Gnesen, whose Diocese Boleslaus was in, to reprimand the king. But everyone was too frightened. Finally, they brought the case to Bishop Stanislaus, who was frightened of nothing other than not serving his Lord the best way he knew.

Stanislaus had no problem berating the king. He told him, as he had before, that he would have to change his behavior, only this time he would be excommunicated.

This caused an animosity between the king and the Bishop, which took on outrageous proportions. A miracle was the result of the venom the king spewed at Stanislaus. The church had purchased land from a man who died shortly thereafter. The king saw this as a way to get at Bishop Stanislaus. He had the dead man's family claim that the land was never paid for. In a set-up trial, the king would not allow any of Bishop's witnesses to be heard. Finally, Bishop Stanislaus brought the dead man to life there in the courtroom, to testify that he had indeed been paid. This gave Stanislaus tremendous popularity with the people, but made the king so outraged, he had to get rid of him.

After that defeat, the king became worse, if that is possible, not only in his lust for women, but in his hatred for the Bishop and the Church. He did everything he could to persecute them. Finally, St. Stanislaus had no recourse but to excommunicate the king, which was a terrible humiliation. A plot was hatched to murder St. Stanislaus. The king sent his men into a small chapel outside of town, which is today the Church of St. Stanislaus. He ordered his men to go in and kill the Bishop. They went in, but came out quickly. They told the king they could not get near the Bishop, as he was protected by a brilliant, heavenly light.

The king, driven by hatred, grabbed the sword from one of his men, ran into the church, and killed the Bishop during the consecration of the Mass. Then his men cut him up into little pieces, and spread the parts of his body all over the city. The idea was that he would be eaten by crows and vultures. However, heavenly eagles[1] picked up all the pieces of his body and brought them to the Cathedral. The authorities of the Church then buried St. Stanislaus in the Chapel of St. Michael.

It's not a sure thing that the king was dethroned as a result of his murder of the Bishop of Krakow, but it is known that he lost his throne not long after. You see, in Poland, the kings were appointed, not by heredity, but by the people. And as they could appoint a king, I'm sure they could also impeach a king. That's what happened to Boleslaus II. A tradition came out of this terrible act of the King's, which

---

[1]The symbol of Poland is the eagle

stayed with the Polish people as long as there was a Monarchy in Poland. Every future king, on the day of his coronation, had to walk in pilgrimage from the Church of St. Stanislaus, to the Cathedral, in penance for the hideous crime committed by his predecessor.

Bishop Stanislaus was proclaimed Saint two hundred years later, by Pope St. Gregory VII in 1253. He has been named the Patron Saint of Poland.

Eleven Nuns of the Woods of Nowogrodek - 1943

We only spent a short time in Poland; we listened to the eyewitness accounts of wholesale massacre of these brave people, first by the Communists, then by the Nazis, and again by the Communists. We can't help but wonder what kind of brainwashing had to be done to the troops of the Nazi and Soviet Union armies, to get them to believe that everyone else in the world except them was so much garbage, to be discarded at will, and slaughtered in any cruel and inhuman manner. We do know that Hitler instituted an indoctrination program for the Nazi military, claiming that they were the Aryan[2] race, and better than anyone else. By comparison, the rest of the world was just so much trash. Brother Joseph of our Ministry brought to our attention just recently that Poland had always blocked Germany from Russian attacks just by the nature of its geographical location. When the Russians would attack the Germans, or vice versa, the battles always wound up being fought on Polish soil.

A statistic we read about World War II maintains that close to 30,000,000 people were killed during that war, and *over half of them were civilians.* So much for the reported skill and bravery of those crack Nazi troops. It doesn't take much of either to mow down unarmed, defenseless people with machine guns. They did their best work against unarmed men, women and children. And let us not forget our priests and nuns. They were not only unarmed victims; they even prayed for their attackers.

One of the most outrageous and senseless massacres of the Polish people we have learned about was the slaughter of 11 helpless nuns of the Order of the Holy Family of Nazareth in the woods of Nowogrodek, on August 1, 1943. During the war, this was part of Poland. The Soviet Union took it over after World War II, and is today part of Byelorussia. This also gives you some idea of how these people have been footballed around by tyrannical bullies during this century alone.

---

[2]Descendants of prehistoric people, who spoke that language. It has no ethnological value, although Hitler claimed it to mean a *Caucasian of non-Jewish descent.* This, however, was not true

The Sisters of the Holy Family of Nazareth were founded for the express purpose of ministering to the family. They are consecrated to the Holy Family. Two Sisters came to Nowogrodek in August, 1929. It had been the prayer of their Bishop, Zygmunt Lozinski, who had been born in the small town. He wanted them to open a school there, and the Mother Superior was more than happy to accommodate him. But there was a slight problem. He was the only one who wanted them in the town. The people didn't want them. It was an uphill fight from the very beginning. They couldn't find a place to call their own. They were blocked by people in power of the town. There were many Protestants and Jews. They were suspicious of the little ladies in black. When they appealed to their superior in Rome, and to the Bishop, they were told to stand their ground, stick with it.

These dear Sisters were so filled with the love of Jesus and Mary. They put up with all the distrust, and coldness of the people. They persevered. By October, two more came, and they were given half a house. It was so small, they had to have the kitchen and bedroom in the same room. But they persevered. The Bishop came to bless their humble quarters. When he saw how they lived, he said to them,

"Oh, you little flock, you were not accepted in town, you had to seek refuge in the last of the houses outside town as if in a stable. Be glad and rejoice for from here will appear the same Christ of Bethlehem. Through you, little flock, Christ will act and radiate until you enter the glory of the Father. You will return to Jerusalem, your city, and become its glory and adornment. **The town will accept you and it will be proud that it possesses you....**" That was to prove to be a prophecy.

Little by little, the locals could see why they were there, to love and teach as Jesus and Mary did. Gradually, the walls crumbled. The little band was accepted. They were even given a nickname, *the eleven prie-dieux.* Prie-dieux is a French word for a kneeler. The eleven Nuns would go to the kneelers to the left of the main altar in the Church of the Transfiguration in Nowogrodek and pray. People came to look forward to seeing them there. Over the years, it became sort of a tradition, *the eleven prie-dieux,* the eleven Nuns praying at the kneeler. If one was missing for whatever reason, great concern was manifested by the townspeople. The question was always raised, *"Is she well?"* *"Should I bring her some hot soup?"*

Another tradition of the Nuns which became expected of them, was the way they walked up the hill to the *Fara,* as the Church of the Transfiguration was called. It was a steep incline, but they seemed to glide up the hill, single file, in their black habits, which were down to the floor.

"First, several of them cut across the road. Then one after another, they ascended the narrow path to the top of the hill which wasn't high; it was a small elevation. The climb to their destination wasn't easy. Yet, to those who

observed them it seemed as though they were gliding along, almost as if they were flying up the hill like birds. Perhaps their wide habits, their pleated collars and their wind-blown veils made them look so picturesque."[3]

They came to be a strong part of the community. The fortitude of these nuns would be an important factor for the spiritual and emotional survival of the little village when the war began.

September 1, 1939, the Nazis attacked Poland from Germany. While Nowogrodek was in eastern Poland, and the Nazis attacked from the German border into western Poland, the danger was very real. It manifested itself in an unexpected way. On September 17, 1939, the Russians crossed the border into eastern Poland and occupied it. The war had begun for the people of Nowogrodek. The Nuns had to leave their school and their convent. They were not allowed to wear their habits. They had to beg in the town for a place to sleep and board. But they had a motto. *"Wherever they were, that was their convent. Wherever they lay their heads, Christ the King was present."* Things were so bad under Russian rule, they almost wished the Nazis would come in and take over. That is, until the Nazis did come in and take over.

Within two years, the governing of Nowogrodek changed hands, from Soviet butchers to Nazi murderers. By June, 1941, the people of the little village saw what a real threat a crack team of armed torturers could do to unarmed men, women and children. The most immediate and obvious result of the Nazi takeover was the sight of Jews taken out of their homes, brought to the center square, and murdered. That was definitely the Nazi modus operandi. However, the nuns were allowed to put their habits back on. They were able to pray in the Church. Perhaps the Nazis wanted to be

---

[3]Eleven Prie-Dieux, by Maria Starzynska, Pg 9

able to identify them easily. Right after that, the persecution and atrocities began. In addition to the fifty jews slaughtered in the center of town, while the band played a Johann Strauss' waltz, the Nazis routed out any communist sympathizers, and immediately shot them.

Watching executions, something most of the inhabitants of the little town had never witnessed in their lives, was becoming an everyday event. The people became numbed to what was happening. The situation went from intolerable to unbearable as the years went by. Jewish people were arrested for no reason, taken in the back of the Nazi barracks, and murdered. Other arrests of the men of the town, very often took place in the middle of the night. The frightened voices of the men, screaming voices of their wives and the muffled sound of children, all became normal for that little town. The men would be taken off, never to be heard of again. The Nazi nightmare was in full swing.

This was the situation on July 25, 1943. A group of men, mostly engineers and factory workers were arrested by the Gestapo. It was pretty well expected that they would be killed. But an unusual thing happened. The Commissar of the town, named Straub, complained bitterly to the Gestapo and SS that his authority was being belittled. He wanted to be the one to pass judgment on local people. Secretly, he wanted to hold them in the palms of his hands in fear, their entire lives depending on his whim. Actually, the Nazis would have understood that. They would have worked with him. But he gave them the excuse that he needed the men who had been arrested to work in the various offices and institutions. He even flew to Minsk to appeal to a higher authority to have the sentence changed, so that he would have these men to work for him.

Nobody in the town knew anything about this. All they knew was that husbands and loved ones were arrested. They would either be killed, or sent to far-off concentration camps. A great fear overcame them. Then, when days passed, and the prisoners had not been removed from the town, curiosity took over.

A Mrs. Broniszewska enters the picture. We're not sure if she had a husband or relative in the group of men who had been arrested. One day, she went to Mass at the Fara. The Nuns of the Order of the Holy Family of Nazareth were at that Mass as well. After the Mass, Mrs. Broniszewska followed the nuns to their home. There was conversation about the situation in the town since the Germans had taken over. There was also very casual discussion about the men who had been taken prisoner. All the Sisters expressed their concern over the safety of these men, most of whom had families. Sister Stella, the superior, made a comment, very off-handedly, very innocently, *"How I would like to give my life to save them."* The other sisters joined her, also very wistful, stating *"And I, too. And I, also. Why should only Sister Stella do this? We also..."* Nobody was really paying any attention to what they were saying, except Mrs. Broniszewska. But perhaps that was enough.

At this, Mrs. Broniszewska left them. The following Saturday, late in the afternoon, Sister Imelda and Sister Stella were in the church, preparing for the Forty Hours Devotion, which was to take place the following week, in honor of the Transfiguration of the Lord. A civilian Nazi came to the church. He said all the nuns, and Sister Stella, the superior, were to report to the commissar's office that evening at 7:30. A surge of fear went through the Mother Superior. After the man left, Sister Imelda asked her what she thought it meant.

Sister Stella shared her fears that the nuns were being taken away to work in Germany, at least the youngest and strongest. The others might be sent somewhere else, based on their strength and age. All of this was speculation, however. She couldn't think of any other reason why they

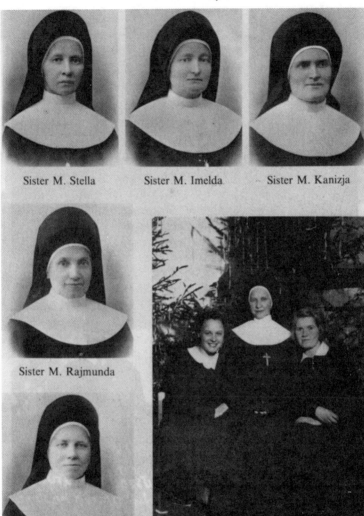

Sister M. Stella   Sister M. Imelda   Sister M. Kanizja

Sister M. Rajmunda

Sister M. Daniela

It's the Christmas season 1939. Sister Stella is photographed with two of her students.

Sister M. Heliodora

Sister M. Gwidona

Sister M. Boromea

Sister M. Malgorzata went out into the woods, where she could see digging had already gone on. She began to dig and discovered the sisters were buried there. She marked the spot with a cross and twigs and visited the place for two years until their bodies were exhumed.

Sister M. Kanuta

Sister M. Sergia

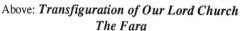

Above: **Transfiguration of Our Lord Church The Fara**

Sister M. Felicyta

would be summoned. She couldn't bring herself to consider that the little community might very possibly be broken up. But she obediently gathered up her flock of twelve together at the Church. Fr. Zienkiewicz, the local Priest, who would be himself a fugitive in a matter of days, held a prayer service and blessed all the Nuns. He encouraged them not to be late. It didn't take much to rile the Nazis up. He assured them of his prayers. Sister Malgorzata, an older Nun, was chosen to stay with him to pray, while the rest went down to the commisariat to get to the bottom of this.

The nuns who went to the Commissar's office that night of July 31, 1943 were as follows:

Sister M. Stella - Age 54 - Mother Superior of the group - a teacher by profession.

Sister M. Imelda - Age 50 - graduate of a Teachers' college

Sister M. Rajmunda - Age 50 - three weeks short of her 51st birthday

Sister M. Daniela - Age 48

Sister M. Kanuta - Age 47

Sister M. Gwidona - Age 43

Sister M. Sergia - Age 42 - 18 days short of her 43rd birthday

Sister M. Kanizja - Age 38 - six weeks short of her 39th birthday

Sister M. Felicyta - Age 37 - one month short of her 38th birthday

Sister M. Heliodora - Age 37

Sister M. Boromea - Age 27

They traveled the road from their convent into the town. They passed friendly places, like the Church of St. Michael where they always bowed their heads and made the Sign of the Cross. Other places, which had always been happy places, were now fearful places. The town square, where many executions had taken place; Smolenski Street, where the Nazi soldiers were billeted, and the office of the Commissar was located, these had become frightening places. Neighbors begged them not to venture down into that part of town, but they went cheerfully, singing as they walked along, these brave women of Poland. When they arrived at the Commisariat, they were swallowed up inside the bowels of the building. They were never seen again alive.

No one knows exactly why what happened, happened. A solid reason was never given. It was never even admitted that they were murdered, much less why. They were Nuns; what could they do? They had no weapons. How could they jeopardize the great Nazi war machine? How could Hitler, or any of his henchmen possibly have been afraid of these women in black, unless they were afraid of the Nuns' Boss, the Man on the Cross, whom they could not destroy?

After many years, people came forward and gave enough details to piece together the events of the evening of July 31, 1943, and the early morning hours of August 1, 1943. We figured out what happened, but initially, we could not figure out why. Finally, we were given the reason. The men who were arrested would have to be executed, unless someone could be gotten to take their place. The Sisters agreed to give up their lives for the lives of the men who were being held prisoner. The Commissar needed the men; the gestapo could not lose face by giving in to his demands. The killing of the Nuns would make a suitable compromise. They took the men's places, just like St. Maxmilian Kolbe took the place of a fellow prisoner, just two weeks short of two years before.

About an hour after the Nuns reported to the office of the Commissar, they were taken out of the building, and loaded onto the back of a truck. It headed in the direction of the woods of Nowogrodek. They went out a short distance, and then turned around. They came back to the office of the Commissar, and the Nuns got out again. They were taken to the basement of the building, where they stayed until the middle of the night, somewhere around 3 am. They were very cramped in the basement. There was not enough room for all of them to lay down on the floor, so they took turns.

They were brought out into the woods. They asked to remain in their religious dress, to die with dignity. They were allowed to say goodbye to each other. The Mother Superior, Sister Stella, blessed each of them. They were kneeling in the same position that they did in the Fara, the Church of the Transfiguration. Only now, rather than kneeling on the prie-dieux, in front of the Altar, where Jesus in the Blessed Sacrament was smiling on them, they were kneeling on the ground, before an open hole, a grave dug for eleven.

When Sister Stella finished blessing them, the first shot rang out. She was shot in the head. She fell into the grave. Then Sister Imelda was shot in the head. She fell into the grave. The other nine Sisters were shot through the chest; they all fell into the grave. There was a great hush in the woods after all the noise of the rifles, killing the Nuns. The sound of the silence was piercing. The sun began to rise about this time. The soldiers moved slowly and methodically. They filled the new grave with dirt; then got into the truck and headed back for their barracks, a good night's work done. They had fought a valiant battle against a vicious enemy and had been victorious. A really important question has to be, did they sleep that night, or any night in the near future? It is said, the next day a drunken soldier could not get the image out of his mind. He kept repeating, *"How they went. You should have seen how they went - those Sisters."*

The older Sister, Sister Malgorzata, waited at the convent the entire night, with the priest, Fr. Zienkiewicz. The eleven Nuns never came back. A few days later, the Priest was advised that the Nuns had been killed out in the woods. He told Sister Malgorzata. She went into hiding, and discarded her religious clothing, as did Fr. Zienkiewicz. Five weeks later, she went out into the woods, on the pretext of looking for mushrooms. She had a little shovel with her. When she got to the spot in the woods where she could see that digging had recently gone on, she began to dig with her little mushroom shovel. Not far down, she felt a leg. She tore the stocking from the body. It had identification. It was Sister Sergia. She knew her comrades were truly dead. She marked the spot with a cross made out of twigs, and left. She kept coming back from time to time to tend the grave of her companions.

The Priest, who had successfully escaped the town, came back again, after a year. The Nazis had already left. Now the Russian troops were in Nowogrodek. Sister Malgorzata told him about finding the grave. He went with her and a small group of people, and blessed the grave. It was determined that that area had become a common grave for other religious, especially two Priests who had disappeared early in the Nazi occupation, and had never been heard from again.

At war's end, the poor people of Nowogrodek were told that this town was no longer in Poland. The boundary lines had been moved quite a distance. So the land they had been born in, lived in, suffered in, was not theirs anymore. They had to be deported. Sister Malgorzata and the priest feared the grave of the eleven brave Sisters would be covered over by brush. That, coupled with the fact that they were all being deported, no one would know anything about the Nuns or their bravery, or their grave. It would all be forgotten.

On March 19, 1945, the common grave was exhumed. The bodies of the eleven nuns were brought into their beloved Fara, the Church of the Transfiguration. There was a solemn Mass of Burial, and the eleven were put in their usual position, at the left side of the Altar, near the Prie-

Dieux. Then, they were put into eleven individual little coffins, and buried on the church grounds.

The town will accept you and it will be proud that it possesses you...."

The prophecy of the bishop, when they first arrived in 1929, was fulfilled.

Honor was given them, by those who loved them. That's not the end of the story, however. Liberation came to Poland. In 1990, a request was made to open the cause for Beatification for Sister M. Stella, and her ten companions, brutally murdered by the Nazis on August 1, 1943. The reason given for their martyrdom was hatred for the Church.

The burial place of the Eleven Nuns remains from 1945 - 1989

The Cross marks the spot of the Martyrdom of the Eleven Nuns

The cause was opened. The bodies of the Nuns were brought in from their tombs outside the Church to a special chapel built inside the church. On September 27, 1991, they were brought into the Church, and placed in a common grave. After forty six years outside the Church, they were finally home. They will never be forgotten.

Fr. Jerzy Popieluszko
Martyr of Solidarity - 1984

Fr. Jerzy's last homily was *"Conquer Evil by doing good!"* This was the final straw for his adversaries. They had to kill him. That sounds a little ridiculous, but there's more truth to it than meets the eye. That statement, and all it implies, is very dangerous and threatening to all that Communism holds sacred. How does an opponent fight against that philosophy. It reminds us of something Jesus said:

"You have learned how it was said, 'an eye for an eye and a tooth for a tooth.' But I say this to you; offer the wicked man no resistance. On the contrary, if anyone hits you on the right cheek, offer him the other as well; if a man takes you to law and would have your tunic, let him have your cloak as well. And if anyone orders you to go one mile, go two miles with him. Give to anyone who asks, and if anyone wants to borrow, do not turn away.

"You have heard it said, 'You must love your neighbor and hate your enemy.' But I say this to you; love your enemies and pray for those who persecute you."[4]

Fr. Jerzy Popieluszko was a victim of an angry, dying dinosaur, lashing out at the very *One* who killed him. It would take almost six years after Jerzy's death for the dinosaur, Communism in Poland, to breathe its last, but the turning point began with the murder, the martyrdom of Fr. Jerzy Popieluszko.

Jerzy was born on the Feast of the Triumph of the Cross, September 14, 1947. He would prove to be a super-strong catalyst in bringing about the Triumph of the Cross in his life, and in the lives of the people of Poland. He was born in the northeastern part of the country. He had the influence of two important role models, which tyrannical governments have been trying to destroy from the beginning of civilization, his *grandmother*, and a *good Priest*. In this instance, the Priest was St. Maxmilian Kolbe.

You see how the Lord works. The martyrdom of Maxmilian Kolbe in Auschwitz has been considered by many, the waste of a brilliant mind. And while the Lord doesn't cause these things to happen, the Lord has been able to use the murder of Kolbe by the Nazis to work in His favor in many ways. The fact that he was a role model for Jerzy Popieluszko and many other young men was only one facet of how our Saint Maxmilian has worked diligently for the Lord as a result of his Martyrdom.

As for the grandmother, they have always been God's way of teaching the young about their Faith. They have been soldiers of the Lord, and bad enemies of the evil one. In Communist China, one of the first things that is done to a child is to remove him from any contact with his grandparents. As a boy, Jerzy found many issues of the

---

[4]Matthew 5:38-45

Franciscan magazine, "The Immaculata" at his grandmother's home.

As much as Jerzy felt drawn to the Franciscan community at Niepokolanow,[5] he entered the Diocesan Seminary in Warsaw in 1965. A standard part of the Communist propaganda where seminarians were concerned, was to draft them into military service at the beginning of their seminary training. For Jerzy, this took place in his second year of training for Theology and Philosophy at the seminary. They jammed their minds with anti-clerical teachings, and anti-religious propaganda. They subjected them to the worst hardcore elements the military had.

Jerzy fought the program with all he was worth. He openly professed his Faith, and made a point of observing all religious observances, even though he paid a heavy price of persecution from his communist superiors. Possibly because of ill-treatment in the service, or because of living conditions in Poland in general, he came out of the army with heart problems, thyroid and other infirmities. But that didn't hold him back. He was on fire for his Church. He wanted more than anything to be a Priest, and serve Our Lord Jesus through his brothers and sisters.

He was not bold or an extrovert. He was really rather quiet, and didn't push his way into anything. He was a great lover of people. Everyone who knew him in the Seminary, his instructors, fellow seminarians, the former rector, who had since become Bishop, Wladyslaw Miziolek, talked about his sensitivity, his quiet and peaceful approach to problem solving, and his relations with his colleagues as well as his superiors. He took St. Maxmilian Kolbe as his role model, and then went on to become a role model himself.

He was ordained on May 28, 1972. He threw himself into his priestly duties. This was why he was born; this is

---

[5]City of the Immaculata

what he lived for. He worked in various parishes, as well as taking on many other activities, such as the National Consultation Group for Health Services in the diocese of Warsaw. Among other things, this entailed recruiting, training and scheduling medical students to handle the thousands of people who came to Warsaw during Pope John Paul II's visits in 1979 and 1983. It was a mammoth undertaking, which would give ulcers and premature gray hair to anyone else. But to Fr. Jerzy, it was exactly what he wanted. Although he was very quiet and reserved, he enjoyed being with people, ministering to people, defending the rights of people.

He was transferred to the parish of St. Stanislaus Kostka in Warsaw in May of 1980. But the Lord was just gearing him for the major job He had for him. In August, 1980, Solidarity, the workers' movement, was born in Poland. All over the country, there were mass anti-government demonstrations.

We have to take a moment to clarify the semantics of *"mass demonstrations"*. Word went out all over the world that these Polish anti-government super-activist demonstrations were going on. What was really happening was that thousands of workers at the factories went on strike and prayed the Rosary, or attended Mass. They had giant prayer meetings. The communist propaganda machines translated that into massive anti-government rallies. They sounded just like the American media who twist accounts of people praying the Rosary, outside abortion clinics, into mass demonstrations of raving activists, trying to block the way for innocent pregnant little girls from getting abortions.

It was determined that a priest was needed to celebrate Mass for the Solidarity, and be their spiritual director. No one ever thought this would be a dangerous job for Jerzy. He would celebrate Mass, give a homily, and spiritual advice. They neglected to consider one important thing, the man to whom they gave the job. Jerzy went out to the factory where a strike was being held in Warsaw. A large Cross was erected. Fr. Jerzy celebrated Mass. During his homily, he inspired the workers, aroused them to greater determination. By the end of the Mass, he was not just the Priest celebrating Mass for them; he was Fr. Jerzy Popieluszko, their supporter and Spiritual Director.

Fr. Jerzy stayed with them for the next fifteen months during that strike. During the most difficult times, when Lech Walesa and the leaders of Solidarity were sent to internment camps, as well as the factory workers in Warsaw, Fr. Jerzy worked untiringly for the union during the trials. He did anything and everything he could. He got legal help for them, baby sitters, food, clothing. *He became the pastor for nine million workers!* He also became a thorn in the side of the government. The persecution began, hot and heavy. He was constantly being harassed by the government.

The more they came after Jerzy, the bolder his homilies became. He was supported by the Cardinal Primate, Cardinal Josef Glemp. But his fellow priests worried about having him celebrate Mass in their churches. They were afraid of his following. Every time he would celebrate a Solidarity Mass, thousands would attend. His homilies were incendiary. The priests in the churches where the Masses were celebrated often worried about repercussions from the government. They tried not to let him give homilies wherever possible. But the people loved Fr. Jerzy. He was a folk hero.

Solidarity was declared illegal, and outlawed. Fr. Jerzy retaliated. In a homily in August, 1982, he criticized the government, and at the same time, gave hope and courage to the people. *"On a December night last year, in a violent and painful manner, the agreements from Gdansk[6] and Silesia were*

---

[6]Gdansk, the shipyards, where Solidarity started

broken. It was a blow and a wound that is still bleeding. It is not mortal, because you cannot hit mortally something immortal. Hope cannot die. Solidarity was and is the hope of millions of Poles, and that hope is made stronger because it is connected with God in prayer."

It was on December 13, 1981 that the communists declared Martial Law in Poland, and outlawed Solidarity. They began in earnest to destroy Solidarity and all its proponents. Fr. Jerzy became a prime target. They began by attacking him with false accusations of illegal political activity. The communist newspaper accused him of sedition, of trying to overthrow the government. They took offense because he accused them of *hypocrisy, anti-democratic legislation, anti-human legislation, depriving the people of the basic human freedoms.*

Fr. Jerzy had to become a target of the Department IV, the communist equivalent to the Gestapo or KGB. They turned their people on Fr. Jerzy. Threats of all kinds were leveled against him. Harassment from every level of the government was thrown at him. He was as much as told he would be murdered.

The month prior to his martyrdom, Fr. Jerzy was warned that he had to stop bringing groups to Czestochowa, the major Marian shrine of Poland. Our Lady of Czestochowa is to the Polish people, much like what Our Lady of Guadalupe is to the people of Mexico. She has been the major force which has given them hope over the centuries that they would overcome the tyranny and persecution to which they had always been subjected. No matter what happened, whether it be the Nazis of World War II, or the Communists after the war, they knew they could count on Our Lady to make it right. However, this was not in keeping with the Communist policy of complete despair, lack of hope of any kind, which they had tried to instill in the people these last forty years.

Fr. Jerzy shared with a fellow priest that his life was threatened, and he didn't know how long he would live. However, rather than backing off from his work with Solidarity, he accelerated. He couldn't allow himself to be frightened into stopping what he believed the Lord was calling him to do.

And so we come to that fateful evening of October 19, 1984, the last time that Jerzy Popieluszko was seen alive. He went to the Church of the Holy Polish Martyr-Brothers in Bydgoszcz, quite a distance from his parish in Warsaw, almost 200 miles away. He began his Homily by quoting Pope John Paul II's words at the shrine of Our Lady of Czestochowa on June 23, 1982: *"I thank you Mother, for all those who remained faithful to their conscience and who, fighting with their weakness, gave strength to others. I thank you, Mother, for all those who do not yield to evil but conquer evil with good."*

He continued on in this vein for his entire talk. He said things like:

"Only he can conquer evil who is himself rich in goodwill."

"...We have to maintain our human dignity to be able to increase the amount of good and conquer all that is evil and to be guided in our lives by justice."

"To conquer evil with good means to be faithful to the truth."

"To conquer evil with good, we ought to have the virtue of courage."

"To conquer evil with good, we are not allowed to use violence."

We're not sure if it was because of this homily that he was marked for assassination, or if the decision to kill him had been made prior to this time. It is so impossible for our logical minds to accept how such a homily could be threatening to anyone, except possibly those who have embraced evil, and joined the ranks of Satan. Whatever the case, he was slated for execution, and this was the night it was to happen.

It is believed that his killers were in the congregation that night. They followed him and his driver, Waldemar Chrostowski, as they began their trip back to Warsaw. They kept their distance for about an hour. Then, as Fr. Jerzy and his driver approached an isolated stretch of road, they overtook them, and stopped them. They wore police uniforms, and stopped the car under the pretense of checking out the car. They took the driver out of the car, handcuffed and gagged him, and put him into the murderers' car.

Then they made Fr. Jerzy get out of the car. They immediately began beating him. They beat him unconscious, and threw him into the trunk of their car. They drove at breakneck speed. The driver took a chance at a turn in the road to jump out of the car. He rolled down a hill, and was saved. The killers continued driving to a predetermined destination. At given times, Fr. Jerzy regained consciousness, and tried to get out of the trunk of the car. He kicked and yelled. They stopped the car, beat him some more, gagged him, and tied his neck to the back of his feet, so that as he moved, he choked himself. They continued to torture him until they came to a bridge of the River Vistula, about halfway to Warsaw. They tied huge stones to the body of Fr. Jerzy, around his neck, around both feet, and around his hands. They threw him off the bridge into the river.

For the people who loved Fr. Jerzy, they feared and prayed for 11 days. They began all-night vigils around his church, St. Stanislaus Kostka in Warsaw. They posted signs, begging for the release of Fr. Jerzy. At first, they were sure Fr. Jerzy was being harassed and possibly tortured by the government. It wasn't until after the first week that they began to fear for his life. On October 30, 1984, their worst fears were confirmed. Fr. Jerzy's body was found in the

Vistula river. The people staged a massive demonstration of sorrow and anger against those who had killed him.

Three days later, on November 3, 1984, an impressive funeral was given to this lover of the Polish people, this lover of justice. The Cardinal Primate, Josef Cardinal Glemp, plus his Bishops, and over a thousand priests gave a lasting tribute to their brother and supporter. There were people all over, outside the church, in the courtyard, in the streets leading up to the church, as far as the eye could see. Hundreds of thousands of Polish brothers showed up. They would not let this travesty, this brutal, senseless killing of their priest, go unnoticed.

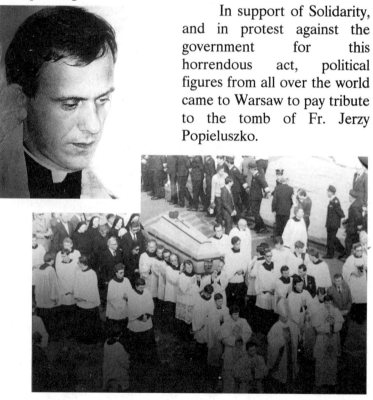

In support of Solidarity, and in protest against the government for this horrendous act, political figures from all over the world came to Warsaw to pay tribute to the tomb of Fr. Jerzy Popieluszko.

His Holiness and Brother Priest, Pope John Paul II, Mother Teresa of Calcutta, Vice President Bush of the United States, Vaclav Havel, President of Czechoslovakia, Margaret Thatcher from England, Foreign Minister Andreotti of Italy, Lech Walesa, future president of Poland and brother in Solidarity, and many many more.

Lech Walesa was very close to Fr. Jerzy Popieluszko. He gave the eulogy at Fr. Jerzy's funeral. He said, *"We will always remember Fr. Jerzy, his teachings and his service. He was a good man, a courageous man, spiritual pastor and champion of the national cause. In his life, he gave testimony to the unity of the Church and the Nation.....Poland ....will not perish and she has not perished....Solidarity is alive because you gave your life for it."*

We can't say that the death of Communism in Poland was sealed with the martyrdom of Fr. Jerzy Popieluszko, but it surely began. There was such a fear on the part of the government, of such heroes as Karol Wojtlya (Pope John Paul II), Lech Walesa and Fr. Jerzy Popieluszko, they would stop at nothing to destroy them. But they came to know that there were too many for them to kill. The battle for liberation was gaining momentum more and more until the country was finally liberated without a drop of bloodshed.

†

We believe our dear Pope, John Paul II, stated all that could be said about the tenacity and courage of the people of Poland in a speech to Lech Walesa on his official visit to the Vatican on February 5, 1991 as President of the Republic of Poland. He remarked, *"We remember the sacrifice and tears of the Polish people, men and women, who were fighting for a free Poland: workers, educated people, priests, monks and nuns, farmers - all of them. Their symbol remains forever Solidarity, Fr. Jerzy and the Crosses of Gdansk, and also you, Mr. President."*

In our hearts and minds, we can't help seeing little
school children of Poland, proud and strong, loving. We are
given such hope for our Church and our world when we look
at the fully habited Nuns of all ages, convents full, singing
and working for Our Lord Jesus. We remember the Priests,
reverent, filled with the Holy Spirit and the love of their
brothers and sisters. We look back on a Sunday morning
when our van pulled up to a church in Kalvarya, while Mass
was going on. There were people outside the Church, in the
parking lot. When the Consecration was prayed over the
loudspeakers, they all went down on their knees in honor of
Our Lord Jesus, Who was coming on the Altar.

The people of Poland have paid an awfully high price to
be able to do the things that you and I not only take for
granted, but very often can't be bothered with. I can't help
comparing these fervent brothers and sisters, thankful for
the gift of being *permitted* to kneel during the Mass, with
those of us in the world who are fighting over whether we
are *required* to kneel. How ironic it is. We pray Lord, that
we accept the example from our brothers and sisters, the
Martyrs of Poland.

Pope John Paul II at Fr. Jerzy's grave, June 14, 1987

Martyrs of Auschwitz

"Jesus remember me when You come into Your Kingdom." We were staying in the *Convent of the Sisters of the Holy Family of Nazareth*, in Krakow, Poland. The good sisters wanted the little pre-school children to sing and perform skits for us.They were so proud of their little charges.

Edith Stein (Rt) and sister Erna

The children went from love songs to Jesus and Mary in Polish, to the only song they knew in English: *"Jesus remember me when You come into Your Kingdom."* Little did the sisters know why we were crying. As we scanned their precious innocent faces, all we could see were the precious innocent faces of children who, fifty years before, had gone to their horrible deaths in the Nazi death camps of Adolf Hitler. For you see, just two days before, we had walked the *Way of the Cross through Auschwitz.*

Our guide at the Concentration Camp said that no one leaves Auschwitz unchanged. *She warned us that we would never forget Auschwitz!* And she was right! For many years, we had avoided the ugly graphic truth of man's inhumanity to his fellow man. In the Holy Land, we avoided the *Monument to the Holocaust.* Whenever we visited Germany, we said our Rosary and the prayers for the dead as we passed quickly by *Dachau.* But stop and go inside? No way! I remember one time, when our daughter wanted to go inside Dachau, I said *"I'm so sorry, but I can't!"*

When we wrote of Saint Maxmilian Kolbe, I found myself very emotionally connected with him, a Pole (and I am not Polish), a Franciscan (and I am not a Franciscan), a Priest and a Martyr. But as I wrote on the life of this

Above: *Left building - Experiments on women conducted there*
Middle wall - The wall where they shot the prisoners
Right building - Building where St. Maxmilian Kolbe died

Above: *The Crematorium at the Auschwitz deathcamp*

phenomenal human being who would have been declared a Saint, even if he had not chosen to give his life for another, I found myself weeping uncontrollably, as his story went from my fingers to the word processor to the pages of our book: *"Saint and Other Powerful Men in the Church."* I knew then that we had to go to Poland! I wanted to discover our connection with Maxmilian Kolbe and the people of Poland, and especially His Holiness Pope John Paul II.

But still, I was not looking forward to Auschwitz. How would I be able to go to Cell Block 11, and stand in the room and look upon the spot where Maxmilian Kolbe was injected with a lethal dose of poisonous acid? How could I stand where he had stood with the other prisoners outside of Cell Block 17 in the scorching heat for twenty four hours? I didn't want to go! Oh my God, did the Jews, and the Poles two years before them, want to go?

Auschwitz - "Work Makes us Free!"

Entrance to Auschwitz death camp with sign over the gate that reads, "Work Makes us Free"

That lying, blasphemous sign stares you in the face, as you approach the entrance to Auschwitz. As you walk through the gate, the silent screams of those who went before you greet you, and you are in the midst of horror. Gray somber buildings flank each side of the dirt road on which unknowing victims walked to their death. They stand as mournful remembrances of the torture chambers that had been within. When the former army barracks could no longer contain all the poor people arriving in cattle cars (trains), the Nazis used the prisoners to build second floors on the buildings. And when they couldn't kill the prisoners fast enough, they had them build more buildings so that they would be able to handle the huge extermination program they had undertaken. It is inconceivable that anyone would be so inhumane as to use prisoners to build the means that would be used for *their* torture and death, and that of their families and friends. But these soldiers, who had once worshiped God, had managed to block Him out of their lives; and when mankind turns his back on God, he is capable of anything.

Even the sky was gray! The rocks seemed to scream out accusingly: *"Where were you when Christ died once more on the Cross?"* We want to tell you briefly of a Nun whose only sin was that she was born Jewish.

Blessed Edith Stein

Saint, Carmelite Sister,
Convert from Judaism,
Author, Philosopher,
Scholar, Humanitarian.

Edith Stein was born in Wroclaw, Poland (formerly known as Breslau, Germany) on October 12, 1891. Edith Stein's parents were Jewish. They had come to Wroclaw, searching for a better life for themselves and their children. The year that she was born,

Edith's birthday fell on the holiest day of the Jewish calendar, The Jewish Day of Atonement - *"Yom Kippur"*.[1] As this is of such importance to their Hebrew Faith, Edith's mother took it as a sign, her child was highly favored with Yahweh. This was one of the reasons she so treasured Edith. Another reason was the special part she played, the day her husband left for work, for the last time. The day was unusually hot. Edith (twenty- one months old), nestled in her mother's arms, called out to her father. He turned around and waved to them. That was the last memory she had of her husband. They were never to see him alive again, as he died of a sunstroke that day.

Her mother became the head of the family, working and yet very much the mother in control of the home and her responsibilities as a parent. She was a strong woman, a religious woman, going to Synagogue with the older children on the Jewish High Holy Days. She was not Orthodox, however. She kept her store open on Saturday which was the Sabbath, and work was not permitted according to Jewish law. The family also prayed in German, not in Hebrew. So, the sad truth was with so many that the Nazis killed, the German Jews considered themselves *Germans*! They loved Germany. They loved their homeland! It is as if someone in our government said that you are not an American because you are Catholic. They were Jews by religion, but they considered themselves loyal citizens of Germany.

Edith Stein was always a brilliant student. When she turned seventeen, she entered a Girl's High School in Breslau. At the same time, in another part of Germany, another teenager was failing an entrance exam to the Academy of Arts and already blaming it all on the Jews.

---

[1]Penny was born September 23rd. That year, *"Yom Kippur"* fell on her birthday.

Adolph Hitler was reading anti-Semitic literature and planning his revenge on those who dared to pass grades, who had stores and professions. It wasn't important to him that these people had saved and scrimped to give their children educations, and their children had worked equally industriously to attain high grades in school and success in life. They had something he wanted and he hated them for it, and he plotted to take everything away from them, initially their possessions and then ultimately their lives. Two teenagers - one a Saint and the other damned to Hell for all eternity.

Edith Stein always had a very strong bond with her family. They cared for one another. She had all the joy of life with brothers and sisters and loads of aunts, uncles and cousins. They would be an integral part of her formation into a warm, compassionate adult. The other teenager, the young Hitler, an orphan without a family was already an angry dissident. Feeling no commitment to anyone but self, he was hiding in Vienna, trying to avoid being drafted into the Austrian Army.

Edith Stein entered the University of Breslau in 1911. She registered in the Department of Psychology and for two years she was unable to pray. She called this her period of *atheism*. First of all, Psychology, at that time, did not acknowledge man had a soul. Did she get caught up in that lunacy? [I remember, a couple of weeks after our son entered college, he came home and said there was no God!] Edith had always been an *individual*, strong willed, with her own mind. The Lord will use this later on when she will need these qualities to bring about His Will.

She loved to learn, and there was excitement in this new challenge. What had happened to her was what we have seen happen to other young people entering universities. Suddenly the enemy attacks with *pride*; we forget *Who* gave us the intellect we have, and Who it is Who gives us the desire to do something with that intellect. We turn to man, whether a professor we admire or fellow students, or give credit to ourselves. We no longer look up, but down, and like Peter, if we do not turn to Him Who is the Giver of all things good, we find ourselves drowning.

But Edith looked for answers in Psychology. When she found it was unable to provide itself with a solid intellectual grounding, she turned to Philosophy in her pursuit of truth. We know God never gives up on us. Even as we are forgetting Him, turning away from Him, rejecting Him, He is placing people in our path who will lead us back to Him. Edith Stein turned away from her God; she believed as long as she and her friends stuck together, they could overcome the evils she saw taking over the world. But God was going to have none of that. He had plans for her.

God placed her among Jewish intellectuals who had become Christians. Although she considered herself an atheist, she found herself seeking truth, and she later wrote that anyone seeking truth is in reality longing to find God, whether he knows it or not. God would not have an easy time with her. Being brilliant, she had little tolerance for those who thought differently than she. The intellectuals in the University she attended, were studying supernatural truths which they considered as real as other phenomena. She began to study under the renowned philosopher Husserl who taught her that *"knowledge, as the name implies, depends on knowing. It is in knowing that we possess the truth."* Although she never spoke of converting, she was on her way to Christ, in seeking the truth.

We cannot help reflect on the paths the two were taking, the Martyr and the Murderer. As Edith Stein was reaching out, trying to discover the *truth*, Hitler was captured, arrested and brought to the Austrian Consulate. He joined the army. He later said that he learned more in the Army about the problems of life than he could have ever hoped to learn in thirty years in a university. Edith served as a Red Cross nurse, compassionately, lovingly administering to soldiers of the Austrian Army infected with spotted fever, dysentery and cholera.

One of Edith's friends, Adolf Reinach, joined the Army. This friend died at the front. But before he did, he converted to Christ at the front. When asked what was one of the motivating forces that led her to Christ, she answered, it was the faith, Adolf's wife had in the power of the mystery of the Cross. When Edith reached out to his wife at the funeral, instead of a grieving widow, she found a woman filled with peace. Adolf's wife was able *"to console Edith, rather than be consoled by Edith because of her faith in a loving God."*[2] Although she had found the Crucified Lord, Whom she would follow to *her* cross, in the witnessing of this Christian, it would be five years before she would convert.

Edith was always involved with humanity, her fellow human beings. In High School, she campaigned as a suffragette. In 1918, she supported the German Democratic Party. She became very interested in the political climate of Germany.

Meanwhile, Hitler in 1919 was writing, in his first manifesto: Because of the *crimes* the Jews had committed, which he listed, they were to be *removed from their midst.* [Later, in 1942, Rudolf Hoss[3] stated in his diary: *"The Jews are the sworn enemies of the German people and must be eradicated. Every Jew that we can lay our hands on is to be destroyed now during the war, without exception. If we cannot obliterate the biological basis of Jewry, the Jews will one day destroy the German people."*[4] And then on January 20, 1942, in Berlin there was a conference attended by high ranking officials of the Third Reich. Eichmann and Heydrich were

---

[2]The Story of Edith Stein by Freda Mary Oben, PhD
[3]Commandant of Auschwitz
[4]Auschwitz - Voices from the Ground

present when they decided that 11,000,000 Jews were to be exterminated.]

Most of her friends had converted to the Lutheran Faith, and it is believed what held her up from converting was, she really did not know which Church she should join. When she read St. Teresa of Avila's autobiography, she said that she knew this was the *truth*, that the Catholic Church contained *the Truth*, our Lord Jesus Christ, Himself. She had just *happened* on this book. But she found she could not put it down, reading through the night to the next morning. Without sleep, but full of excitement and resolve, she immediately bought a Catholic Catechism and a Missal. As St. Teresa of Avila had been influenced by St. Augustine, we see the never-dying words of truth, only now through St. Teresa, influencing another future Saint.

Edith walked the difficult path between her loyalty to her mother and Judaism, and her growing awareness of this God Who was growing inside her. To her family, Catholicism was a cult steeped in superstition. They pictured Edith kissing Priests' shoes and *"going around on her knees"*. Her mother believed differently. Although she did not want Edith to become a Catholic, she saw that God was placing His Hand on her daughter and she dare not interfere.

January 1,[5] 1922, Edith Stein was baptized.

"On the wall, by the font, there is a plaque dedicated to her. It depicts the scene from 1 Kings 19:17. A loaf of bread and jug of water have been placed at the feet of the sleeping Elijah by the Angel who bids him: 'Get up and eat or the journey will be too long for you.'" It goes on to suggest *"that it is the heavenly Bread awaiting Edith at the baptismal font, the*

---

[5]January 1st is the Feast of the Solemnity of Mary. So, we can see the Mother of Jesus and her hand in bringing this other daughter of Abraham to her Son Jesus. Edith will always have a relationship with Mary. January 1st is also the date that Bob and Penny *came back to Jesus* and the Church.

Eucharist, which alone enabled her to ascend the Mount Horeb of her life through the gas chamber, where she died for her people and her faith."[6]

Her life changed after her baptism. This well-known intellectual left the university and taught in a remote Dominican school for the next eight years. Edith would have become a Religious immediately after she was admitted into the Church, but her spiritual director would not permit this, as he judged she could do so much more out in the world through her role as a prominent lay woman. Besides, he argued this would be too much for her mother to accept, on top of her converting to Christianity. Edith began to lead the life of a Religious, reading the Office daily, and the Psalms. She not only poured through Holy Scripture, relating with it, she faithfully digested her Breviary. She was passionately in love with the entire liturgy of the Church.

She lost none of her sense of humor, though, or her concern for others. All the pride, she had had, turned into humility. All her impatience with others, turned into patience and gentleness. The girl who had always been good was now *holy*.

Jacques Maritain wrote: *"How can one describe the purity, the light which shone from Edith Stein at the time of her conversion, the total generosity which one felt in her which was to bear fruit in Martyrdom?"*[7]

Now, tracking Hitler, we find he is made leader of the National German Workers' Party. After he unsuccessfully tried to overthrow the government, he was imprisoned; there he wrote *Mein Kampf*. How would he be able to stir up hate and division? *Lay blame.* Tell the German people that the Jews were *not* created by God. [Don't we excuse the killing of unborn children saying they are fetuses, not human

---

[6]The Story of Edith Stein by Freda Mary Oben, PhD
[7]The Story of Edith Stein by Freda Mary Oben, PhD

beings?] Hitler proclaimed that only the *Aryan* was formed in the true image of God, and the Jew was molded in the image of the *other*, the direct opposite of God. Where did he get the authority to make such a statement? What did he base this on? On what foundation did this demented structure stand? How did he dare say that *any* of God's children were not created by Him? How anyone, with an ounce of brains, and a soul, could accept this ludicrous statement as anything but the ravings of a madman, I don't know. But for whatever reason, some did, and the end began.

Edith pursued knowledge of her Catholic Faith, recognizing that her intellect was not an enemy to believing in Christ, but a gift from the Father to enable her to help others to understand Him. She turned to St. Thomas Aquinas, and his text "*De Veritate*" (On Truth) translating it into German.[8] She soon became sought after as a lecturer.

January 30, 1933, Adolf Hitler became Reich Chancellor of Germany. She was asked to step down from her position at the University. She was an embarrassment to them because she was *Jewish*. She became aware of the impending persecution of her people and herself, as well. Two months later, there was an anti-Jewish boycott instituted, covering all of Germany. Seeing the threat to both Christians and Jews, she pleaded for a private audience with Pope Pius XI. When that failed she wrote to him, warning him that the fate of the Jews would also be suffered by Catholics, as well. She prophesied this as early as 1933. Was the Pope hoping that Hitler would not succeed? Did he think that Christians could not follow anyone as demonic as he? No one knows. It is believed he never received her letter.

---

[8]the first translation from Latin to German

Edith Stein could have fled from Germany, as many German Jews had, seeing the handwriting on the wall. In fact, prior to this, she had been considering teaching in London. There was also a teaching position offered to her in South America where her brother Arno was living. She could have been with him. Instead, she chose to go to the Cross for her people. She wrote in her essay: "*The Road to Carmel*" that she had spoken to *her Savior* and told Him that she recognized it was *His* Cross that the Jewish people were being made to carry. She wrote that those who understood must accept it with all their heart, for those who did not understand.

After thirteen hours spent in prayer in Church, Edith Stein made her decision to enter the Carmel. She chose the Carmelite Order because she believed, with them, that she was called to share joyfully and freely in Christ's Redemptive suffering. She offered up her prayer and her life for not only the persecuted (the Jews) but the persecutors (the Nazis). She felt that if she did not pray and offer her life for the immortal souls of the Nazis, and for the remission of their sins, as the Savior had done for all mankind, who would? She was living out St. John of the Cross' words that: "*God sustains and is present substantially in every soul, even that of the worst sinner.*" She wrote to friends telling them not to be afraid for her, as "*God works out all things for good.*"

Not only was Edith to look toward the Cross for her people, but she was to walk the *painful* Way of the Cross when her family objected so vehemently to her becoming a Nun. Her mother was 84 years old. She grieved that she would never see her again, as Edith would be fully cloistered. Edith was questioned by her niece: *Why did she have to become a Nun? Was she denying her people?* Edith gently explained to her little niece, she was not entering to escape persecution as a Jewess. Because although she was a Nun, she would always be part of the Jewish people.

On the Feast Day of St. Teresa of Avila, October 14, 1933, Blessed Edith Stein entered the Carmel in Cologne. We can try to experience the joy she felt at being, at last, able to enter the Carmel and live the life of a contemplative, a way of life she so ardently desired. But as all of us know, who have had to leave precious loved ones to serve the Lord, it is bitter herbs mixed with sweet honey. Edith Stein, did you feel the pain that your mentor St. Teresa, felt when you said goodbye to *your* beloved family?

"while leaving my father's house, I knew I would not, even at the very moment and agony of my death, feel the anguish of separation more painfully than at that moment and time."[9]

Blessed Edith Stein took the Religious name "*Teresa Benedicta a Cruce*", Teresa Blessed by the Cross. She shared with her Spiritual Director that she chose the name because it represented the one who had led her into the Church and the Carmel, St. Teresa, and the role that she (Edith Stein) chose: to her Lord through the Cross.

All her life, Edith Stein was an asset to everyone who knew her or came in contact with her. In community, she became a source of joy to the other Nuns who were not only aware of her humility, but of her warmth and her great sense of humor. Like with all the greats (for example St. Anthony), she tried to hide her great intellect, never flaunting it, never talking down to the other novices.

She never forgot her Jewish roots. She had begun writing "*Life in a Jewish Family*" while she was still at home, putting down on paper the emotional pain of separation from her loved ones, both spiritual and physical. She also wanted to write this as a tribute to her mother, giving her full credit for all she had ever been, was or would be. "*The commandment Honor your father and mother*" was one that

---

[9]from the chapter on Teresa of Avila in Bob and Penny's book: "*Saints and Other Powerful Women in the Church*"

Edith Stein took very seriously. She also wanted to share with the youth, who had been deluded by Hitler and his henchman, the true makeup of the Jewish people, not the devious tainted picture that had been painted, so that they could be manipulated into hating and harming the Jews.

Again, we come to the two who started about the same time: Martyr and murderer. Hitler wrote "*Mein Kampf*" and it has become a book of infamy. Edith Stein wrote a translated Psalm 61 into German and today it is included in the official prayer book used at all Daily Masses in Germany: Hymn #302.[10]

Edith Stein took her first vows in 1935. When asked how she felt, she replied "*Like the Bride of the Lamb*". That year, the Nurenberg Statues imposed grim decrees: Jews were no longer considered citizens and lost all legal rights; Marriage to Jews by Germans was prohibited, punishable by law. With Spring of 1936, there were new beginnings, only they were not the beautiful blooms that please the Lord but the strangling weeds of hate and division. The Nazis marched into the Rhineland, and with them Hell!

1936 was to be a year of pain and joy. When her mother died of cancer, and Edith could not be with her, she thought surely she too would die. Not even the joy of celebrating the Feast Day of the *Exaltation of the Cross* and her renewing her vows, could stop the ache in her heart. She later said that, as she was standing in her choir stall awaiting the renewal of her vows, she felt the presence of her mother beside her. Edith Stein and her mother had such a close relationship, it transcended time and space. [We believe that love never dies. That great love, we have known on earth, will be poured down on us from our loved ones until we are reunited with them in Heaven. I feel the presence of my son as closely as when he was on earth.]

---

[10]The Story of Edith Stein by Freda Mary Oben, PhD

Her sister Rosa, who had been a believer for many years, was baptized that Christmas. And so, the Way of the Cross, once again led to Resurrection, as Edith witnessed new life for her sister. Rosa was being born anew, as they were celebrating the coming, the birth of the Messiah, the King of the Universe into the world.

Edith could see that the pieces were coming together; the Cross, the inevitable Cross! Edith completed her great philosophical work "*Finite and Eternal Being*", but it could not be published under her name, because she was Jewish. When they suggested bringing it out under the name of a Nazi sympathizer, she refused. This great book, like all great books could not be buried; in 1950 it was finally published and won world-wide acclaim.

Like lava from an erupting volcano, Hitler and his forces of destruction spread to Austria in March of 1938 and on to the Sudetenland in September of that same year. As he was fulfilling his vow to the enemy of God, Edith Stein was taking her final vows. In April of 1938, when she stood before the altar of God and her whole community, she abandoned herself totally to our Lord through His Mother.

Often she was spotted praying before the picture of *Our Lady of Sorrows*. It was not that she was praying for suffering. We believe that she knew that one day she was to walk that Way of the Cross with Mother Mary and her Son. She believed that only by standing with Mother Mary at the foot of the Cross, your eyes on the Crucified, can you win souls for Jesus. She wrote:

"Today I stood with you beneath the Cross,
And felt more clearly than I ever did
That you became our Mother only there.
Even an earthly mother faithfully
Seeks to fulfill the last will of her son.
But you became the handmaid of the Lord;
The life and being of the God made Man

Was perfectly inscribed in your own life.
So you could take your own into your heart,
And with the lifeblood of your bitter pains
You purchased life anew for every soul.
You know us all, our wounds, our imperfections;
But you know also the celestial radiance
Which your Son's love would shed on us in Heaven.
Thus carefully you guide our faltering footsteps,
No price too high for you to lead us to our goal.

"But those whom you have chosen for companions
To stand with round the eternal throne,
They here must stand with you beneath the Cross,
And with the lifeblood of their bitter pains
Must purchase heavenly glory for those souls
Whom God's own Son entrusted to their care."[11]

Ten days before the "*Kristallnacht*", Edith Stein wrote that like Queen Esther, she was ready to give her life for her people. It was the beginning of the end; synagogues were torched, the Jews' homes and businesses demolished. They didn't know what to do! It was mass havoc and desolation. The parents tried to keep their fear from their children. They were like people sleep-walking. They never, for one moment, thought this could happen!

But they had hope! As they were rounded up and led to the trains, they thought they were going to another area to start life anew. They even had to buy their own train tickets! Many purchased from the Gestapo, homes in the new village where they were relocating. They even had deeds to their new homes with them, and some had legal papers showing ownership of businesses they had purchased. They tried to bring all their treasures. They carried all they could, as they were being jammed into cattle cars. They

---

[11]The Story of Edith Stein by Freda Mary Oben, PhD

were heartbroken leaving the village of their birth and their families before them, parting from friends and often family, but it was not new with the Jewish people and they would survive.

Thirty to forty thousand Jews were sent to concentration camps on that infamous day when God held His Face in His Hands and cried. Wasn't His Son's sacrifice enough? How could His children do this to His other children? The madman Hitler had told the German people that he was just relocating the Jews to another place. He never mentioned killing them; that's why many Germans had a problem believing this outrageous act against God ever happened. But Hitler and his demonic master-minds had already set up these camps as far back as 1933.[12]

Edith feared for the lives of the Nuns at the Carmel where she was, and the Nuns feared for her life, so on December, 1933 she left for the Carmel in Echt, Holland. There, she spent her time bringing joy as well as spiritual direction to the novices she was teaching. In those days Nuns who did manual tasks such as gardening, cooking and laundering were not allowed to use the library. As she was in charge of professions, she pleaded, all the Nuns and novices and postulants be allowed to read books, even those engaged in physical labor. Permission was denied. But it gives us a glimpse into the never-ending care this Jewish convert had for others. Like the other Jewish Convert - Mother Mary whom she admired so, she was involved with all God's children.

Although she never showed it outwardly, always cheerful, her writings and poetry show the agonizing she did over the way the world and Hitler were heading. She was not far from wrong! On January the 30th, 1939, Hitler

---

[12]Catholics, Priests and Nuns, citizens of countries they had invaded were imprisoned and executed in Concentration Camps years before the Jews.

threatened the Jews with total annihilation, if they were the cause of another war. March 25th of that same year, Hitler declared "*Poland should be totally subjected.*" He was just freeing the Germans under Polish rule, and besides it all really belonged to the Third Reich. He was only planning to regain land from the Poles which really belonged to Germans. It is amazing how many countries conveniently justified Hitler's words and actions with his premeditated and obviously warped reasoning. They looked away, as the blood began to run down the streets. And the wailing of the "women of Jerusalem" could be heard, and is still heard if one has ears to hear and eyes to see.

In Warsaw, we stood before the Monument, rising high into the sky, remembering the brave *Uprising of the Warsaw Ghetto.* It was a tribute to the Jews who had fought bravely but futilely when the Nazi Gestapo came to get them. There, on the Arch which still hovers over the spot where the Jews were forced to board trains to torture and death, a sign warns:

"Those who ignore history are bound to repeat it"

On Palm Sunday (at that time it was called Passion Sunday), Edith Stein wrote to her prioress:

"*Dear Mother, I beg your Reverence's permission to offer myself to the Heart of Jesus as a sacrificial expiation for the sake of true peace; that the Antichrist's sway may be broken, if possible, without another world war, and that a new order may be established. I am asking this today because it is already the twelfth hour. I know that I am nothing, but Jesus wills it, and He will call many more to the same sacrifice in these days.*"

June of 1939, Edith Stein wrote her last will and testament. She joyfully and peacefully offered herself as a sacrifice: "*for the Glory of God, for the Sacred Heart of Jesus and the Immaculate Heart of Mary, for the intentions of*

Mother Church,[13] *for peace in the world and the salvation of the German nation, and for her family both living and dead.*" This she declared as a testimonial of her complete abandonment to "*God's preordained will*".

September 1, 1939, Hitler invaded Poland. The rest of Europe had turned its face away, as Hitler took country after country; they made excuses for the evacuation of Jews, the enslavement of Czechoslovakia, Austria, and the Sudetenland. Their thinking had been, with each conquest, that the beast would be satisfied. They started with the concept: Better *one* than all. But the *one* turned into *another one* and then *another one*, until he walked into Poland! A few days later, she wrote: "*Hail Cross, Our Only Hope.*"

Edith Stein's sister Rosa came to the Carmel in Echt, in 1940. She became keeper of the door, welcoming, and also screening those who wanted to speak with the cloistered Nuns. She desired, like her sister, to become a *Religious*. But before she could become a Carmelite Nun, Hitler invaded Holland in May of 1940. Therefore, she became a Third Order Carmelite. September 1st of 1941, although one (Edith) was a Religious and the other (Rosa) a Third Order Carmelite, both sisters were ordered by the Gestapo to wear a yellow star of David, inscribed "*Jew*". It didn't matter, they were converts to Catholicism.

When Hitler started his persecution of the Jews, all the Christian churches protested. They were warned that if they continued speaking out against the treatment of the Jews, Jewish *converts* would be rounded up and placed in Concentration Camps. All the Christian denominations ceased, at once. All the Churches that is but the Roman Catholic Church. And so, the persecution spread to Priests,

---

[13]So like Saint Catherine of Siena who "*offered herself as a willing sacrifice when she had had a vision ....in which the ship of the Church crushed her to death.*" from the chapter on Saint Catherine of Siena in "*Saints and Other Powerful Women in the Church*"

Bishops, and Religious, those who had converted and those who dared defend them. Edith Stein's words to Pope Pius XI were coming to pass; the slaughter of the innocent was covering Christian and Jew, alike.

Edith and her sister were required to report to the Gestapo periodically. One time, when they entered Gestapo headquarters, Edith Stein greeted one of the soldiers with the traditional German salutation: *"Praised be Jesus Christ!"* The officer just stared at her. He didn't say a word. What was he thinking? Was it so long ago that anyone had greeted him with these words? Was her salutation bringing back days long forgotten when men and women loved one another, all were Germans, all were one regardless of religion? Edith Stein said that she had no choice but to utter these words; it was as if she could see, in the eyes of this soldier *the battle being waged between principalities and powers,* the raging struggle of Lucifer against Christ.

The prioress of the Carmel wrote to *Le Pâquier Carmel* in Switzerland, requesting they admit Edith and her sister Rosa. The Carmel only had room for Edith and she would not leave her sister behind. What were Edith's thoughts as she waited? She began to delve into St. John of the Cross; her writing began to show clear evidence that Edith was, in addition to other holy attributes, a mystic. Some of her writings were: *"Ways to know God"* and *"Science of the Cross".* She wrote:

"Thus the bridal union of the soul with God for which it was created is purchased through the Cross, perfected with the Cross, and sealed for all eternity with the Cross."

Eventually the Carmel found a place for Rosa, a home for Third Order Carmelites near *Le Pâquier.* They had only to await permission from the Dutch authorities.

Edith Stein did not want to die. She carried the Scripture passage on her person: *"When they persecute you in one town, flee to the next."* But she did not shrink from persecution and dying; she prepared herself for that eventuality, as each day and each piece of the puzzle fell into place.

July 1, 1942, the Nazis decreed that Jewish Catholic children were no longer permitted to go to Catholic schools. This robbed them of *all* education, as other schools were not open to them. The Bishops in Holland wrote a pastoral letter to be read at all Masses, protesting this treatment of innocent children. They also came out *strongly* against the deportation of Jews from their native land. It was read at all Masses on July 26th. On August the 2nd, the Nazis ordered all Dutch Jews, converted to Catholicism, be arrested! Now that included, as well, any Dutch Catholics of Jewish descent. The Nazis considered anyone who had any Jewish blood, no matter how little or from how far back in their ancestry, a Jew. Edith Stein and her sister were picked up that evening. Dutch citizens stood at the front of the Carmel, incredulous, grief-stricken, helpless. They heard Edith Stein say to her sister Rosa:

"Come let us go for our people."

The two sisters were taken to three camps; the first two were Dutch camps: Amersfoort and Westerbrook. A guard from Westerbrook later testified that Edith went among the prisoners praying and consoling them, giving them hope in that God Who never forgets us. Imagine their surprise to hear a Catholic Nun speaking to them as a Jewess, reaching out to them, understanding, loving, focusing on them and not herself. When the mothers became crippled by fear and hopelessness, Edith Stein cared for their children. They were so overcome by fear that they did not know if their children were eating! Edith bathed them, dressed them, fed them, and nurtured them with her generous love. As she was filled with peace, she transmitted that peace to all around her. It brought a little bit of Heaven into the darkness of the hell all around them.

On August 7th, the two sisters Edith and Rosa Stein were transported from Westerbrook to Auschwitz! They, with thousands of helpless Jews were jammed mercilessly into cattle cars to make the long ride to hell. Many died before they arrived in Auschwitz. There was no air in the cars, no facilities to relieve oneself, no water or food for days. When one died, the others had to remain with him in the same car.

[A man gave this testimony, in 1982. He said he had been a worker on a mail truck when he was conscripted into the German Army. While he was being transported to Russia, for special duty, he said that his train stopped to be refueled, in a railroad yard in Breslau. A train pulled up alongside, and stopped. When the guard opened up the door of one of the cattle cars, he saw people heaped on one another like bundles of rags, and others squatting, swaying back and forth listlessly. There was an unbearable stench coming from within the cars. He could hear the moaning and wailing of men and women, interrupted only by the pathetic crying of little children.

He testified, there was a Nun among them dressed in brown, with a yellow Star of David on her breast. He said that maybe it was because he looked at them sympathetically, she spoke to him: *"It's terrible. We don't even have containers to relieve ourselves."* Then looking forlornly off into the village of Breslau, she said: *"This is my home; I'll never see it again....We are going to our death."* Trying to contain his feelings, he asked her if the other prisoners knew. She responded, *"It's better for them not to know."* He identified the Nun in brown, as *Edith Stein*. He said that the train was marked as going to Poland.

In 1948, when he was returning from camp, he said that he read about Edith Stein and when he saw her picture, he knew that this was the Nun he had seen and spoken to in Breslau.]

Scene of Auschwitz death camp from the Guard Tower

When at last they arrived, a welcoming band greeted them with German folk songs. They were told to disrobe completely. They were handed soap and towels. A sign read *"Clean is Good!"* They were led to cottages where they were told, they would be deloused. The mothers with an instinct only a mother has, tried to hide their children under the clothes, until they would come out from the *showers*. When the guards caught them and asked them why, they replied, they were afraid the disinfectant would harm the children. They were assured this was nonsense, and so the mothers led their children into the cottages with them.

When some of the prisoners became aware of their fate and refused to enter the gas chambers, they were clubbed and thrown in. The guards carefully silenced anyone who gave the slightest evidence of hysteria, lest they incite a riot. They really had very little to fear; most were too weak from the long, arduous trip to stand up, no less fight.

For Edith and her sister and all the others who had survived the days of unbearable heat locked inside the airless cars, the walk from the train stop to the cottages was a long, hard one. [When we were at Auschwitz, we looked down from the guards' post in the watch-tower. Our guide pointed out the distance the sisters and the Jews had to walk; it was *miles* from the platform to the cottages.] Edith thought that the guards would choose them to work in Germany. That's what they did with strong, able-bodied women. And so, I wonder if she knew the fate that awaited them. Was there possibly a ray of hope that they would survive?

It was the beginning of the implementation of their perfect plan! The Nazis had to devise a method of disposing of the Jews and their political prisoners, in the fastest, most efficient way. They learned, all too soon, that they could not handle the hundreds of thousands who were being herded into the camps, so their next plan was to exterminate them! They came upon a plan to use *Cyclon B*, a bitter, extremely poisonous gas that was supposed to kill those trapped within, in fifteen to twenty minutes. Before they died, their lungs, their throats, their esophagus', were set on fire by this powerful acid. It was a horrible death.

But when Edith and her sister arrived, the Nazis had not yet perfected this method of exterminating defenseless men, women and children. The guards had not thrown enough cans of cyanide in the air-tight, sealed cottage, and so, when they opened the door twenty-four hours later, they were still alive. They threw in more cans.

We stood on the spot where the cottage once stood, the torture chamber where Edith and her sister, along with so many other Martyrs, went to their horrible death. All that remains is a small sign where a harmless looking cottage became a house of horror. Less than twenty feet from the cottage was a mound of bones that had survived over fifty years, there as a witness to man's inhumanity to man. When the Nazis could not cremate the bodies fast enough, to keep up with the mass annihilation, they piled the dead bodies, forming funeral pyres. In this large field, we saw Crosses where the bodies of Christians had been burned and Stars of David where the Jews had been.

Bob and Penny Lord at site of Edith Stein's death - Auschwitz

    Because she and all those who had been chosen to die [approximately 1/2 had been judged unfit to work and therefore killed.] were killed immediately, there were no records. It would appear that the world would never know what had happened that dark and ugly day. But the Lord would not allow His bride to be lost in a maze of shadows of the valley of death. Our faithful Father in Heaven wants her story to be told, as well as the events that led up to such a massacre of humanity. The world is poorer because we have been cheated of loving, talented, committed Saints like Edith Stein, Sister Teresa Benedicta a Cruce. The Lord will not allow them to die in vain. Their cries will not be silenced. God will not allow us to ignore history. Why? Because He loves us.

    Who was Edith Stein? As with Saint Maxmilian Kolbe, Edith Stein would have been nominated for Sainthood even if she had not died a Martyr's death. Her writings, so long suppressed under the Nazis have now been published not only in German but have been translated and published in English.

"Those who ignore history are bound to repeat it"

Edith Stein was one of 6,000,000 Jews, and 4,000,000 Christians who were murdered while the world looked the other way.

On the first day of the month of Our Lady, the Jewish Convert she so dearly loved and admired, May 1st, 1987: **Edith Stein**, *Sister Teresa Benedicta a Cruce* **was beatified by John Paul II.**

The Lord will not allow her song to Mother Mary to go unsung:

"Today I stood with you beneath the Cross,
And felt more clearly than I ever did
That you became our Mother only there.

"....those whom you have chosen for companions
To stand with round the eternal throne,
They here must stand with you beneath the Cross,
And with the lifeblood of their bitter pains
Must purchase heavenly glory for those souls
Whom God's own Son entrusted to their care."[14]

†

"One day this will have to be atoned for."

Blessed Edith Stein died, as a Jewess and Catholic Nun, for the Jews who were being persecuted because of their belief in the One God, and as a German for the Germans who were persecuting the Jewish people, saying if she did not pray and do retribution for the Germans, who will?

Who will die for *those persecuted*, today, because of His Name and who will die in reparation of the sins committed by *those who persecute* those who defend His Name? Who

---

[14]The Story of Edith Stein by Freda Mary Oben, PhD

are the persecuted, today? And who are those who persecute those who follow Him through His Vicar on earth? Who will pray for those who lead so many innocent lambs to the slaughter of their souls with their false theology, claiming it is the teaching of the Church?

St. Maxmilian Kolbe

We wrote an extensive chapter on St. Maxmilian Kolbe in our book, "*Saints and Other Powerful Men in our Church*," in which we followed his life in detail. We made a television program as part of our series of the same name, in which we shared very emotionally about this Saint. We went to Poland to videotape the City of the Immaculata built by Maxmilian Kolbe, where he had the largest Religious community of Franciscans in the world. We also went to Auschwitz, the Nazi death camp, where Kolbe and Blessed Edith Stein were murdered. This aspect of the life of Maxmilian Kolbe is what we want to share with you in this book, his Signal Grace[15], his inspired courage which enabled him to give up his life for a stranger.

"I am a Catholic Priest."

How does a man give up his life for someone he never met before? This *man* has been called by many titles: Saint of World War II, Holy Prisoner, Saint of Concentration

---

[15]Mother Angelica calls Signal Grace that special grace Our Lord Jesus gives us through the Holy Spirit, which enables us to suffer outrageous tortures, and die for our Faith. Everyone we've written about in this book could be said to have been given *Signal Grace*.

Camps, Saint of the Press, Saint of Aviation, Saint of
Progress, Saint of the Poor. But I think the one he would
prefer is "Catholic Priest."

The devil uses any means to kill us. For so many years,
in the United States, the Polish people have been the brunt
of very poor ethnic jokes. It is true, every new group coming
into our free society inherits the suffering, the minority
before them endured. It's like being a freshman in college.
The only difference is, the freshman is only degraded for a
year not a lifetime. It gets so bad that the minority, to
become one of "the guys," often pokes fun at *itself!* And
then, most tragically, everyone believes it and the world is
cheated of an extraordinary people.

But God loves us! God sent us a *Pole*, a charismatic,
powerful, intelligent, talented, loving leader, Karol Wojtyla,
our Pope John Paul II. Through him and the interest the
world has in him, we have become aware of the history of a
brave, faithful, bright, true people of God. We find
ourselves getting upset when someone tells an *innocent*,
cutting joke about a *Polack*. It's like they're attacking us!

I would like to dedicate this chapter to our Pope and a
young man whose name is *Robert Ziminsky*. He happens to
be our grandson. We have tried to share with Robert, the
centuries of *Italians* in his life who make up part of the fine
man he is becoming. Now, Rob, we pray this will bring you a
part of your ancestry we knew nothing about. Through the
life of this Polish, Franciscan Priest, we bring you hope in
what man can be, and the courage to bring that hope to
others.

It is with much thanksgiving to our Lord and His
Mother, Mary Immaculate, *Niepokalanow* who play such a
great and integral role in this chapter, that we begin our walk
alongside our brother Maxmilian Kolbe.

The Journey to Life, Death and Resurrection

*Printing press located at Niepokalanow, City of the Immaculata
that is still used to spread the Good News*

It was 1940. Father Maxmilian had been preparing his
brother friars for the time when he would leave for his final
walk to *Calvary*. When he wrote and published his *Knight of
the Immaculata*, he knew his arrest would be any day. Loyal
Poles who were working inside the Gestapo offices, kept
warning him to leave Niepokalanow, but he wouldn't!

The Gestapo had noticed his many gifts. *Why not use
them for the Third Reich! He could influence the stubborn
Poles to cooperate, especially through his press. How to go
about this?* They told Father Maxmilian that the High
Command had heard of him and were pleased with him.
They would be even more appreciative (with all the
privileges that would bring), if he would apply for German
citizenship. It was obvious, with his name, he had German
blood.

No one knows of the temptations Satan might have put into Father's mind and heart. *He could continue his work. His sons (friars) needed him. He certainly could do more alive than dead!* If he had accepted their offer, how different things might have been. What a price to pay for life on earth, even doing *good things*, if the end result is the loss of your soul and the souls of others. His love for his Mother in Heaven was sacred. He could not see himself betraying Her, and doing less than Her Son Jesus, saving his own life at the cost of his Poland. And so, he said: "*No!*" Father Maxmilian had *lived*, a son of Poland, and he would *die* a son of Poland.

Bob and Penny Lord signing the guest log book in
St. Maxmilian Kolbe's office at Niepokalanow

February 17th, 1941, at 9:45 in the morning, they came to arrest him. Two cars pulled up and entered the Niepokalanow. Five Gestapo officials got out, four with uniforms and one in plainclothes. As they approached the house of the Religious, a brother phoned Father Maxmilian, who was in his room. Father had been expecting this moment, but when he answered the phone, the brother said, his voice *trembled* with his "yes." But only for a moment; regaining his composure, he said:

"*All right, my son.*" Then he gave him *their* greeting, "*Mary,*" for the last time.

The night before, he had said:

"*What indescribable happiness! What a great grace it is to be able to seal one's ideal with one's life.*"

Was brother thinking of this, as the Gestapo called out Maxmilian's name and that of five other Priests? Satan was not finished tormenting him. "Isn't that a German name?" the Gestapo asked? Once again, Father Maxmilian proclaimed:

"*Perhaps some of my grandparents may have come from Germany, but I was born in Poland and therefore I am Polish.*"

Father and the other five Priests were taken to Warsaw and kept in prison. Now, the Gestapo had a problem. Father Maxmilian was not one of the thousands of unknown Priests who would be arrested and killed. He was known worldwide and highly acclaimed. They would have the whole church down on them, unless they could provide some kind of justification for their action.

And the Church came; his Provincial as well as a Nun, who worked for the Gestapo, came, putting their necks on the block. Nothing would dissuade the authorities. They used a trumped-up charge signed by a former brother, who had been expelled by Father Maxmilian because of some wrongdoing, while at Niepokalanow. In highly legalistic terminology, it alluded to a plot supposedly hatched by Father Maxmilian against the Germans occupying Poland. Anyone, who knew Father, would call this *impossible*! But the Gestapo said, since the papers were signed, nothing could be done.

The brother later testified, he didn't understand what was in the papers. Not knowing the German language, trusting it said what they said it did, he signed. So, they condemned an innocent man with a *forgery*.

As the days passed into weeks, in prison, Father Maxmilian spoke repeatedly of dying a Martyr's death for the Faith.   One of the brothers in the prison objected, complaining, "You, Father, speak of Martyrdom for the Faith, while there are *many*[16] people who are in concentration camps perishing; this is not for the Faith but for the country."

Father's answer, wisely and prophetically was:

"Son, I tell you that if it is thus, the Martyrdom is certainly for the Faith".

All wars are religious wars.   The war is *always*, not between countries or people, but between God and Satan. And certainly, this war, with its inhumanity against God's children was not political to *Him*. Ask parents whose sons or daughters died, if it was political.   They'll tell you, it was *personal*. So, when anyone of us is hurt, God is hurt and so is His Faith.

Auschwitz - Roll Call of Hell

On May the 28th, 1941, Father Maxmilian, although suffering seriously from tuberculosis, was transported along with 320 other prisoners, to *Auschwitz*. He was treated no better because he was a *Religious*. Rather, they were harsher on the *Religious*, taking some kind of delight, determining how much torture they could take before cracking.

Father Maxmilian was given a number, 16670; he was assigned to block 17. The guards pushed, kicked and beat Father when he was too ill to walk. He struggled, as he tried to haul the wheel barrels full of gravel, they needed to build the crematorium walls.   Oh, they were not past using prisoners to build their own means of torture or death.

---

[16]meaning many who were not Catholic.

No matter how they brutalized him, how they tried to humiliate him, the could not force Father into hating them. He had so much love in his eyes, they made him lower his eyes so they wouldn't have to look into them.

Auschwitz or *the Death Camp*, as it was more commonly called, was originally to be for the extermination of *Jews*. Then, the Third Reich added to their Martyred number: the Danish, French, Greek, Spanish, Flemish, Yugoslavian, German, Norwegian, Russian, Rumanian, Hungarian, Italian and Polish undesirables, whose only crime was they were leaders or intellectuals.

Although its horror was not singularly its own, it had the reputation of being the most efficient of all the concentration camps, building up to a record of *exterminating 3500* enemies of the state in 24 hours. They became so good at their job, the sign above the entrance gate reading *"Work makes one free,"* they were capable of killing prisoners on arrival. Many they did; others they saved for slave labor; others they had *fun* with; their action: to degrade, to see how low they could make a human stoop with enough torture.

I think, the saddest testimony I ever heard was from a survivor of the concentration camps. He told how parents would have their children go before them, into the *showers* (the Nazis jokingly called the gas chambers), so they would not be frightened, the parents reassuring them, it was all right, they would be following.

A fellow prisoner testified that nothing they did to Father Maxmilian could break his spirit. He would lift up the other victims, repeating:

"No, No, these Nazis will not kill our souls, since we prisoners distinguish ourselves quite definitely from our tormentors; they will not be able to deprive us of the dignity of our Catholic belief. We will not give up. And when we die, then we die pure and peaceful, resigned to God in our hearts."

He infuriated the Nazis as he worked to keep the Poles and the European Jews from being reduced into groveling animals, turning on each other. To punish him, the guards would save the most demeaning work for him. At one time, they even set their vicious dogs on him.

They used Father to carry corpses to the crematorium. A former prisoner testified: one time, when he (the prisoner) was asked to carry a young man's horribly ravaged body, his ripped open stomach, evidence of just part of the torture he'd suffered before dying, he was so repulsed by the sight, he did not have the strength or the stomach to lift him. Then he heard a gentle voice, hardly above a whisper: *"Let us take him."* As they carried the young man to the crematorium, he could hear the prisoner helping him, *"Holy Mary, pray for us."* Father Maxmilian was calling to his Mother, and as She did with Her Son Jesus as He carried His Cross, Her eyes sustained him.

One day, Father fell under the weight of the wood he was carrying. Face down, in the mud, unable to get up, the picture I see before me is, again, the one of Jesus on the way of the Cross, when He fell the third time. Was that the picture before Father Maxmilian? Was that how he was able to get up? With his last ounce of strength, each day, he carried his sufferings, taking on the sins of *his* jailers upon his wounded body, as his Jesus before him. He said over and over again:

"For Jesus Christ, I am prepared to suffer still more."

But soon, they beat his weary, broken body to such a point of breaking, he landed, more dead than alive, in a hospital. His tuberculosis got so bad, he was, again, like Jesus before him, dying of asphyxiation, unable to breath. They determined he had *pneumonia.*

His face had begun to show the scars of his mistreatment, and his voice, betrayed by the dryness from too much heat and too little water, was robbing him of his speech. But yet, a fellow Priest testified, he was an inspiration to everyone. He was never too weary, too tired, too broken, too sick to hear confessions.

He was happy to be in the hospital because so many there needed a Priest. One of the prisoners had somehow gained the trust of the guards and they would let him out. He would return, hiding food under his clothes, which he shared with the other prisoners.

One day, he sneaked in some hosts. *Now, it was immediate execution, if a Priest was caught celebrating Holy Mass. Even those men, who had become monsters, knew the Power of Jesus.* Father took the hosts, said the words of consecration and he brought Jesus in the Holy Eucharist, the Bread of Life, to his fellow patients. He celebrated Holy Mass not once but twice. At times, he took what little bread he had and consecrated it, distributing the Lord to all. But, he never would accept any of the other prisoners rations, saying *"You need them. You must live."* Father Maxmilian, Priest! When he left the hospital, he was assigned to Cell Block 14.

A prisoner escaped! The shrill sound of the alarm pierced the still, dark night. The prisoners lay frozen, praying they would not be part of those chosen to be executed. According to the barbaric law of the camp, when *one* inmate escaped, *ten* men from his cell were chosen to starve to death, in the underground bunker. They rounded up all the prisoners and had them stand at attention, for three hours, in the prison yard. Then, they marched them in to have their meager supper, all that is but the men of *block 14!* Instead, they were forced to helplessly look by, as their rations were dumped into the canal.

The next day, they were lined up in the scorching sun, as the rest of the prisoners went off to work. They were given nothing to drink or eat. Their condition became so unbearable, many of them collapsed and not even the guards' brutal beatings could arouse them.   They just dumped them, one on top of another, in a heap.

As night approached, the rest of the prisoners came back. They were lined up, facing those of *block 14*, so they

 could witness what happens when someone escapes. They stood there, helpless to ease the fear they saw in their fellow inmates eyes, as they stared across at them.   And then, the dreaded announcement: *"Since the fugitive has not been found, ten of you are condemned to death."*   Commander Fritsch took delight as he passed back and forth, before the prisoners of *block 14*.

He could see the fear in their eyes; he could read their minds, *Oh God, don't let it be me.*

"Good-by, friends; we will meet again where there is justice," was joined by another sobbing, "Long live Poland!" "Good-by! Good-by, my dear wife; good-by, my dear children, already orphans of your father," cried out Sergeant Francis Gajowniczek.

A prisoner from *block 14* stepped out of the lineup. It was Father Maxmilian! He had been assigned to block 14, had endured all the torture and was still standing.   He walked slowly and calmly toward the commandant.   He stopped in front of Fritsch. The sight was blinding! There was a hush that went through the men lined up.   No one, in the history of the camp, had ever done anything like this before.

They stared; they tried to take their eyes away, but they couldn't or wouldn't. Suddenly they were not afraid of this man who reduced men to animals; he no longer posed a threat. The man before him, chest caved in, little more than hanging flesh on thin bones, had the upper hand. The commander was stunned, frozen. Was he afraid at what or who it was, he saw? Did he remember from a thousand lifetimes ago, his mother telling him about the Savior who gave His life for him?

Here was a man who had traded his God in for a lie and he looked frightened. Facing him, was one who death could have no victory over, one who dared to love *Him* with all his heart, mind and soul, totally abandoning himself to Him. He had loved others through *Him*, in *Him*, with *Him*, even this monster in front of him. This one who so exemplified the *Sacrificial Lamb* who died, forgiving them, saying "*They know not what they do*", frightened him!

The commander found his voice; regaining his composure, he barked, "What does this Polish pig want?"

Father Maxmilian, pointing toward Sergeant Francis Gajowniczek, answered:

"*I am a Polish Catholic Priest; I am old; I want to take his place because he has a wife and children...*"

Father Maxmilian was 47 years old!

The underground bunker, *block 11*, was a *chamber of horror*. It was closed in by a wall twenty-one feet high; prisoners were to have no communication from the outside. Upon entering, inmates knew they would only leave as corpses, on their way to the crematorium. Only a few Poles came in any kind of contact with the bunker, those who the Nazis needed, to carry out bodies and etc. This is how we have any idea of what went on.

They led Father and the other nine to *bunker 11*. They stripped them of all their clothing and left them, sneering, "We will dry you up like tulips!" A Pole later testified: when they went down to the bunkers, it sounded as if the Angels were accompanying the prisoners singing hymns to Jesus and

Mary; instead of curses, the Rosary and Litanies of prayers resounded through the dungeons, petitioning God for mercy in what He *would* give them and thanking Him for what He *had* given them. The other bunkers, having joined the little Priest in *bunker 11* were heard echoing his love song to Mary and Her Son Jesus. They were so immersed in their praise and worship, they often did not hear the guards until they shouted at them to be quiet!

When the door opened, the prisoners pitifully begged for some water and bread. Those who were strong enough to make it over to the door were kicked in the stomach, and when they fell, if they did not die, they were shot right there. Conditions got so bad, the prisoners drank their own urine (as was evidenced by the empty and dry pails that had been left for them to relieve themselves).

Father encouraged the other innocent prisoners not to give up hope, to pray that the escaped prisoner would be found and they would be freed. For himself, he asked nothing. He even got to the guards, who came in each day to check up on the prisoners. They had never experienced such love and compassion. For some, it was more than they could handle; was he showing them what man could be like, according to God's plan? They called him a real gentleman.

Father Maxmilian lived longer than the rest, consoling them and praying with them until they mercifully gave up their last breath. Two weeks passed; prisoners died one after the other. At the end of the third week, there were four left; Father Maxmilian was one of them! So, needing the bunker for more prisoners, they called in the director of the hall of the sick, the infamous and wicked Boch. He lifted the arms of the prisoners left. As they looked up at him, helplessly, he injected them with poisonous *acid*.

One of the Poles testified he had been with the Nazi officers in the block. He saw Father Maxmilian, a prayer on his lips, love and forgiveness in his eyes, hold out his left arm to the killers. He said he couldn't stand it anymore and he (the Pole) left, with the pretense he had work to do. When he returned, he found Father Maxmilian sitting, his body leaning against the wall, his beautiful eyes open, and his head bent to the left side. He did not look as if he had died a horrible death. He was radiant, he looked serene as if he had fallen asleep or was just dreaming with his eyes open. He was beautiful! When You died, Jesus, You died that all men could live, once and for all. Now, another son was called to give up his life that *a* man could live and that son, Your brother Father Maxmilian Mary Kolbe said "yes!"

Father Maxmilian died on the vigil of the Feast of the Assumption of our and his Lady into Heaven. What the world, with the world's eyes, saw was an emaciated body brutally tortured, wasted away, desecrated by his forced nakedness - more bones than flesh. But witnesses testified when they saw him, he was shrouded in a flood of light, almost transfigured. He looked as if he were in ecstasy. Had Jesus and Mary come to accompany him home?

It was Friday, August the 15th; men came for his body and placed it in a box. It was taken to the ovens. They had been burning for him, day and night, as they had for others. There was a silence that screamed through the camp. Love had been there. Compassion had lived in their midst. Hope had battled fear. God had been present among the godless. *He*, through His Priest, had entered this holocaust, had brought the dead to new life, and it would never be the same!

"I would like my ashes to be scattered to the four winds," a prayer he had often said, was on this day, the day celebrating the Feast of Her Assumption into Heaven, *answered* by the Lady he had always loved, his Mama, his Queen, his Niepokalanow.

But his desire *"to decrease while Christ increase"* was *not* to be granted by his Father in Heaven. He would not disappear *"without a trace."* On the vigil Feast of the Assumption, 1941, a man died, a Pole, a Catholic Priest and a son of Mary.

His story needed to be told. In this world, where man sometimes sinks to a level beneath the animals, we need a Father Maxmilian Mary Kolbe. We are in the time of Maxmilian Mary Kolbe. We are in the time of Mary. We are in the time of Pope John Paul II.

We may be in the time of new Martyrs. A modern day *dry Martyr,*[17] Pope John Paul II, another Pole, on October 10th, 1982, raised a knight of Mary to Sainthood, and in Heaven, Mary said *"This day, son, you have lived your motto 'Totus Tuus' (all yours, Mary)"* Thank you!

Below:
Candles in the cell where St.
Maxmilian Kolbe gave up his life

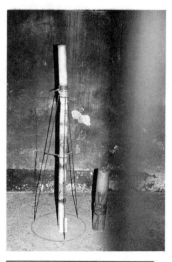

Above:
St. Maxmilian Kolbe accepted the
crown of Martyrdom

---

[17]One who does not actually die a Martyr's death, but suffers from the torture and ill treatment inflicted by his tormentors.

Acknowledgements

Excerpts were reprinted from the following books with permission of these copyright holders:

The Irish Martyrs - Msgr. Patrick Corish - Copyright 1989
Veritas Publications 7/8 Lower Abbey St. Dublin, Ireland

17 Irish Martyrs - Veritas Publications - 7/8 Lower Abbey St. Dublin, Ireland - Photos and Sketches

Fr. Jerzy Popieluszko - Fr. Antoni Lewki - Copyright 1991
Warsaw, Poland

Edith Stein - Freda Mary Oben, PhD - Copyright 1988
Alba House - 2187 Victory Blvd. - Staten Island, NY 10314

Carmelite Digest - Oakland, Ca

The Meaning of Maryknoll - Albert Nevins MM - 1954
Catholic Foreign Mission Society - Maryknoll, NY

Lives of the Saints - Butler, Thurston, Atwater - Copyright 1980 Christian Classics - PO Box 30 Westminster, MD 21158

Romero, a Life - James R. Brockman Copyright 1989
Orbis Books - Maryknoll, NY

Martyrs - Donald Atwater - 1957 - Sheed & Ward, NY

Mexican Martyrdom - John O'Connor OSA - Copyright 1936
Tan Publications - PO Box 424 - Rockford, IL 61105

Blood Drenched Altars - Bishop Francis Kelley Copyright 1935 - Tan Publications - Box 424 - Rockford IL 61105

Eleven Prie-Dieux - Starzynska, Maria - Copyright 1992
Sisters of the Holy Family of Nazareth - Rome, 1992

Bibliography

Attwater, Donald - *Martyrs* - Sheed & Ward NY 1957

Brockman, James R - *Romero, a Life* - Orbis Books NY 1989

Butler, Thurston, Atwater - *Lives of the Saints*
    Christian Classics - Westminster, MD 1980

17 Irish Martyrs - Veritas Publications Dublin 1992

Corish, Patrick J - *The Irish Martyrs*
    Veritas Publications - Dublin, Ireland 1989

Kelley, Francis Bishop - *Blood-Drenched Altars*
    Bruce Publishing Co. Milwaukee, WI 1935 (TAN)

Lewik, Antoni Fr. - Fr. Jerzy Popieluszko

Lord, Bob & Penny - *The Many Faces of Mary*
    Journeys of Faith - Slidell, LA 1987

Lord, Bob & Penny - *Scandal of the Cross and Its Triumph*
    Journeys of Faith - Slidell, LA 1992

Lord, Bob & Penny - *Saints and Other Powerful Men in the Church* - Journeys of Faith - Slidell, LA 1990

Lord, Bob & Penny - *Saints and Other Powerful Women in the Church* - Journeys of Faith - Slidell, LA 1989

Marshall, Peter - Manuel David - *The Light and the Glory*
    Fleming Revell Company - 1977

Nevins, Albert J. MM - *American Martyrs from 1542*
    Our Sunday Visitor - Huntington, IN 1987

Nevins, Albert J. MM - *The Meaning of Maryknoll*
    Mc Mullen Books - NY 1954

Oben, Edith Mary Ph.D - *Edith Stein*
    Society of St. Paul - Staten Island NY 1988

O'Connor, John OSA - *A Priest on the Run*
    Veritas Publications, Dublin 1992

Parsons, Wilifred, SJ - *Mexican Martyrdom*
Mac Millan Co - New York 1936 (TAN)
Starzynska, Maria - *Eleven Prie-Dieux*
Sisters of the Holy Family of Nazareth - Rome 1992
Valkenburg Augustine O.P. and Fenning Hugh O.P.
Two Dominican Martyrs of Ireland
Dominican Publications - Dublin Ireland 1992
Forristal, Desmond - *Dominic Collins* - Messenger
Publications - 37 Lower Leeson St. Dublin 2, Ireland 1992

Journeys of Faith

To Order: 1-800-633-2484 - 1-504-863-2546

Books

Bob and Penny Lord are authors of best sellers:

This Is My Body, This Is My Blood;
Miracles of the Eucharist $8.95 Paperback only
The Many Faces Of Mary, A Love Story $8.95 Paperback $12.95 Hardcover
We Came Back To Jesus $8.95 Paperback $12.95 Hardcover
Saints and Other Powerful Women in the Church $12.95 Paperback only
Saints and Other Powerful Men in the Church $14.95 Paperback only
Heavenly Army of Angels $12.95 Paperback only
Scandal of the Cross and Its Triumph $12.95 Paperback only
The Rosary - The Life of Jesus and Mary $12.95 Hardcover only
Martyrs - They died for Christ $12.95 Paperback only

Please add $3.00 S&H for first book: $1.00 each add'l book - Louisiana. Res. add 8.25% Tax

Videos and On-site Documentaries

Bob and Penny's Video Series based on their books:
A 5 part series on the Miracles of the Eucharist filmed at EWTN
A 9 part Eucharistic Retreat series with Father Harold Cohen
A 14 part series on The Many Faces of Mary
A 10 part series on Saints and Other Powerful Women in the Church
A 12 part series on Saints and Other Powerful Men in the Church
Many other on-site Documentaries based on Miracles of the Eucharist, Mother Mary's Apparitions, Saints and other Powerful Men and Women in the Church, and the Heavenly Army of Angels. Request our list of videos and audios.

Pilgrimages

Bob and Penny Lord's ministry take out Pilgrimages to the Shrines of Europe, the Holy Land, and the Shrines of Mexico every year. Come and join them on one of these special Retreat Pilgrimages. Call for more information, and ask for the latest pilgrimage brochure.

Lecture Series

Bob and Penny travel to all parts of the world to spread the Good News. They speak on what they have written about in their books; the Body of Christ, through the Miracles of the Eucharist, the Mother of Christ, through her apparitions, and the Church of Christ, through the lives of the Saints both men and women and what they are saying to us today. If you would like to have them come to your area, call for information on a lecture series in your area.

Good Newsletter

We are publishers of the Good Newsletter, which is published four times a year. This newsletter will provide timely articles on our Faith, plus keep you informed with the activities of our community. Call 1-800-633-2484 for subscription information.